PROGRAM ISSUES IN
DEVELOPMENTAL DISABILITIES

PROGRAM ISSUES IN DEVELOPMENTAL DISABILITIES

A Guide to Effective Habilitation
and Active Treatment

Second Edition

James F. Gardner
Chief Executive Officer
Accreditation Council on Services for People with Developmental
    Disabilities
Washington, D.C.

and

Michael S. Chapman
Director
Office for Community Program Development
The Kennedy Institute
Baltimore, Maryland

with invited contributors

·P A U L·H·
BROOKES
PUBLISHING CO.

Baltimore • London • Toronto • Sydney

Paul H. Brookes Publishing Co.
Post Office Box 10624
Baltimore, Maryland 21285-0624

Designed and Produced by Stony Run Publishing Services (Baltimore,
   Maryland)
Typeset by Brushwood Graphics, Inc. (Baltimore, Maryland)
Manufactured in the United States of America by Victor Graphics, Inc.
   (Baltimore, Maryland)

Library of Congress Cataloging-in-Publication Data

Program issues in developmental disabilities: a guide to effective habilita-
   tion and active treatment/[edited by] James F. Gardner and Michael S.
   Chapman; with invited contributors.—2nd ed.
      p. cm.
   Includes bibliographical references.
   ISBN 1-55766-029-8
   1. Mentally handicapped—Rehabilitation—United States. 2. Mental
retardation facilities—United States.   I. Gardner, James F., 1946–
II. Chapman, Michael S.
HV3006.A4P76   1989
362.1'968—dc20

89-22057
CIP

Contents

Contributors

Michael S. Chapman, M.Ed.
Director
Office for Community Program Development
The Kennedy Institute
707 N. Broadway
Baltimore, Maryland 21205

James F. Gardner, Ph.D., M.A.S.
Chief Executive Officer
Accreditation Council on Services for People with Developmental
    Disabilities
8100 Professional Place
Suite 204
Landover, Maryland 20785

Larry J. Goldberg, J.D.
Assistant Attorney General
Attorney General's Office
Maryland Department of Health and Mental Hygiene
300 W. Preston Street
Baltimore, Maryland 21201

Solomon G. Jacobson, Ph.D., M.P.A.
Consultant in Human Services Development
1234 Massachusetts Avenue
Suite 723
Washington, D.C. 20005

Chaya M. Kaplan, L.C.S.W.
Project Manager
The Community Training Center
The Kennedy Institute
707 N. Broadway
Baltimore, Maryland 21205

Cynthia Shima Kauffman, M.Ed.
Director
Department for Family Support Services
The Kennedy Institute
707 N. Broadway
Baltimore, Maryland 21205

John O'Brien
Responsive Systems, Inc.
58 Willowick Drive
Lithonia, Georgia 30038

Nancy R. Weiss, M.S.W.
Director
Department for Community Services
The Kennedy Institute
707 N. Broadway
Baltimore, Maryland 21205

Preface

The Health Care Financing Administration (HCFA) intends the 1988 conditions of participation for intermediate care facilities for the mentally retarded (ICF/MR) to be client centered and outcome directed. The regulation focuses on the person residing in the ICF/MR, not on the facility. The emphasis in the provision of habilitation services should be on what the individual receives rather than what the facility delivers. Also, the regulation stresses the importance of outcomes—the increased skills and behaviors that individuals develop as a result of habilitation services.

In addition, HCFA intends through the new regulation to provide facilities with greater freedom in operating their programs. As a result, the current ICF/MR conditions of participation are less prescriptive than the previous requirements. HCFA has focused provider attention on client outcomes and given the facilities greater latitude in designing the delivery of habilitation services to accomplish those ends.

The first edition of this book was written as part of a 3-year grant of national significance from the Administration on Developmental Disabilities to provide training to state survey and independent professional review team members. The training focused on contemporary issues in the field of developmental disabilities as they related to the implementation of the 1977 ICF/MR regulations. The current edition is intended for personnel responsible for program development and implementation in the ICF/MR as required in the 1988 regulation. The change in the subtitle from *A Resource Manual for Surveyors and Reviewers* to *A Guide to Effective Habilitation and Active Treatment* reflects the wider audience and greater emphasis on effective programs for people with developmental disabilities.

The second edition of *Program Issues in Developmental Disabilities* is intended to assist facilities in the design of habilitation programs that meet the ICF/MR regulation. The content of the chapters of this edition is not derived from the requirements of the new ICF/MR regulation. Rather, the authors have identified the best habilitation and active treatment practices that focus on client outcomes and that facilitate compliance with the conditions of participation.

The authors designed this guide for personnel responsible for effective habilitation and active treatment. The guide covers a basic conceptual and theoretical framework for understanding the application of habilitation and active treatment in the ICF/MR. The book also offers specific and concrete suggestions for the design and implementation of active treatment programs that meet the requirements for effective habilitation. The focus of the book is on implementation of quality habilitation programs. The authors believe that quality habilitation programs will meet and surpass the requirements of most licensing, certification, and accrediting organizations.

Senior staff and midlevel managers, program coordinators, and qualified mental retardation professionals can use the guide in designing habilitation programs and in supervising the staff who implement the programs. The guide will provide new staff with the basic requirements for providing quality active treatment programs. Team leaders and facilitators, behavioral specialists, quality assurance coordinators, and other specialized staff will benefit from the specific discussion of habilitation requirements in their individual areas of professional responsibility.

This second edition of *Program Issues in Developmental Disabilities*, like the first edition, is not an implementation guide for the federal regulation. The book is not intended as an analysis of the regulation. The reader can best obtain an understanding of the new regulation by reviewing and analyzing the conditions of participation themselves.

Program Issues in Developmental Disabilities provides habilitation approaches and methods that are consistent with the conditions of participation and that reflect the intent of the new regulation. This approach reflects the authors' belief that programs incorporating the best in habilitation and active treatment methods will, as a matter of course, meet the ICF/MR regulation as well as any other accreditating or licensing requirements.

Chapters in the book address issues that may not be covered in the federal regulation. For example, the federal regulation does not require an agency mission statement. However, the authors believe that mission statements provide the agency and staff with a set of values, purpose, priorities, and a sense of direction. The mission statement is a critical requirement for the provision of effective habilitation programs. In a similar manner, while active treatment has a specific definition, the authors extend the definition of active treatment to cover appropriate organizational systems. This enables the provider of service to place active treatment within the context of the whole organization.

As a third example, Chapter 2 addresses the legal rights of persons with developmental disabilities with an emphasis on persons residing in the ICF/MR. The chapter addresses the legal rights arising from the United States Constitution, federal and state statute, and case law. The chapter does not analyze the legal requirements or legal status of the ICF/MR conditions of participation. Finally, the discussion of the normalization principle does not attempt to interpret the ICF/MR standards in terms of the normalization principle. Rather, the narrative attempts to indicate how the ICF/MR can incorporate aspects of the normalization principle into daily practices and routines.

The terminology in the second edition of *Program Issues in Developmental Disabilities* reflects the new federal approach to the ICF/MR requirements. Prior to 1988, the federal requirements for the ICF/MR program were commonly referred to as the *regulations*. The 1988 changes in the ICF/MR program were contained in a new *regulation*. The *regulation* contains eight *conditions of participation*. Each of the *conditions of participation* contains a number of *standards*.

Chapter 1 provides an introduction to the book and discusses the major themes that have developed since the publication of the first edition in 1980. The support services model is contrasted with the continuum model and the development of family support services and supported employment are introduced. The chapter covers other issues of concern such as aging, mental health needs of persons with developmental disabilities, community integration, and the growth of community-based services.

In Chapter 2 emphasis is placed on the constitutional, statutory, and case laws protections of legal rights of people with developmental disabilities. The major sources of legal protection are explored, and the chapter provides practical information on how habilitation program staff can increase attention on the legal rights of residents of ICFs/MR.

Much of the content of Chapter 3 was carried forward from the first edition. That original discussion by John O'Brien was particularly effective in focusing staff attention on major points of normalization theory and those aspects of facility practice that were under their control and could be changed.

Chapter 4 focuses on the individual with developmental disabilities and challenging behaviors. Strategies for developing effective nonaversive intervention programs are presented. In addition, the chapter presents strategies for evaluating program effectiveness.

Chapter 5 treats the interdisciplinary team as an exercise in small group dynamics. Successful habilitation programs require effective interdisciplinary teams that conduct business in an efficient and effective manner. Team facilitators, program coordinators, and qualified mental retardation professionals will find the chapter particularly important.

Chapter 6 provides a discussion of active treatment and sets forth a conceptual framework from which agency staff can systemically view active treatment. It provides a model for use by agencies in the development of its program.

The importance of mission statements is discussed in Chapter 7. The significance of mission statements as a driving force behind active treatment services is presented. To be successful, all staff must know the agency's purpose and direction, and what goals they are working toward.

Chapter 8 presents information on the assessment process within the active treatment model. Three levels of assessment are presented for consideration. The need to understand clearly the individual with developmental disabilities provides the basis from which program plans are developed.

Chapter 9 discusses the team process as it relates to the development of an individual program plan. Strategies for developing strength, interest, and needs lists as well as for developing effective goals and objectives are presented.

The development of effective implementation strategies is discussed in Chapter 10. Developing an effective program is a planned process. In this chapter, specific steps in program development are presented and discussed.

Chapter 11 deals with the last phase of the active treatment sequence. The focus of the chapter is on the application of theory to practice and the design of simple yet effective methods for monitoring and evaluation. The focus on implementation of proven data collection methods will be of interest to all habilitation program staff.

The new regulation does not discriminate between large and small facilities. The implementation of the regulation in the small community-based program offers many challenges. These challenges and the strategies to address them are presented in Chapter 12.

Quality assurance, the focus of Chapter 13, is a facility responsibility. The facility must determine the level of quality that will be required in its habilitation services. The chapter provides practical suggestions for designing and implementing a facility quality assurance program.

The final chapter reviews the history of Medicaid reform and the ICF/MR program. Quality enhancement is discussed in terms of a long-term commitment on the part of the ICF/MR. Quality enhancement includes such endeavors as strategic planning, organizational development, staff training, and internal monitoring and evaluation.

Acknowledgments

We would like to extend our appreciation to the authors of the first edition: William Bricker, Marcia Burgdorf, Philippa Campbell, Kenneth Crosby, Karen Green-McGowen, Wade Hitzing, Diane Iagulli, Linda Long, Roann Nichols, and John O'Brien. Their work provided a model from which the second edition was developed. We also wish to recognize the contributions of Theo Lasinski for her review and analysis of the entire manuscript.

To Our Families:

Diane Jean Gardner
Kathy Michelle and Tracy Lynn Gardner

Sally Kees Chapman
Lauren Reed and Katherine Logan Chapman

I
FOUNDATIONS

1
Introduction
A Decade of Change

James F. Gardner

When the first edition of *Program Issues in Developmental Disabilities* was published in 1980, the regulation for intermediate care facilities for the mentally retarded (ICFs/MR) was still new. The institution was the focal point for services for persons with developmental disabilities. Deinstitutionalization, normalization, and the least restrictive environment (LRE) formed the foundations for the design and delivery of service to people with developmental disabilities.

In the following decade a new vocabulary emerged. A growing recognition focused on the importance of the physical and mental health needs of people with developmental disabilities. Attention was directed toward persons with a dual diagnosis of developmental disability and serious psychiatric disability. People described as "technology dependent" and "medically fragile" entered community-based service programs.

The importance of support systems in enabling families to care for persons with severe disabilities was a major factor in the formation of a wide range of family support programs. The provision of these support services enabled thousands of persons to make the transition from segregated day activity programs to competitive employment.

Medicaid emerged as the major source of financial support for residential services. The Home and Community Based Waiver and the proposed 1989 Medicaid reform legislation (S. 384, H.R. 453) attempted to redistribute Medicaid funds to community-based programs. The debate over the wisdom of deinstitutionalization ebbed as the small community-based program became the center of the service delivery system.

INTENT OF 1988 ICF/MR REGULATION

The ICF/MR program also underwent change in the 1980s. At the beginning of the decade the Health Care Financing Administration

(HCFA) issued new guidelines for facilities serving 15 or fewer persons. In addition, HCFA began to rewrite the ICF/MR regulation in 1982. The regulatory rewrite incorporated a review of the literature in the field of mental retardation and developmental disabilities and extensive comment on and review of drafts of the regulation at each stage in the review process.

The new ICF/MR regulation, which became effective October 3, 1988, establishes conditions of participation, a format that is consistent with the regulation for skilled nursing facilities under Medicaid and Medicare. HCFA condensed more than 20 pages of old conditions into 9 pages of new conditions.

The new regulation establishes eight conditions of participation. The facility must be in compliance at least at the "condition level" to be eligible for Medicaid certification. If a facility complies with all conditions of participation but falls short of standards for one or more conditions, it must achieve full compliance through a plan of correction within 12 months.

The new regulation contains the following conditions of participation and standards:

483.410 *Governing Body and Management*
   a.   Governing body
   b.   Compliance with federal, state, and local laws.
   c.   Client records
   d.   Services provided under agreements with outside sources

483.420 *Client Protections*
   a.   Protection of clients' rights
   b.   Client finances
   c.   Communication with clients, parents, and guardians
   d.   Staff treatment of clients

483.430 *Facility Staffing*
   a.   Qualified mental retardation professional
   b.   Professional program services
   c.   Facility staffing
   d.   Direct care (residential living unit) staff
   e.   Staff training program

483.440 *Active Treatment Services*
   a.   Active treatment
   b.   Admissions, transfers, and discharge
   c.   Individual program plan
   d.   Program implementation
   e.   Program documentation
   f.   Program monitoring and change

483.450 *Client Behavior and Facility Practices*
   a.   Facility practices—Conduct toward clients
   b.   Management of inappropriate client behavior

     c. Time-out rooms
     d. Physical restraints
     e. Drug usage

483.460 *Health Care Services*
     a. Physician services
     b. Physician participation in the individual program plan
     c. Nursing services
     d. Nursing staff
     e. Dental services
     f. Comprehensive dental diagnostic services
     g. Comprehensive dental treatment
     h. Documentation of dental services
     i. Pharmacy services
     j. Drug regimen review
     k. Drug administration
     l. Drug storage and record keeping
     m. Drug labeling
     n. Laboratory services

483.470 *Physical Environment*
     a. Client living environment
     b. Client bedrooms
     c. Storage space in bedrooms
     d. Client bathrooms
     e. Heating and ventilation
     f. Floors
     g. Space and equipment
     h. Emergency plan and procedures
     i. Evacuation drills
     j. Fire protection
     k. Paint
     l. Infection control

483.480 *Dietetic Services*
     a. Food and nutrition services
     b. Meal services
     c. Menus
     d. Dining areas and service

The 1988 regulation is intended to sharpen the focus on individuals with a developmental disability and put less emphasis on facilities. The survey team will pay attention to the specific programs and services rendered to each individual in accordance with the individual program plan. The emphasis is placed on the active treatment the individual must receive rather than on the services the facility must be capable of providing.

The new regulation also stresses the rights and protections of individuals living in the ICF/MR. Two important themes flow through the client protection condition of participation. The first is that facilities must actively ensure rights rather than passively permit individuals to exercise their rights. The second is that the facility must train individuals to use and exercise their rights. For example, the right to financial resources is meaningful only if an individual is taught how to control and spend money. The facility is expected to teach individuals their rights and how to exercise them.

The regulation stresses that active treatment is a process that takes place across program settings, during morning, day, and evening, in formal and informal settings. As such, all facility staff are responsible for the provision of active treatment all day long. All staff who interact with the individual on a formal or informal basis are obligated to provide active treatment.

Finally, the 1988 regulation stresses changes in individual skill and behavior rather than the process of service delivery. HCFA has provided the facility with considerable flexibility in deciding how to provide active treatment services. The qualified mental retardation professional will focus attention on changes in individual skill and behavior. The important issues will be the individual outcomes. The new standards stress individual and staff performance rather than compliance with process. The intent of the new ICF/MR regulation was to develop federal standards on contemporary practice in residential programs for individuals with developmental disabilities. The development of these standards took place during a time of rapid change in the field of developmental disabilities.

DEINSTITUTIONALIZATION

The term *deinstitutionalization* has generally contained three elements. The first element is the transfer of persons with developmental disabilities from institutions to community-based care systems. The second is the effort to prevent new admissions to institutions. The third is the concerted attempt to improve conditions in the institution (Bachrach, 1985).

While deinstitutionalization has decreased the number of persons residing in large custodial facilities, the process has not been without difficulties. In spite of the growth of community-based service systems, during the 1960s and 1970s both persons with developmental disabilities and those with serious psychiatric illness were "dumped" into the community without adequate support services or supervision. During the same period, the lack of community-based services resulted in the admission of persons to institutions.

Institutional reform remains unfinished, but much has been accomplished since the mid 1970s. Implementation of the ICF/MR standards, compliance with the standards of the Accreditation Council on Services for People with Developmental Disabilities, and an emphasis on individualized program planning have accelerated the trend from custodial care toward habilitation and training.

During the period 1977–82 states spent over 1 billion dollars for capital construction and renovation of state institutions primarily to gain and retain federal financial participation through the ICF/MR program (National Association of State Mental Retardation Program Directors, 1980). Advocates for community-based programs argue that, in effect, the ICF/MR consolidated the institutional model of service delivery by encouraging institutional improvement for small numbers of persons with developmental disabilities (Lakin & Bruininks, 1985).

The professional community has generally supported the policy of deinstitutionalization. The reaction of parents has, however, been mixed. Some parents became concerned over new public policy based on normalization and least restrictive environment when the policy was applied to their own children. Many parents believe that the institutional setting offers physical safety, permanence, medical care, and treatment programs (Conroy, 1985; Spreat, Telles, Conroy, Feinstein, & Colombatto, 1987).

Deinstitutionalization has also resulted in varying degrees of social integration in local communities. Preliminary evidence suggests that support services may develop at a slower rate in rural communities than in urban settings. Shalock, Harper, and Genung (1981) noted the lack of mental health services in rural areas. Slater and Black (1986) found that persons with developmental disabilities in rural areas participated in significantly fewer recreation, counseling, and sheltered employment activities than did persons in urban areas.

By the mid 1980s, however, a consensus emerged that persons with developmental disabilities, regardless of the degree of impairment, could best be served in community-based programs (Haney, 1988). Those programs offered the greatest potential for social integration, use of generic services, and employment opportunities. This consensus reflected the decade-long guiding principals of normalization, least restrictive environment, legal rights, and individualized service plans.

The design and operation of quality community service systems has ended the deinstitutionalization debate. To debate deinstitutionalization when community-based service systems meet the specialized needs of persons with developmental disabilities is unnecessary. The debate has shifted to a discussion of how to finance and develop comprehensive community-based programs and how to maintain standards of quality in service delivery.

GROWTH OF COMMUNITY-BASED SERVICES

The institutional census declined from 149,176 in 1977 to 100,421 in 1986 (Braddock, Hemp, & Fujiura, 1987). During this period a gradual decrease occurred in state funding for institutions as federal funding increased. In FY 1977 federal ICF/MR reimbursements represented

24% of institutional spending, but by FY 1986 that figure had grown to 46% (Braddock et al., 1987).

The small (less than 15 person) ICF/MR has played a role in the growth of the community-based service system. Nine states in FY 1986 were budgeting 25% or more of their total ICF/MR resources on the small programs (Braddock et al., 1987). These states included:

Alaska	37%
Connecticut	31%
District of Columbia	48%
Florida	27%
Indiana	44%
Michigan	44%
Minnesota	29%
North Dakota	25%
Rhode Island	45%

In 1982 Lakin and Hill (1984) identified 9,714 residents in small ICF/MR programs. By June 1986 that number had increased to approximately 19,900 persons (Braddock et al., 1987).

In the early 1980s the Home and Community Based Waiver and the Community and Family Living Amendments indicated the commitment to community-based services. The Home and Community Based Waiver permitted states to offer community services through Medicaid to persons who would otherwise require care in an ICF/MR (Gardner, 1986). The Community and Family Living Amendments introduced in Congress in 1983 and supported by the Association for Retarded Citizens of the United States would have phased out Medicaid funding for institutions over a 10- to 15-year period.

Community-based service systems will continue to face significant difficulties through the new century. Wages for community program staff are substandard. The poor salary and the increasing age of the work force combine to produce a shortage of qualified personnel. In addition, the turnover rate remains high, and monitoring the quality of decentralized residential and employment sites can prove difficult.

THE ISSUE OF AGING

During the past decade the American population has grown older. The number of persons age 65 and older increased from 16.7 million in 1960 to 25.9 million in 1980 (Rice & Feldman, 1985). Some national estimates indicate that the number of persons over 65 will double from 25 million currently to 50 million by the year 2025 (Krauss & Seltzer, 1986). While the projections of life span for persons with developmental disabilities are uncertain, there is general agreement that their increased longevity will be similar to that of the general population.

Some question remains, however, about the extent to which the aging process is complicated by the presence of a developmental disability and whether older persons with developmental disabilities have different needs and service requirements from their younger counterparts. The uncertainty is caused, in part, by a lack of uniformity in the definition of "elderly" or an agreed-upon age for the elderly. During the last decade, however, numerous researchers have begun to address the program issues raised by an increasing number of persons who are both elderly and developmentally disabled.

A distinct possibility exists that both small and large facilities during the next decades will address the needs of persons who are both significantly more disabled and older than their counterparts in the 1970s. Yet whether aging people with developmental disabilities currently need, or in the future will require, highly structured residential settings is not at all clear.

Different patterns of service utilization exist between older and younger persons with developmental disabilities. Elderly persons are more likely to receive specialized medical services, but less likely to be involved in a day program where they would receive physical or occupational therapy and recreational services than younger persons (Krauss & Seltzer, 1986).

Elderly persons with developmental disabilities have fewer residential options than do younger persons. Foster family care, large residential programs, and boarding homes are more frequent service options than semi-independent and independent living for them (Krauss & Seltzer, 1986).

The implication for the ICF/MR program is that the target population for services will become increasingly older during the next decades. The ICF/MR will have to provide active treatment to a population that is older than in the past. The challenge for the ICF/MR is to continue to refine program practices and services to reflect the changing needs of the population.

PHYSICAL HEALTH

The growth in the community-based service system has resulted in many state institutions serving people with considerably more complicated health needs than a decade ago. Those persons now remaining in large ICFs/MR are more severely retarded, have more ambulation and other mobility problems, and have more complicated medical conditions than the institutional population of a decade ago (McDonald, 1985). However, this change is not an argument for institutional care for the medically fragile. Indeed, Hill, Bruininks, and Lakin (1983), in a study of over 2,000 persons with developmental disabilities living in community residential programs or in institutions, found no statistically significant difference in the prevalence of chronic health problems in the two types of facilities.

Ample evidence indicates that for any medically fragile person in an institutional setting, there is a corresponding medically fragile person in an integrated community setting. The issue is not where people with health complications should live; rather, the challenge is to provide the necessary range of coordinated health care that addresses significant needs, such as ongoing monitoring of seizure disorders, physical therapy, and orthopedic interventions for multiple joint contracture, or specialized nutrition protocols (Crocker & Yankauer, 1987).

MENTAL HEALTH NEEDS OF PERSONS WITH MENTAL RETARDATION

The diagnosis of mental health problems among persons with mental retardation remains unclear. Some persons with mental retardation are diagnosed as having a psychiatric illness. Other persons, without a formal diagnosis, display maladaptive behaviors. The problems of diagnosis, classification, and measurement are made more difficult because of the effects of both mental retardation and mental health on behavior and performance (Borthwick, 1988).

Confusion regarding terms such as problem behaviors, maladaptive behaviors, mental illness, and severe emotional disturbance makes it difficult to generalize from studies of behavior among persons with diagnoses of mental retardation and mental illness. Authorities have estimated that 20% to 40% of persons with mental retardation in a range of service programs exhibit serious behavior problems. The rate for more serious behavioral and emotional dysfunction that might yield a diagnosis of mental retardation and mental illness is considerably lower. Various studies have indicated that between 5% and 13% of persons with mental retardation also have a diagnosis of mental illness (Bruininks, Hill, & Morreau, 1988). Some authorities, however, note that over 25% of individuals with mental retardation have a mental illness (Menolascino, Wilson, Golden, & Ruedrich, 1986).

Despite the lack of precision in definitions, professionals agree that serious maladaptive behaviors in persons with mental retardation are related to events and circumstances such as out-of-home placement, reduced opportunities for social integration, decreased prospects for employment, and leisure in community settings.

In addition to the problems of classification and diagnosis and unconnected and uncoordinated service systems, persons with a dual diagnosis become locked into a single service system. Unfortunately, professionals have tended to share many of the same misconceptions and biases toward persons with mental retardation and mental illness as the rest of society. Psychotherapists generally view persons with mental retardation as uninteresting, unattractive, and unresponsive to traditional therapy. Providers of services to persons with mental retardation view persons with mental illness as unpredictable and dangerous.

During the past 20 years, however, a transformation has occurred in the provision of community-based services for both persons with mental illness and those with developmental disabilities. During the 1970s state developmental disabilities administrations began the movement toward community services. A decade later state governments began to alter the patterns of care to persons with mental illness.

In the past decade significant advances in research into the biological basis of mental illness have provided new avenues for treatment and habilitation. Strong evidence of the genetic basis of schizophrenia and other chronic mental illness and the effectiveness of newer psychoactive medications have made community-based service systems more feasible (Menolascino et al., 1986). There is also some evidence that persons with mental retardation often display depressive symptoms of sadness, loneliness, and crying, and that an association exists between low levels of social support and depression among persons with mental retardation (Reiss & Benson, 1985).

The recent research in the causes and management of mental illness and the evolution of state-of-the-art service programs clearly argues against separate service systems for persons with a dual diagnosis. People with a dual diagnosis of mental retardation and mental illness should be supported within the array of service settings for mentally retarded and mentally ill persons (Stark, Menolascino, Albarelli, & Gray, 1988).

THE SUPPORT SERVICE MODEL

During the past two decades the community has replaced the institution as the locus of services to persons with developmental disabilities. The movement from the institution to the community began with the "halfway house" at the institution and progressed through the "group home" to the alternative living unit (apartment). The new models, however, never replaced the more restrictive programs; rather, they became additions to the evolving continuum of services. The continuum approach was based on the belief that persons with the most severe disabilities can be appropriately placed in the more restrictive settings (e.g., a pediatric nursing home). Persons with less severe needs should live in less restrictive settings (e.g., a co-resident apartment). Other persons with disabilities will live in residences spread across the continuum. With proper funding the continuum will be comprehensive with no gaps in service. As people with disabilities gain skills, they would move through the continuum to less restrictive residential services (Davis & Trace, 1982; Minnesota Governor's Planning Council on Developmental Disabilities, 1983).

In reality, the continuum model does not work. Movement along the continuum does not take place. Bruininks, Hauber, and Kudla (1980) found that approximately one half of community residential programs reported no movement in or out in the previous year. In addition, limited state and federal funding results in an underdeveloped continuum, with most of the resources directed toward the most restrictive end. As a result, the continuum becomes blocked.

During the late 1970s and the early 1980s the support service model evolved as an alternative to the continuum. The major design characteristics of this model (Davis & Trace, 1982) are:

1. People are placed in the least restrictive setting and given all the supports needed to succeed.
2. Supports are gradually withdrawn as they are no longer needed.
3. Because the setting is modified to meet their needs, people move less often. More funds go to service rather than to facilities.
4. The use of generic resources is greater.

EVOLUTION OF FAMILY SUPPORT SYSTEMS

The growth of the support services model was particularly evident in the increased focus on family support services (Rowitz, 1985). Family support approaches were consistent with the philosophy of normalization, the deinstitutionalization movement, and mainstreaming in public education. The three guiding principles pointed to the need to keep children at home rather than designing services that substituted for the family. Support for the family rather than substitution for the family characterized the growth of these programs.

By 1983–84 family support programs were identified in 49 of the 50 states (Agosta, Jennings, & Bradley, 1985). The programs either provided money to families to pay for medical and habilitative supplies and services or funded providers to deliver the services.

A major characteristic of the family support programs was the emphasis on an ecological intervention (Weiss, 1984). Families with children with developmental disabilities have many needs and concerns. Some are related to the child's disability; others are not. The child with a developmental disability is approached as a member of a family with a diversity of strengths, resources, and needs. Family functioning cannot be interpreted as a narrow response to a child with a developmental disability. Instead, the response to the child is influenced by the coping resources and support services available to the family (Crnic, Friedrich, & Greenberg, 1983). Extended family and informal social contacts can decrease stress and increase the parents' ability to cope with the needs of a child with a developmental disability.

The family support programs also reflected an important change in the relationship between parents and professionals. A greater willingness to conduct programs *with* families rather than *for* them developed. Professionals recognized the legitimate need for support by families caring for a child or parent with a severe disability. Rather than viewing the impact of the child on the family as a problem, the family was viewed as a potential resource for the child. The family, particularly the parents, emerged as primary partners with the professionals in the provision of service to children with developmental disabilities.

SUPPORTED EMPLOYMENT

By the early 1980s residential services had evolved beyond the institutional setting to a diverse set of options ranging from group homes to apartments, specialized foster care, family support, and independent living. However, no corresponding change was evident in the provision of day habilitation, vocational training, or employment services. Yet within a few years, 1983–85, supported employment emerged as a major service option to persons with developmental disabilities.

Supported employment is defined in the 1984 amendments to the Rehabilitation Act (PL 98-524) as paid employment that is:

1. For persons with developmental disabilities for whom competitive employment is unlikely and who, because of their disabilities, need intensive, ongoing support to perform in a work setting.
2. Conducted in a variety of settings, particularly where persons without disabilities are employed.
3. Supported by an activity needed to sustain the paid work of persons with disabilities, including supervision, training, and transportation.

Most states operating supported employment programs have adopted four additional criteria for supported employment as set forth by the U.S. Department of Education, Office of Special Education and Rehabilitative Services (Jackson & Associates, 1985):

1. *Severe disability.* The supported employment program is intended for those individuals with severe disabilities who need a range of support services to maintain employment. The program and available support services are not designed for persons who might benefit from short-term training that leads to competitive employment.
2. *Ongoing support.* Ongoing support is provided at the place of employment. The supports are necessary to sustain paid employment.
3. *Integration.* Social interaction with peers who are not disabled or paid staff must be frequent. The site meets the test for integration when eight or fewer persons with disabilities work together. The location cannot be adjacent to another disability program, and

nondisabled workers must be present in the work area or the vicinity.

4. *Employment.* The individual must be paid for work. Emphasis is clearly on wages, benefits, working conditions, and work performance rather than on skill development. A regular opportunity to work must be present and the paid work must exceed 20 hours per week (Bellamy, Rhodes, Mank, & Albin, 1988; Gardner, Chapman, Donaldson, & Jacobson, 1988).

The concept and practice of supported employment were adopted so quickly because the foundations were well developed. The first foundation was the evidence that people with severe disabilities were capable of working. Marc Gold demonstrated that university research and training methodologies could be applied in the community (Gold, 1976). The Association for Persons with Severe Handicaps advocated for the development of community programs through new teaching techniques. Finally, Thomas Bellamy and his colleagues at the University of Oregon had designed new vocational training programs for persons with severe mental retardation beginning in the late 1970s (Bellamy et al., 1988).

The second foundation was the realization that many students who entered school as a result of the passage of the Education for All Handicapped Children Act of 1975 (PL 94-142) would soon graduate. Parents and advocates began to ask whether the states were willing to spend large sums of money to educate students and then allow their skills and abilities to atrophy in low expectation workshops and activity centers (Bellamy et al., 1988; Gardner et al., 1988).

The third foundation for supported employment was provided by the emphasis on integration that flowed from the normalization principle, least restrictive environment, and PL 94-142. The concern for the benefits derived from integration, development of social skills, informal supports, and greater learning opportunities led some authors to argue for placement in community jobs as an alternative to the traditional vocational rehabilitation service (Rusch, 1986; Wehman, 1981).

The fourth foundation was the realization that the concepts of preparation for, sequenced skill development, exit criteria, and flow-through actually presented barriers to movement through the vocational continuum (Gardner et al., 1988).

1. *Preparation for.* Day programs adopted the educational premise that the purpose of the program was to prepare the person for the next level program. Continual training (preparation for) became an end in itself.

2. *Sequenced skill development.* An assumption existed that skill development was sequential and that the next skill in the chain was the skill to be learned. The deficit automatically became the learning objective, even if other ways were present to accomplish

the functional task. The assumption was commonplace that counting, money recognition, and sight vocabulary were necessary preemployment skills.

3. *Exit criteria.* The day programs established exit criteria, and it became incumbent upon the individual to earn his or her way out of the program. Rather than focus on the requirements of specific jobs in the community and teach those skills, the day activity centers stressed the skills needed to exit the program.

4. *Flow-through.* People seldom successfully prepared for the next level program, learned the sequence of skills, and exited from one program to a less restrictive program. The flow-through to employment became blocked. Bellamy and associates estimated that an individual who entered the continuum at age 21 would emerge from the continuum at age 77 (Bellamy et al., 1988).

Even as the evidence accumulated that the continuum did not work, the states were expending considerable money in the programs. Between 1979 and 1984 the number of people in day programs funded through state mental retardation and developmental disabilities administrations increased from 105,000 to 185,000. This represents a 76% increase over a 5-year period. At the same time the per capita costs of the programs increased 65% from $3,000 to $4,963 (Bellamy et al., 1988). State mental retardation and developmental disability agencies approached supported employment as an alternative to continued increases in resources for traditional day programs.

CONCLUSION

During the 1980s the emphasis on deinstitutionalization faded as the growth of community-based services pointed to the future of programs for people with developmental disabilities. However, in approaching the last decade of the century, the problems of low salary, shortages of labor, high turnover, and management of decentralized programs must be resolved.

Also during the 1980s a renewed emphasis focused on persons who are both elderly and developmentally disabled, as well as persons with physical health problems and those with a dual diagnosis of mental retardation and mental illness. The ICF/MR in the next decade will be providing services to a relatively greater number of these people than in the past. Active treatment and other program protocols will need to be calibrated to meet the needs of the changing population.

The ICF/MR program, with greater flexibility in provision of services, will be challenged to incorporate the support service model. The successful linkage of active treatment and the support service model will maintain the ICF/MR program during the 1990s.

REFERENCES

Agosta, J., Jennings, D., & Bradley, V. (1985). Statewide family support programs: National Survey results. In J. M. Agosta & V. J. Bradley (Eds.), *Family care for persons with developmental disabilities: A growing commitment* (pp. 94–112). Boston: Human Services Research Institute.

Bachrach, L. L. (1985). Deinstitutionalization: The meaning of the least restrictive environment. In R. H. Bruininks & K. C. Lakin (Eds.), *Living and learning in the least restrictive environment* (pp. 23–36). Baltimore: Paul H. Brookes Publishing Co.

Bellamy, G. T., Rhodes, L. E., Mank, D. M., & Albin, J. M. (1988). *Supported employment: A community implementation guide.* Baltimore: Paul H. Brookes Publishing Co.

Borthwick, S. A. (1988). Section 1: Epidemiology introduction. In J. A. Stark, F. J. Menolascino, M. H. Albarelli, & V. C. Grey (Eds.), *Mental retardation and mental health: Classification, diagnosis, treatment, services* (p. 1). New York: Springer-Verlag.

Braddock, D., Hemp, R., & Fujiura, G. (1987). National study of public spending for mental retardation and developmental disabilities. *American Journal of Mental Deficiency, 92*(2), 121–133.

Bruininks, R. H., Hauber, F. A., & Kudla, M. J. (1980). National survey of community residential facilities: A profile of facilities and residents in 1977. *American Journal of Mental Deficiency, 84*(5), 470–478.

Bruininks, R. H., Hill, B. K., & Morreau, L. E. (1988). Prevalence and implications of maladaptive behaviors and dual diagnosis in residential and other service programs. In J. A. Stark, F. J. Menolascino, M. H. Albarelli, & V. C. Grey (Eds.), *Mental retardation and mental health: Classification, diagnosis, treatment, services* (pp. 3–29), New York: Springer-Verlag.

Conroy, J. (1985). Medical needs of institutionalized mentally retarded persons: Perceptions of families and staff members. *American Journal of Mental Deficiency, 89*(5), 510–514.

Crnic, K. A., Friedrich, W. N., & Greenberg, M. T. (1983). Adaptation of families with mentally retarded children: A model of stress, coping, and family ecology. *American Journal of Mental Deficiency, 88*(2), 125–138.

Crocker, A. C., & Yankauer, A. (1987). Basic issues. *Mental Retardation, 25*(4), 227–232.

Davis, M. J., & Trace, M. W. (1982). *The support model: A new approach to providing a continuum of service.* Unpublished manuscript, Ellsworth Community College.

Gardner, J. F. (1986). Implementation of the home and community based waiver. *Mental Retardation, 24*(1), 18–26.

Gardner, J. F., Chapman, M. S., Donaldson, G., & Jacobson, S. (1988). *Toward supported employment: A process guide for planned change.* Baltimore: Paul H. Brookes Publishing Co.

Gold, M. (1976). Task analysis of a complex assembly task by the retarded blind. *Exceptional Children, 43*(0), 78–84.

Haney, J. I. (1988). Empirical support for deinstitutionalization. In L. W. Heal, J. I. Haney, & A. R. Novak Amado (Eds.), *Integration of developmentally disabled individuals into the community* (pp. 37–58). Baltimore: Paul H. Brookes Publishing Co.

Hill, B. K., Bruininks, R. H., & Lakin, K. C. (1983). Characteristics of mentally retarded people in residential facilities. *Health and Social Work, 8*, 85–96.

Jackson & Associates. (1985). *Executive summary, National Leadership Institute on Supported Employment.* Unpublished paper, Olympia, Washington.

Krauss, M. W., & Seltzer, M. M. (1986). Comparison of elderly and adult mentally retarded persons in community and institutional settings. *American Journal of Mental Deficiency, 91*(3), 237–243.

Lakin, K. C., & Bruininks, R. H. (1985). Social integration of developmentally disabled persons. In K. C. Lakin & R. H. Bruininks (Eds.), *Strategies for achieving community integration of developmentally disabled citizens* (pp. 3–25). Baltimore: Paul H. Brookes Publishing Co.

Lakin, K. C., & Hill, B. K. (1984). *Expansion of the Medicaid ICF/MR program over a five-year period, 1977–82.* (Working paper 25.) Minneapolis: University of Minnesota, Center for Residential and Community Services, Department of Educational Psychology.

McDonald, E. P. (1985). Medical needs of severely developmentally disabled persons residing in the community. *American Journal of Mental Deficiency, 90*(2), 171–176.

Menolascino, F. J., Wilson, J., Golden, C. J., & Ruedrich, S. L. (1986). Medication and treatment of schizophrenia in persons with mental retardation. *Mental Retardation, 24*(5), 277–283.

Minnesota Governor's Planning Council on Developmental Disabilities. (1983). *Developmental disabilities and public policy: A review for policy makers.* St. Paul, Minnesota: The Governor's Planning Council on Developmental Disabilities.

National Association of State Mental Retardation Program Directors. (1980). *Trends in capital expenditures for mental retardation facilities: A state by state survey.* Arlington, VA: Author.

Reiss, S., & Benson, B. A. (1985). Psychosocial correlates of depression in mentally retarded adults: 1. Minimal social support and stigmatization. *American Journal of Mental Deficiency, 89*(4), 331–337.

Rice, D. P., & Feldman, J. J. (1985). Living longer in the United States: Demographic changes and health needs of the elderly. In M. P. Janicki and H. M. Wisniewski (Eds.), *Aging and developmental disabilities: Issues and approaches.* Baltimore: Paul H. Brookes Publishing Co.

Rowitz, L. (1985). Social support: The issue for the 1980's. *Mental retardation, 23*(4), 165–167.

Rusch, F. R. (1986). *Competitive employment issues and strategies.* Baltimore: Paul H. Brookes Publishing Co.

Schalock, R. L., Harper, R. S., & Genung, T. (1981). Community integration of mentally retarded adults: Community placement and program success. *American Journal of Mental Deficiency, 85*(5), 478–488.

Slater, M. A., & Black, P. B. (1986). Urban-rural differences in the delivery of community services: Wisconsin as a case in point. *Mental Retardation, 24*(3), 153–161.

Spreat, S., Telles, J. L., Conroy, J. W., Feinstein, C., & Colombatto, J. (1987). Attitudes toward deinstitutionalization: National survey of families of institutionalized persons with mental retardation. *Mental Retardation, 25*(5), 267–274.

Stark, J. A., Menolascino, F. J., Albarelli, M. H., & Grey, V. C. (1988). Executive summary. In J. A. Stark, F. J. Menolascino, M. H. Albarelli, & V. C. Grey (Eds.), *Mental retardation and mental health: Classification, diagnosis, treatment, services* (pp. xi–xviii). New York: Springer-Verlag.

Wehman, P. (1981). *Competitive employment: New horizons for severely disabled individuals.* Baltimore: Paul H. Brookes Publishing Co.

Weiss, H. B. (1984). Preface. In C. Payne (Ed.), *Programs to strengthen families: A resource guide* (pp. 1–6). Chicago: Family Resource Coalition.

2
Legal Rights of Persons with Developmental Disabilities

Larry J. Goldberg

The legal rights of persons with developmental disabilities arise under federal and state statutory and constitutional law and administrative regulations. The rights of individuals with developmental disabilities to treatment in the least restrictive environment, to safety, to education, and to freedom from undue restraint have been the subject of many federal and state lawsuits since the early 1970s. The constitutional rights of institutionalized persons with mental illness or mental retardation, first established by the courts at that time, (see *O'Connor v. Donaldson, 1975; Wyatt v. Stickney,* 1971), were further defined by the United States Supreme Court a decade later (see *Halderman v. Pennhurst,* 1981, 1984; *Youngberg v. Romeo,* 1982).

This chapter focuses on the civil rights of persons in intermediate care facilities for the mentally retarded (ICFs/MR). It examines judicial interpretation of these rights and the implications of these rights for providers of services to persons with developmental disabilities residing in ICFs/MR. As the provision of services to persons with developmental disabilities has improved, their legal rights have become more narrowly defined and more carefully regulated.

BACKGROUND

The legal rights of persons with developmental disabilities rest in the United States Constitution, in federal and state statutes and regula-

---

The opinions expressed herein are those of the author and do not necessarily reflect any official position of the Maryland Attorney General's Office.

tions, and in case law. Legal rights evolve as the Supreme Court's interpretation of the Constitution changes and as federal and state law is modified.

Constitutional Requirements

The Fourteenth Amendment to the United States Constitution guarantees equal protection and due process rights to persons with developmental disabilities. These constitutional rights form the basis for many of the judicial decisions in the disability area as well as legislation establishing the rights of this group of individuals. Equal protection requires that, despite the mental and physical differences of persons with developmental disabilities, they cannot, on the basis of these differences, be discriminated against or be treated differently from individuals without disabilities. They must have equal access to benefits and services available to citizens generally.

- Individuals in wheelchairs cannot be denied the right to vote because a polling place is not accessible.
- Individuals testing in the profound range of mental retardation cannot be denied training in an ICF/MR because their level of disability is more severe than that of others residing in the facility.
- Deaf children cannot be excluded from receiving an appropriate education because of the absence of interpreters or staff trained in sign language.

Due process requires that individuals be treated fairly and that they be given notice and an opportunity to protest the failure of a state to provide adequately for their rights.

- A person must have a hearing prior to the proposed restriction of his or her liberty.
- Children with handicaps have the right to a hearing prior to any change in their educational placement.
- Prior to commitment to an institution on the basis that a person charged with a crime is not criminally responsible as a result of mental retardation, that individual has the right to a court hearing.

In a residential setting due process would require that an individual receive the type of care or treatment that the facility is intended to provide.

Protection from Inhumane Treatment

In the *Willowbrook* case the plaintiff challenged conditions such as overcrowding, understaffing, and an unsafe environment in Willowbrook State School in New York (*NYSARC v. Carey*, 1975). The court held that individuals residing in a state facility have the right to protection from inhumane treatment, which constitutes cruel and unusual punishment under the Eighth Amendment. This decision found that impermissible treatment existed not just when physical deterioration took place, but when conditions frustrated the full development of a person's capabilities (*NYSARC v. Carey*, 1975). A consent decree was signed in the case that mandated the immediate hiring of additional staff and the improvement of conditions at the institution.

Youngberg v. Romeo

The Supreme Court, in *Youngberg v. Romeo* (1982), further defined the constitutional rights of involuntarily committed residents of a state ICF/MR. These rights include: 1) adequate food, shelter, clothing, and medical care; 2) reasonable personal safety; 3) freedom from undue bodily restraint; and 4) adequate training to ensure the enjoyment of these rights. In addition, decisions regarding these rights must be made by appropriate professionals who are qualified to make such judgments. The issue of a general constitutional right to treatment in the least restrictive environment did not arise in *Youngberg*, as the plaintiff was not pursuing the right to receive treatment in the community.

Post-*Youngberg* cases have further interpreted the constitutional rights of persons in ICFs/MR. In one case (*Thomas S. v. Morrow*, 1986), the court of appeals, in light of *Youngberg*, affirmed the right of a mentally retarded institutionalized adult to a detailed treatment plan, a case manager, suitable support services, and periodic evaluations. Several courts have faulted states for their failure to meet constitutional and federal requirements (see *ARC of North Dakota v. Olson*, 1982; *Clark v. Cohen*, 1985).

STATUTORY REQUIREMENTS

Statutory sources of legal rights include laws and regulations enacted by the United States government, the 50 states, and the territories of the United States. This section focuses on the major laws enacted by the United States government.

The Civil Rights of Institutionalized Persons Act

The Civil Rights of Institutionalized Persons Act (CRIPA) (PL 96-247, 1980) was enacted by Congress in 1980. The statute itself created no substantive rights but granted authority to the United States Attorney General to file a lawsuit when he has reason to believe there is a pattern of flagrant conditions that violates the civil rights of individuals in institutions and causes them grievous harm. The statute covers publicly operated institutions, such as mental health institutions, mental retardation facilities, nursing homes, juvenile facilities, and prisons and jails. The civil rights protected in the statute, for residents of mental retardation facilities, include federal constitutional as well as statutory rights. An example of the latter would be those rights guaranteed by Section 504 of the Rehabilitation Act of 1973 (29 U.S.C § 794, as amended) that prohibits discrimination on the basis of handicap.

The resolution of cases involving ICFs/MR under CRIPA has included the negotiation of consent decrees. These decrees give the state the opportunity to correct voluntarily deficient conditions identified by the Attorney General. Such decrees have been negotiated in Maryland, Colorado, Connecticut, and Louisiana. Where the federal and state governments have failed to come to an agreement, lawsuits have been filed. (This has occurred in Oregon and New Mexico.)

Section 504 of the Rehabilitation Act of 1973

Title V of the Rehabilitation Act of 1973 (PL 93-112, 1973) has been described as the civil rights act for individuals with disabilities. Its protection is similar to that established by the equal protection clause of the Constitution. It imposes affirmative action and nondiscrimination requirements on public and private employers, educators, and service providers. Section 504 of the act offers the broadest protection of the rights of individuals with disabilities:

> No otherwise qualified individual in the United States shall, solely by reason of his handicap, be excluded from the participation in, be denied the benefits of, or be subjected to discrimination under any program or activity receiving federal financial assistance or under any program or activity conducted by any Executive agency . . .

The act prohibits discrimination on the basis of handicap in programs that receive federal financial assistance, including educational institutions, hospitals, ICFs/MR, and many others. The act and the implementing regulations (45 C.F.R. Part 84) establish no right to treatment in ICFs/MR where none previously existed. But they do require that recipients of federal financial assistance provide effective benefits or services in a manner that does not limit or have the effect of limiting the participation of qualified handicapped people in the program. Further, adjustments to programs must be made to accommodate individuals' disabilities. At least one case has held that discrimination on the basis of severity of handicap in an ICF/MR is a violation of Section 504 (*Garrity v. Gallen*, 1981).

The Education for All Handicapped Children Act

The Education for All Handicapped Children Act (PL 94-142, 1975) requires public school systems to provide a free, appropriate public education to handicapped children, ages 3 to 21. It provides states with money for special education and imposes clear procedural due process and substantive requirements on how that special education should be provided. The law covers children who need special education and related services because of their handicaps. It includes those with mental retardation, deafness, visual impairments, serious emotional disturbances, chronic health problems, and other impairments and disabilities. Under the act every handicapped child has a right to specifically designed instruction to meet his or her unique needs. The act also includes the right to related services that may be necessary to help the child benefit from the special program. Moreover, this education must take place in the least restrictive environment.

To the maximum extent appropriate, handicapped children must be educated with children who are not handicapped (i.e., mainstreamed), thereby eliminating the stigma of being educated separately. Special classes and special school placements are appropriate only when the handicap is of such nature or severity that placement in regular classes with the use of supplementary aids and services will not meet the educational needs of the child satisfactorily. This requirement has had a positive impact. Children who previously were forced to reside in institutions due to lack of services are ensured a greater opportunity to receive those services in a regular educational setting.

The school system must devise an appropriate individualized education program (IEP) for each handicapped child. The IEP is a written report that identifies and assesses the child's disability, establishes long- and short-term learning goals, and states which services the school must provide to help the child achieve them. Parents have the due process right to appeals and hearings regarding any decision made about their child's educational placement, program, or services. This includes the right of access to all records used by the school to make placement decisions regarding the child.

Several court cases have interpreted the rights of children under this act. In one case the court relied on the statute to support many of its orders establishing the educational and training rights of children in that state's ICF/MR (*Garrity v. Gallen*, 1981). In another the Supreme Court held that a free, appropriate public education was not one that maximized a child's potential but rather guaranteed some benefit from the child's IEP (*Board of Education v. Rowley*, 1982). More recently the Supreme Court held that no change in placement could occur until all due process protections had been accorded the parents and child. This was true even in the case of a dangerous or disruptive emotionally disturbed child, if that behavior was the result of that child's handicap (*Honig v. Doe*, 1988).

The Developmental Disabilities Assistance and Bill of Rights Act

The Developmental Disabilities Assistance and Bill of Rights Act (PL 94-103, 1975; PL 95-602, 1978) was designed to fund and provide services to more than 2 million persons with developmental disabilities, including severe mental or physical impairments, that begin in childhood. A 1978 amendment expanded the rights accorded under the statute to individuals who became disabled prior to the age of 22. The act provides assistance to states, through a system that coordinates, monitors, plans, and evaluates services to persons with developmental disabilities in order to protect their legal rights. It requires the development of individualized habilitation plans (IHPs) and annual review of these plans. The IHPs are similar to the individual program plans (IPPs) mandated in the ICF/MR regulation and include both short- and long-term goals, measurable behavioral objectives, a description of how these objectives will be achieved, the services to be provided, and the duration of each service. Further, the act created and funds state protection and advocacy (P&A) programs to ensure the legal rights of this group.

The Supreme Court ruled that the Developmentally Disabled Assistance and Bill of Rights Act did not provide a legal basis for a general right to treatment in the least restrictive environment. The "bill of rights" in the act, providing for appropriate treatment, services, and habilitation, was not viewed as a mandatory requirement on states (*Halderman v. Pennhurst*, 1981) (*Pennhurst I*). (In the case of *Halderman v. Pennhurst* [1984] [*Pennhurst II*], the Supreme Court declared that while state law might provide a legal basis for such a general right to treatment, federal courts could not enforce state law. Prior to the question of a general constitutional right to treatment being considered by the Supreme Court in *Pennhurst*, all parties in the case reached a settlement agreement that was entered by the federal district court in Pennsylvania.)

Social Security Act

The Social Security Act provides funding for intermediate care facilities, including those that serve persons with mental retardation and related conditions. ICFs/MR may qualify to be certified by the state and receive funding from the state and the Health Care Financing Administration (HCFA) of the United States Department of Health and Human Services (HHS), as part of the Medicaid program (Section 1905(d) of the Social Security Act, 42 U.S.C. §1396d(d)). In order to do so, they must comply with certain conditions of participation and standards set by HCFA. These standards are set forth in regulations recently amended by HHS, which became effective on October 3, 1988 (see 53 Fed. Reg. 20448, 1988). The conditions focus on the provision of active treatment, clients rights and protections, administrative services, physical environment, and safety and sanitation.

Compliance with Other HHS Regulations

In addition to compliance with the ICF/MR regulation, facilities must also meet the requirements of other HHS regulations pertaining to nondiscrimination on the basis of race, color, or national origin

(45 C.F.R. Part 80), nondiscrimination on the basis of handicap (45 C.F.R. Part 84), and nondiscrimination of the basis of age (45 C.F.R. Part 91). These regulations are particularly relevant to persons in ICFs/MR, in that such factors often give rise to differentiation of treatment among this group. While the other sections do not constitute conditions of participation, the violation of any of their provisions may jeopardize continued federal financial assistance.

REVIEW OF THE STANDARDS

483.420(a) *Protection of clients' rights*
483.420(b) *Client finances*
483.420(c) *Communication with clients, parents, and guardians*
483.420(d) *Staff treatment of clients*

The conditions of participation and the standards for the ICF/MR program are set forth in a federal regulation enacted under the authority of the Social Security Act. The ICF/MR standards, particularly the sections on active treatment, behavior management, and the physical environment have a direct impact on rights. However, this chapter focuses on the legal rights, constitutional requirements, and the federal statute related to the "bill of rights" condition of participation. In addition, many of the suggested program requirements for quality habilitation programs and protection of rights are derived from sources and requirements other than the ICF/MR regulation.

The ICF/MR regulation concerning legal rights covers four sections. The first section, "Protection of Clients' Rights," discusses what the facility is required to do to protect rights, covering issues of consent, financial management, abuse, privacy, pay for work, communication, and personal possessions.

The section on finances describes requirements for accounting for client personal funds, the prohibition of commingling client funds, and financial documentation.

The standards concerning communication cover families, friends, visits, leaves, and notifications.

The standard on staff treatment of clients covers policy and procedure concerning abuse, prohibition of punishment, and allegations and investigations of abuse.

APPLICATION

The ICF/MR regulation addresses issues similar to those covered in legal proceedings. As a result of both legal proceedings and federal regulations, a specific recognition of individual rights has emerged which pertains to persons living in both large and small residential facilities regardless of funding sources, in the following areas:

- Adequate staffing, in terms of both numbers and qualifications
- Medical care
- Psychiatric treatment
- Behavioral training
- Medication policies and practices
- Record keeping
- Appropriate use of seclusion, restraint, and time-out
- The right to be free from physical harm
- Adequate sanitation
- Implementation of adequate life safety measures

In addition, the issues of consent, guardianship, and discrimination have been the subject of great concentration in recent professional literature, as well as in case law.

Right to Safe Conditions of Confinement

One issue addressed in *Youngberg* is the right to liberty guaranteed by the Fourteenth Amendment to the United States Constitution. This right includes safe conditions of confinement. Harm to an individual's well-being arises from several potential deficiencies that might be found within an ICF/MR.

First, harm might result from too few direct and professional care staff. It can also result from staff who are not trained or qualified to provide necessary care or to develop and implement treatment and training programs. The inability of an inadequate or untrained staff to manage violent and self-abusive behaviors often leads to the inadequate supervision of individuals, resulting in injuries, abuse, and neglect. Inadequate or untrained staff in each of the professional disciplines has its own specific impact:

1. Inadequate psychology staff may result in the failure to evaluate clients, design appropriate behavioral treatment or training programs, and instruct staff on how to implement programs, and ultimately in a lack of professionally designed treatment and training programs.
2. Inadequate and/or untrained psychiatry staff may result in the inability to diagnose concomitant mental disorders, prescribe appropriate medications, monitor their use, and detect and act upon adverse side effects of medication.
3. An inadequate number of nurses or untrained nurses may result in the failure to do appropriate health care surveillance or to diagnose illness and disease on a timely basis.
4. The lack of staff trained in physical, occupational, recreational, and speech therapy may result in clients not receiving services that are essential to improve their conditions and often leads to deterioration or risk of harm to the the clients' personal safety.

The lack of adequate treatment and training programs may also threaten individuals' safety by causing acutely aggressive, self-injurious, or violent behaviors, often resulting in physical injury to staff or other individuals. Inadequate individualized programs can also result in the undue use of mechanical and chemical restraints and seclusion without the exercise of professional judgments. This occurs when they are used as a substitute for treatment and training programs, for punishment, or for the convenience of staff.

The lack of adequate health care can cause injuries and accidents. It can also result in the failure to detect illness in a timely manner and to provide access to specialized medical services.

Inadequate health care can also lead to the inappropriate use of psychotropic medications and to the improper use of medications as a chemical restraint to subdue inappropriate or annoying behavior or for the convenience of staff. In addition, substandard health care often leads to the inconsistent monitoring of medications, thereby exposing individuals to dangerous side effects, such as tardive dyskinesia.

The lack of adequate health care often causes poor sanitary practices such as the lack of appropriate feeding, toileting, and food temperatures, which may result in infection, illness, and the spread of disease.

Risks to an individual's safety may also arise from the failure to record data, monitor identified medical and psychiatric conditions, and document the use of restraint, time-out, or seclusion. Finally, poor documentation causes a lack of information necessary to make professional and safe decisions regarding the care of individuals.

Right to Freedom from Undue Bodily Restraint

Individuals with developmental disabilities have an independent constitutional right, according to *Youngberg*, to be free from the unreasonable use of bodily restraints. This right would prohibit the undue use of:

- Mechanical restraint
- Chemical restraint
- Time-out

These techniques may be used only to the extent that professional judgment deems them necessary for the reasonable safety of individuals and staff or to provide needed treatment and training.

Right to Adequate Food, Clothing, Shelter, and Medical Care

The right of individuals with developmental disabilities to adequate food, clothing, shelter, and medical care has been established in *Youngberg* and other case law. Individuals must be provided with:

- Adequate nutrition and eating skills
- Appropriate clothing
- A physical environment that provides for minimally adequate fire safety
- Medical care for all medical conditions requiring treatment, including specialized services, such as physical and occupational therapy

---

Program Checklist

		Yes	No
1.	An official in-service training program exists for all residential, day, and specialized clinical service staff.	—	—
2.	All staff can identify and implement policies and procedures concerning behavior management responses to aggressive, self-injurious, or violent behavior.	—	—
3.	Uniform policy, procedure, and format for data collection and record keeping throughout the facility are in place.	—	—
4.	Staff are trained to recognize illness and adverse reactions to medications.	—	—

Right to Treatment

The major distinction between the constitutional rights guaranteed in *Youngberg* and those required for continued participation in the Medicaid program is the type of treatment to be provided to clients in ICF/MR facilities. *Youngberg* requires adequate treatment and training to ensure an individual's personal safety and freedom from undue bodily restraints. For example, if an individual engages in behaviors that inflict harm upon himself or herself, such as biting, head banging, or scratching, that individual must receive appropriate training to avoid those particular behaviors. An individual must also be trained in self-care skills such as toileting, dressing, or feeding, when necessary to prevent abuse or reduce aggressive behaviors.

The ICF/MR regulation, however, requires, as a condition for participation, active treatment services defined as follows:

(a) Each client must receive a continuous active treatment program, which includes aggressive, consistent implementation of a program of specialized and generic training, treatment, health service and related services . . . that is directed toward—
(i) The acquisition of behaviors necessary for the client to function with as much self-determination and independence as possible; and
(ii) The prevention or deceleration of regression or loss of current optimal functional status (45 C.F.R. §483.440(a)).

This requirement could potentially encompass a whole range of services for an individual including, for example, rehabilitation, medical, behavioral, social, and personal care services if these are deemed necessary for the particular individual to achieve as much independence as possible.

Thus, the requirements in the ICF/MR statute and standards as they relate to active treatment far exceed the constitutional requirements in this area.

Program Checklist

	Yes	No
1. Individuals are provided programs and training to remove the need for restraint and time-out procedures.	___	___
2. Individuals are trained in self-care skills necessary to prevent abuse or prevent aggressive behaviors.	___	___
3. Individuals in the facility receive the full range of services as set forth in the IPP.	___	___
4. Sufficient staff provide the services set forth in the IPP of individuals in the facility.	___	___

Informed Consent, Guardianship, and Confidentiality

Additional issues involving people with developmental disabilities affect ICF/MR providers on a daily basis and must be systematically addressed. These include issues related to informed consent, guardianship, confidentiality, and discrimination.

Informed consent requires that prior to medical treatment an individual has the right to understand the procedure and to be warned about any significant risks or dangers related to it. This enables the person to make an intelligent and informed choice about whether to undergo such treatment. The active treatment regulations stipulate that an individual program plan can be conducted only with the written informed consent of the individual, parents (if the child is a minor), or legal guardian. The doctrine of informed consent implies that the individual to receive the treatment or therapy is competent to give consent. Once individuals reach the age of majority, they are assumed to be their own guardian, with the ability to make informed choices concerning their welfare and finances. Persons with a developmental disability will often be capable of making informed choices about aspects of their care in an ICF/MR.

An issue that arises for many adults without guardians, who cannot give informed consent in particular situations, is what procedure can be carried out to comply with these regulations. Various states have established different procedures to accomplish this purpose. Such procedures can include:

- Formal guardianship proceedings, where an individual or state agency is appointed guardian of the person
- Limited guardianship, which gives the guardian the right to make decisions only as to particular types of procedures or treatment
- Substituted consent provisions, where particular family members, although not formal guardians, may in certain instances give consent to the initiation of particular medical treatment
- Consideration by a state designated agency
- Surrogate decision-making committees, comprised of individuals similar to those who often constitute human rights committees

In case of emergencies where a person's life is threatened, state laws frequently provide that medical care may be provided, without informed consent, upon the certification of the physician that exigent circumstances exist. Under the ICF/MR regulation, informed consent is required not only for medical treatment but also for the participation in research activities, the initiation of behavioral programs to manage inappropriate behavior, and the implementation of programs or practices that potentially abridge client protections or rights.

All records must be kept confidential, and facilities must establish procedures for the release of information upon the consent of the individual, parent, or guardian, where applicable. State law may establish additional situations where release of confidential information may be appropriate and may often authorize release of information to human rights or medical review committees, providers of services to the individuals, licensing agencies, state agencies, and protection and advocacy agencies.

A current issue concerning confidentiality is whether information regarding an individual who has tested positive for the human immunodeficiency virus (HIV) or who has acquired immune deficiency syndrome (AIDS) should be shared with staff working with that individual. A person's right to confidentiality would require that information related to an individual's AIDS status not be shared unless essential for treatment. If that information were shared unnecessarily, the person could be subject to neglect or to discriminatory treatment within the ICF/MR. In a Supreme Court case involving contagious diseases, the Court ruled that such conditions are covered under the antidiscrimination provisions of section 504 of the Rehabilitation Act (School Board of Nassau County, Florida v. Arline, 1987). This decision has a significant impact on individuals with AIDS, who could not be discriminated against in a federally funded program on the basis of such a diagnosis, as long as they meet the requirements for participation in the program. Thus in those circumstances an individual cannot be denied treatment or other services solely on the basis of an AIDS diagnosis, whether or not the person has symptoms of the disease (see opinion of the Office of Legal Counsel, Department of Justice, September 17, 1988).

Program Checklist

		Yes	No
1.	The facility has a written policy and procedure concerning informed consent for adults without guardians.	___	___
2.	All staff can identify situations where informed consent is required.	___	___
3.	The facility has a written policy and procedure concerning contagious diseases and confidentiality.	___	___

Facility Strategies for Promoting Rights

The wide attention focused on the rights of individuals with developmental disabilities by the courts, federal and state legislatures, and administrative agencies makes clear that the protection of these rights is of grave concern. This is true particularly as a result of the vulnerability of these individuals. All providers of services to individuals with developmental disabilities should understand client rights. More importantly, they must promote these rights for each individual residing in the ICF/MR.

Staff Training Programs

To best achieve the protection of individual rights, staff must be trained in the requirements imposed by federal and state statutes and regulations. Orientation and continuing education training should include sessions on individual rights and the staff's responsibility to assist in the promotion and protection of these rights. Staff shall be informed of changes in facility policies and procedures, particularly in the area of physical and chemical restraints, to ensure that implementation is appropriate and consistent with professional judgment. Staff should also be familiar with the active treatment programs of the individuals for whom they are responsible. Allegations of rights violations occur frequently because an individual's program plan is implemented inappropriately.

Finally, training should include functional methods of implementing individuals' rights. Training and skill testing in the physical management of clients should be demonstrated to ensure client safety.

Reporting Violations of Rights

In order to facilitate individual rights, staff must know what action is a violation and the procedure for reporting allegations of violations. A fundamental right protected by the ICF/MR regulation is the right to be free from abuse. Abuse can include physical injury, psychological abuse, inhumane treatment, or sexual abuse. Allegations of abuse might arise as a result of observed, witnessed, or admitted activity. In addition, such allegations are appropriate when a physical injury or condition, either alone or in conjunction with other circumstantial evidence, would lead a reasonable person to believe that the injury or sexual activity had been inflicted intentionally or because of gross negligence.

Allegations of abuse may also result from mental abuse, a form of inhumane treatment. Mental abuse of an individual with a developmental disability consists of treatment that shows an intent to inflict physical or mental suffering, such as taunting the individual about some aspect of the disability such as speech, intelligence, or motor development. Suspected incidents of violations of rights should be reported immediately to the director or appropriate facility personnel. An internal investigation and/or one conducted by an appropriate state agency should be initiated. In cases of abuse, reports to a law enforcement agency are advisable and generally required by state law. The ICF/MR regulation requires appropriate corrective action to be taken in all cases where allegations of violations are sustained.

The Human Rights Committee

Human rights committees frequently advise facilities concerning the legal and human rights of individuals with developmental disabilities. These committees review policies and procedures of the facility to ensure that they do not infringe on the rights of individuals. The committee can advise the director as to whether state law and regulations are being appropriately implemented at the facility. The human rights committee will also review behavior management programs and incidents of restraint, exclusion from programs, or abuse. Finally, the committee can provide a forum relating to an individual's rights for the individual, staff, advocates, and other interested persons. Members of these committees may include consumers/families; professional, administrative, and direct care staff; and members of community or advocacy organizations, including attorneys.

Human rights committees often have the authority to make recommendations to the director of a facility concerning issues affecting individuals' legal rights. For example, if a grievance system is in place, an individual client may file a complaint with the rights committee. The committee then meets to review the complaint and ultimately makes a recommendation to the director. If the director fails to take the action recommended by the committee, an appeal system may be in place, with final authority resting with the director of the state agency responsible for the operation of the service delivery program. These committees fulfill a useful role by providing an independent mechanism to review the actions of the facility, to resolve alleged rights violations, and ultimately to ensure the protection of individual rights.

Advocates and Access to Legal Representation

The federal Developmental Disabilities Act establishes a state protection and advocacy system to ensure the legal rights of individuals with developmental disabilities. The law requires that individuals be educated regarding their right to counsel or independent advocacy and that the facility provide the opportunity and privacy to consult with advocates and/or attorneys. Advocates include individuals who develop a one-to-one relationship with particular individuals, as well as representatives from volunteer associations. These advocates foster communication with administrative, professional, and direct care staff, as well as human rights committees. They also ensure that individual programs are implemented and that people are treated in a way that promotes their safety and well-being and is consistent with existing legal protections.

Attorneys play an essential role, particularly when informal advocacy efforts fail. Advocating on behalf of individuals with developmental disabilities, they may be found in state protection and advocacy agencies and in legal aid and public defender offices. These attorneys serve an important role in representing individuals in any team meetings or administrative hearings related to placement or treatment issues, in judicial proceedings in the event the person is a juvenile, or when the individual is involved in guardianship or criminal proceedings.

Program Checklist

		Yes	No
1.	Staff can demonstrate safe physical management of individuals.	___	___
2.	Staff can identify actions that constitute violations of individual rights.	___	___
3.	The facility has a written policy and procedure for reporting allegations of abuse.	___	___
4.	The facility supports an active and involved human rights committee.	___	___
5.	A majority of the members of the human rights committee are community representatives.	___	___
6.	The facility promotes access and communication between individuals with developmental disabilities and advocates from outside the ICF/MR.	___	___

IMPLICATIONS

For Administrators

Policies and procedures, particularly in the area of individuals' rights, must be developed by ICF/MR administrators. Further, professional and direct care staff must be informed of these policies and procedures to ensure their effective implementation. One area of individuals' rights addressed by *Youngberg* and the ICF/MR regulation is safety and protection from unreasonable risks of harm. This right has several components. In ensuring that individuals are not subject to abuse or punishment (45 C.F.R. §483.420) the facility must have a system to:

- Train staff in management of persons with developmental disabilities
- Ensure the reporting of abuse allegations
- Investigate allegations of abuse
- Analyze incident and injury patterns
- Monitor staff treatment of clients
- Follow up on patterns of abuse
- Implement mechanisms to correct deficiencies
- Inform family members of incidents of alleged abuse

In addition, the facility must have written policies and procedures on the use of drugs and physical restraint, confidentiality, and access to individuals' files and information. Administrators must also ensure adequate professional and direct care staff in an ICF/MR to carry out the mission of the facility. A sufficient number of physicians, nurses, therapists, psychologists, psychiatrists, and direct care staff must provide an appropriate array of services.

Staff must have the ability to implement the goals and objectives of the professional services as part of the individual's daily experience. Specialized clinical staff should provide training to other staff, and training should be available to weekend and other shift staff.

Direct care staff should be precluded from performing support services such as laundry, housekeeping, or cooking chores that might lead to the neglect of individual clients, as demonstrated by unattended clients in need of intervention, services, or toileting.

Finally, sufficient staff must be available to supervise and monitor individuals. Numbers alone are not the key. Rather, the facility must have the ability to organize and evaluate individual needs and make staff available to meet them.

Administrators must also ensure that individuals live in the least restrictive grouping in keeping with their levels of functioning. The facility must ensure that individuals of extremely different ages are not grouped together, thus impeding appropriate training and posing a threat to the safety of younger more vulnerable persons. Physically handicapped persons should be grouped together only if they have the same skill levels, consistent with the requirements of Section 504 of the Rehabilitation Act.

For Specialized Service Staff

Specialized service staff, as part of the interdisciplinary team, should develop active treatment and training programs. The specialized service staff should train the day and residential staff to implement all aspects of active treatment relevant to their provision of effective services.

Competent professionals, sufficient in number, must be hired to deliver services and interventions. The qualified mental retardation professional (QMRP) has primary responsibility for coordinating the individual's IPP. The QMRP must monitor the program itself in addition to the paperwork.

The facility must ensure adequate communication between and among staff regarding individuals' medical treatment and training needs. Specialized service staff must provide necessary information to direct care staff to carry out the individuals' active treatment program on the unit. The communication must also alert staff to health care risks and other issues on behalf of the individual. For example, some procedure must exist to inform staff on the residential unit of events in the work environment so they can be prepared for particular types of behavior or activity of the individual.

The facility must provide adequate medical care to all individuals. Health care staff must take adequate measures to protect clients and prevent illness, disease, and injury. Direct care staff must be trained by professional health care staff to recognize indicators of illness, disease, and injury.

The ICF/MR must ensure that bodily restraints and time-out procedures are endorsed by a qualified professional and administered safely. The ICF/MR must prevent the practice of using restrictive techniques more frequently in units where staffing is not optimal or where there is frequent staff turnover. Restraints should not be used due to deficiencies in staff and programs.

When emergency measures are necessary, staff must attempt to use the least restrictive procedures necessary to control severely aggressive or destructive behavior that places the individual or others in imminent danger. A systematic pattern of using emergency restrictive techniques without their being a part of an approved program must not exist.

ICFs/MR must monitor the frequency with which restrictive techniques are employed. Repeated use over prolonged periods should raise questions among specialized service staff about the individual's receipt of active treatment and the right to be free from unnecessary restraint. Specialized service staff must be able to demonstrate that less restrictive behavioral programs were implemented but did not succeed in managing problem behaviors before beginning more restrictive approaches.

Facility specialized service staff must also ensure that appropriate policies and procedures are implemented regarding the prescription, administration, and monitoring of psychotropic, behavior management, and other drugs. Specialized service staff must guard against overmedication of individuals with developmental disabilities. For example, they must ensure that if drugs are administered to control maladaptive behavior, those behaviors are responsive to the types of drugs being administered.

1. The drugs should be monitored to see whether they are in fact exacerbating the behavior.
2. Polypharmacy should be checked to determine whether it results in exceeding the maximum daily limits for any one drug.
3. Injections should be monitored to ensure that they are not administered too frequently or in excessive doses.
4. The administration of daily medication and PRN (as needed) drugs must be monitored so that the combination of drugs does not exceed maximum recommended daily doses.

The overall rate of psychoactive medication usage in the ICF/MR should be monitored. In instances of a psychiatric diagnosis, specialized service staff should ensure that psychotropic drug therapy is not used outside the active treatment program designed to eliminate specific psychiatric symptoms and behavior thought to be drug responsive.

A system should be in place to guard against the inappropriate use of polypharmacy. Such inappropriate use complicates treatment, makes drug effectiveness difficult to determine and increases the risk of drug interactions and adverse reactions caused by the additive effects of the prescribed drugs. The number of individuals on polypharmacy should be reviewed.

For Direct Care Staff

The facility must ensure that individuals are protected from unreasonable risks to their personal safety caused by the conduct of staff. Direct care staff must receive adequate training in appropriate and effective measures to respond to various individual behaviors. Direct care staff must also be able to demonstrate the skills necessary to implement the IPPs for the individuals for whom they are responsible. Staff members must be competent and knowledgeable regarding individual needs, programs, and progress.

Direct care staff must be able to explain and demonstrate training and data collection procedures. They must also be aware of individuals' activities in outside programs so these can be incorporated into the individuals' programs on their residential units. For example, if a public school implements a manual communication program with an individual, the direct care staff in the individual's living unit must have instruction to implement the program in the residential environment, and vice versa, regarding the public school staff's training in the individual's behavior management program.

CONCLUSION

Both the provision of appropriate treatment to persons with developmental disabilities and the legal protections accorded this group have greatly advanced in recent years. A clear recognition has developed in statutory, regulatory, and case law that individuals in ICFs/MR may no longer receive only custodial care, nor may they be subjected to harm, be denied their right to liberty, or have other unreasonable and illegal restrictions placed upon them. The constitutional protections enumerated in *Youngberg v. Romeo* (1982) are guaranteed to all individuals with developmental disabilities in residential facilities. While these protections do not rise to the level of the federal statutory and administrative rights accorded individuals in ICFs/MR funded by HCFA, the combination of all the protections discussed in this chapter have strengthened the empowerment of these individuals to improve the conditions in which they live and the care and treatment they receive.

To the extent that state facilities continue to be certified by HCFA, with its emphasis on active treatment, persons with developmental disabilities will have a solid basis to ensure their right to protection, adequate staffing, active treatment, effective policies and procedures, adequate health care, and a safe physical environment. ICF/MR administrators, professional staff, and direct care workers will have an ever-increasing responsibility to understand and implement the statutory and regulatory requirements supporting the above rights. This implementation is necessary in order to ensure that their facilities meet HCFA certification requirements, thereby qualifying for continued financial assistance from the federal government to operate their programs.

Advocates for developmentally disabled persons will continue to take an active, analytical look at case law interpreting and further defining the constitutional and statutory protections to be accorded to this group. The development of the law and further reforms in this area will continue to be the subject of much national attention.

REFERENCES

ARC of North Dakota v. Olson, 561 F. Supp. 495 (D.N.D. 1982). [Operation of a state facility for mentally retarded persons must meet minimal constitutional standards.]
Board of Education v. Rowley, 458 U.S. 176 (1982).
Clark v. Cohen, 613 F. Supp. 684 (E.D. Pa. 1985). [Where professionals recom-

mend community services, proper support services must be provided by the state.]

Garrity v. Gallen, 522 F. Supp. 171 (D.N.H. 1981).

Halderman v. Pennhurst, 451 U.S. 1 (1981) (*Pennhurst I*). [Developmental Disabilities Act does not require treatment or habilitation in the least restrictive environment.]

Halderman v. Pennhurst, 465 U.S. 89 (1984) (*Pennhust II*). [Federal court cannot enforce state law, here a state law establishing a right to treatment.]

Honig v. Doe, 108 S. Ct. 592 (1988).

NYSARC v. Carey, 393 F. Supp. 715, 718 (E.D.N.Y. 1975).

O'Connor v. Donaldson, 422 U.S. 563 (1975). [Custodial confinement without something more for nondangerous individuals capable of living in freedom with assistance violates the constitutional provisions of the Fourteenth Amendment.]

Public Law 93-112, *Rehabilitation Act of 1973*, 87 Stat. 355, 29 U.S.C. §§701–796 (1973).

Public Law 94-103, *Developmental Disabilities Assistance and Bill of Rights Act*, 89 Stat. 486 (1975).

Public Law 94-142, *Education for All Handicapped Children Act*, 89 Stat. 773, 20 U.S.C. §§1401–1461 (1975).

Public Law 95-602, *Developmental Disabilities Assistance and Bill of Rights Act Amendments*, 42 U.S.C. §§6000–6081 (1978).

Public Law 96-247, *Civil Rights of Institutionalized Persons Act*, 96 Stat. 349, 42 U.S.C. §§1997a–j (1980).

School Board of Nassau County, Florida v. Arline, 107 S. Ct. 1123 (1987).

Thomas S. v. Morrow, 781 F. 2d 367 (4th Cir. 1986).

Wyatt v. Stickney, 325 F. Supp. 781 (M.D. Ala. 1971), *aff'd sub nom. Wyatt v. Aderholt*, 503 F. 2d 1305 (5th Cir. 1974). [Purpose of involuntary hospitalization is treatment, not custodial care, and failure to provide such violates the Fourteenth Amendment.]

Youngberg v. Romeo, 457 U.S. 307 (1982). [Institutionalized persons with mental retardation have the right to the basic necessities of life, safety, freedom from undue bodily restraint, and minimally adequate treatment to ensure these other constitutional rights.]

3

The Principle of Normalization

James F. Gardner and John O'Brien

The principle of normalization is a foundation for planning and providing services to persons with developmental disabilities. It also provides the criteria for determining the quality of service programs. The principle of normalization can be applied to situations particular to a single individual, to small groups of people, and to large service systems. The normalization principle has been particularly useful in focusing attention on what people with developmental disabilities can achieve and how service systems should be designed to maximize that achievement.

Various authors in the United States and Europe have provided definitions of the normalization principle. Wolf Wolfensberger (1972) provided what has been regarded as the most common and useful definition of the term: "Normalization is the utilization of means which are as culturally normative as possible, in order to establish and/or maintain personal behaviors, experiences, and characteristics which are as culturally normative as possible."

This definition, as John O'Brien (1980) noted, focuses attention on two aspects of any human service program:

1. *What* the program achieves for those it serves ("personal behaviors, experiences, and characteristics" in the definition):
   a. The social competencies people develop
   b. The personal appearance of people in the program
   c. The public image of the people in the program
   d. The quality and variety of the life options people experience

over time (This includes choices of living arrangements, educational opportunities, leisure time pursuits, productive work roles, and other opportunities to participate in the lives of natural families and communities.)

2. *How* the program accomplishes its objectives ("means" in the definition):
   a. The physical settings used in delivering the program
   b. The ways in which people are grouped for various program purposes
   c. The goals of the program
   d. The activities selected to meet program goals, as well as the way they are scheduled
   e. The people who provide the program's services and control the program's direction
   f. The language used to describe the program, as well as the people it serves

Evolution of the Normalization Principle

The normalization principle originated in Scandinavia (Bank-Mikkelsen, 1969; Nirje, 1969). Wolfensberger introduced the term to North America, and many human service agencies incorporated some variation of the early definition into their mission statements and planning processes. Attention to the normalization principle was evident in the formation of the Eastern Nebraska Community Office of Retardation (ENCOR) in 1970 (ENCOR, 1979). The Canadian Association for the Mentally Retarded also engaged the services of Wolfensberger in the development of a plan for comprehensive community services for persons with mental retardation (NIMR, 1974). Finally, the Developmental Disabilities Program of The Minnesota State Planning Agency noted Nirje and Wolfensberger's work on the normalization principle in its 1975 plan for establishing community alternatives for people with developmental disabilities (Minnesota State Planning Agency, 1975). The normalization principle challenged the segregated nature of large congregate residential facilities during the 1970s.

Critics charged that the normalization principle attempted to make people normal (Aanes & Haagenson, 1978) and overlooked individual differences (Throne, 1975). Other critics argued that the normalization principle had not been fully evaluated through scientific study and represented a "slogan" or "fad" (Zigler, 1977). In many instances, however, critics pointed to misuse of the concept in service settings as evidence that the concept itself was flawed (McCord, 1982).

The response to the criticism was, and is still, grounded in the fact that the principle of normalization is not a scientific theory to be proved or disproved. Rather it is a value base that mandates that all people, regardless of disability, be treated as full human beings (McCord, 1982). However, clear research supports the major components of the normalization principle. Finally, normalization is not something that is done to a person. People are not normalized. Rather, the normalization principle provides a series of criteria by which services to people with disabilities can be planned and evaluated.

The confusion over the meaning, interpretation, and implementation of the normalization principle led Wolfensberger in 1983 to propose the term *social role valorization* as a replacement for the principle of normalization (Wolfensberger, 1983). In proposing the alteration, Wolfensberger noted that the two primary goals of social role valorization were the enhancement of the social image and the personal competencies of persons or groups at risk of social devaluation. Despite Wolfensberger's recommendation, the term normalization is generally used.

Stigma of Mental Retardation

People with developmental disabilities suffer from social stigma. American society considers them as significantly different. In addition, society has evaluated the difference negatively (i.e., people with disabilities are devalued). The combination of being both different and devalued produces the stigma of disability.

The distinction between being different and devalued is important (Gardner & Chapman, 1985). People quite commonly can be different but not devalued. Frank Zappa, Elton John, and Malcolm Forbes, for example, may act very differently from other people. However, the differentness is not valued negatively. Like the eccentric millionaire or the reclusive artist, individuals who are valued and accepted are allowed to engage in strange behavior and still remain valued.

People who have a developmental disability and who are devalued are not allowed to act differently. Society does not tolerate differentness in people who are devalued. Normalization theory suggests that the ICF/MR should minimize the perceived differentness of persons with developmental disabilities by encouraging the establishment of behaviors and experiences in persons with disabilities that are similar to those of other people. The normalization principle also stresses the use of valued means (the "How") to achieve goals (the "What").

Vicious Circles

Because people with developmental disabilities are often stigmatized, they are frequently caught in vicious circles (O'Brien, 1980) that unfold in the following sequence (Gardner & Chapman, 1985):

1. Prejudiced beliefs about the capabilities of people with developmental disabilities leads to . . .
2. Low expectations of what they can accomplish, which leads to . . .
3. Withholding of opportunities for learning and decision making, which leads to . . .

4. Limited growth and development, which . . .
5. Confirms the prejudiced belief.

One example of a vicious circle is provided by the diagnosis of Down syndrome two decades ago. At that time most medical and educational authorities believed that children with Down syndrome were unable to learn basic preacademic skills. Because no instructional program would expend resources on children who could not learn, no preacademic education was provided. It was not surprising that the prejudiced belief was confirmed. Children with Down syndrome who were provided no education could not count or recognize basic words.

A second example is provided by residential program staff who do not believe that adolescents with developmental disabilities can make decisions. As a result, the staff provide no opportunities for making small decisions. People with disabilities are prevented from learning from a succession of small mistakes over time. Program staff should not be surprised, then, when the adolescent reaches adulthood and cannot make even the most basic adult decisions.

The Five Dimensions of Normalization

John O'Brien has broken out the normalization principle into five dimensions that cover the major themes associated with the principle. The five dimensions are (Gardner & Chapman, 1985):

1. Community presence
2. Community participation
3. Skill enhancement
4. Image enhancement
5. Autonomy and empowerment

Community Presence

The first dimension of the normalization principle is community presence, considered as physical integration. Potential for participation is increased by closeness to the community. Residence in a neighborhood or community provides a sense of belonging or ownership. People residing in a group home outside the neighborhood cannot make the same claim on services or activities as people on your block.

Community Participation

Community participation, the second dimension of the normalization principle, is a measure of the extent to which people are socially integrated into the community. The mere presence of a small ICF/MR in a neighborhood does not guarantee social integration. People with developmental disabilities can be just as segregated from the community in a small community-based program as in a large institution.

Community participation includes both personal and impersonal interactions. Impersonal interactions take place, for example, while ordering a meal in a restaurant and during work or work training. Personal interactions include the opportunity to have meaningful relationships with friends and family. For children this includes parents, siblings, relatives, and school and neighborhood friends. For adults this interaction extends to friends, relatives, and, perhaps, spouse and children.

Skill Enhancement

Contemporary values support the belief that individual growth and adaptation take place throughout the life cycle. Realistic yet firm expectations should be set for persons living in the ICF/MR. A strong program of active treatment across all areas during all hours of the day, in formal and informal settings, promotes developmental growth.

One common obstacle to growth and development is physical and social overprotection which occurs when programs unnecessarily lower the person's exposure to normative dangers, risks, and growth and learning challenges. All people learn through making a series of mistakes. The series moves in the direction of increasing complexity and potential danger. If people are not allowed to learn from minor failures, they will be ill-prepared to make more important decisions, with potentially dangerous consequences.

A second obstacle to growth and development results from confusing behavior with performance (Gilbert, 1978). Little reason exists to teach a skill or shape a behavior if no opportunity is presented for the individual to benefit from a valued consequence. For example, teaching shopping skills may involve complex behaviors, but unless opportunities are provided for shopping in the community, the behavior produces no valued consequence.

Image Enhancement

The fourth dimension of the normalization principle is the consideration that public perception of the ICF/MR program is as important as its accomplishments. As such, the ICF/MR program should assist people with developmental disabilities to project a positive image. A positive image is vital for two reasons. First, it is human nature to treat people as they are perceived. Thus a person who projects a negative image will be treated in a negative manner. Second, a person who is treated in a negative fashion starts to act accordingly. The self-fulfilling prophecy occurs as the person with the developmental disability begins to act out the negative expectation.

Agency staff have a particular responsibility to act as role models for people with developmental disabilities. For some people, staff may be one of a few role models, or even the only one, exerting a very powerful influence on the person's self-image. The ICF/MR staff will also have a major responsibility for how the person is perceived. By acting in a conscientious and prudent manner, staff encourages similar behavior in others.

Autonomy and Empowerment

In one sense, autonomy and empowerment are issues related to the basic rights of all people: due process, equal protection of the law, freedom from abuse, and the right to medical treatment. Autonomy and empowerment, however, with important meanings quite apart from the legal sense, mean transferring power and control to the person with the developmental disability. The autonomy of these persons can best be ensured by making them the key to developing the individual program plan, allowing them to be present at their individual program plan meetings and reviews. They should attend even if staff question their ability to understand or contribute.

REVIEW OF THE STANDARDS

483.420(a)	*Protection of clients' rights*
483.420(c)	*Communication with clients, parents, and guardians*
483.440(a)	*Active treatment*
483.450(b)	*Management of inappropriate client behavior*
483.470(a)	*Client living environment*
483.470(b)	*Client bedrooms*
483.470(c)	*Storage space in bedrooms*
483.470(d)	*Client bathrooms*
483.470(e)	*Heating and ventilation*
483.470(f)	*Floors*
483.470(g)	*Space and equipment*
483.480(b)	*Meal services*
483.480(c)	*Menus*
483.480(d)	*Dining areas and service*

The standards and interpretative guidelines discuss derogatory and stimatizing language within the context of psychological abuse. There is an emphasis on privacy, access to telephone and mail communications, and the necessity of community participation in small groups.

The standards note the need to ensure that individuals are properly clothed according to age, sex, and cultural norm and that the styles, colors, and design conform with community norms.

The standards also cover interaction between the individual and his or her family through visits to the facility and leaves of absence from the program to stay with relatives.

The active treatment standard discusses self-determination and independence and prevention of regression.

The standard on client behavior and facility practices covers systems for managing behavior and issues of identification, documentation, and least restrictive alternative. Medications and their impact on ability to participate in daily living activities are covered.

The section on client living environment covers normalization-related topics of: age range in living units; adequate living and storage space; and privacy in toilet, bath, and shower areas. Temperature, humidity, and a normal comfort range are included.

The dietetic services standard covers the topics of eating in the dining room, adaptive equipment and utensils, menu requirements, and positioning at the table.

APPLICATION

The normalization principle has many applications to the ICF/MR program and can provide significant guidance in the planning and design of a comprehensive ICF/MR service program. In other instances the range of application may be more limited. For example, a large ICF/MR located in a rural setting without access to community services may be unable to influence either community presence or community participation. In addition, its ability to increase personal competencies may be limited. Opportunities exist, however, for implementing the normalization principle in all ICFs/MR. In particular, the facility can ensure that three vicious circles of dehumanization, age inappropriateness, and isolation are not operating.

Understanding the patterns of devaluation will assist in defining positive practices to ensure that people residing in the ICF/MR experience dignity and individual respect, age appropriate settings and practices, and as much participation in the community as possible.

These are the challenges of the normalization principle for the ICF/MR program, which is not consistent with some of the major components of the principle. Few residential programs for people with disabilities meet all the criteria. However, many policies and practices of the ICF/MR can be altered and moved in the direction of greater conformity with the normalization principle.

Dignity and Individual Respect

Conditions that Enhance Dignity and Individual Respect

Eliminating dehumanizing conditions does not guarantee a person dignity and respect. All program elements should actively promote the development of people's ability to choose, the expression of individuality, and positive, personalized interactions.

Individualization One of the most dehumanizing effects of institutional life is the experience of self as a part of a mass, rather than as an individual. To develop a sense of individual worth, a person needs opportunities for self-expression and time apart from a group. To promote individualization, staff must sometimes redesign programs to meet changing individual circumstances instead of expecting people to change to fit the program. For example, individualization is furthered when:

- Adequate space for people to use personal items of furniture and decorations and to store other possessions and furnishings is provided.
- Space arrangements not only permit privacy but also promote a clear sense of personal space. Staff do not violate personal space without invitation or permission.
- Each individual program plan is developed with the participation of the person served, and, as necessary, family members, a guardian, or advocate. Individual preferences are reflected in the plan as written and implemented.
- People choose their companions for leisure activities and can participate in deciding whether or not they will have a roommate and who their roommate(s) will be.
- Staff interpret and respect individual preferences of people with significant communication difficulties. Priority is given to assisting such people to develop alternative ways to express choice.
- Special equipment to assist posture, mobility, communication, or control is highly individualized. Appliances and equipment are comfortable and well fitting, designed and applied to minimize stigmatizing appearances.

Development of choice Persons with developmental disabilities, especially those who have been institutionalized for long periods, often need systematic assistance to develop their ability to choose. Learning to choose is enhanced when:

- The physical setting offers numerous opportunities for choice and decision making (e.g., controls for water temperature, lights, radios, stereos, television, and cooking and snack preparation equipment are accessible).
- People have access to a variety of different leisure and recreational activities and are expected to choose among them. This includes the option to choose no activity.
- Except perhaps for very young children, people are present at all program planning meetings and reviews that concern them. This should happen regardless of assumptions about the person's ability to understand or contribute.
- People are encouraged to exercise the rights and entitlements of citizenship, including voting, free communication, freedom of movement, and so forth.

Positive interactions Positive staff-client interaction has different characteristics in different settings. In all situations, however, staff interactions can be described as open, direct, and sincere. People are not "talked down to" either by choice of words or tone of voice.

- In a work or structured learning situation, the level of formality is appropriate to the activity and the ages of the participants.
- In the home or residential setting, at least some staff interactions can be described as warm and personal. Staff genuinely share some of their life space and personal time with residents. Few, if any, distinctions are evident between "staff" and "residents"—such as "off limits" areas, staff bathrooms, uniforms, and so forth.
- People of all ages live in a heterosexual world. Children see a range of positive male-female interactions in their residential settings. Young adults have increasing choice of individual relationships with members of the opposite sex. Adults have opportunities to experience personal relationships, including the choice of intimate relationships.

Conditions that Diminish Dignity and Individual Respect

Dehumanizing practices rob a person of individuality, rights, and dignity. They depict people as less than human and deprive them of the opportunity to learn appropriate self-expression. Dehumanizing conditions are particularly oppressive when a person spends 24 hours a day in one setting or in the place a person makes his or her home, since home is where most people experience the most freedom to express their individuality.

Space and settings Dehumanizing interactions are fostered by space arrangements that make it difficult for people to experience personal space and privacy. For example:

- Sleeping arrangements that permit no choice as to whether or not one will share a room or have one's own
- Toileting and bathing arrangements that do not promote privacy
- Food preparation and eating arrangements that encourage "mass feeding" with few menu choices or options to cook for oneself
- Lack of adequate space for personal possessions, including lack of space and opportunity to express one's preference for furnishings and decor

Groupings and practices Dehumanization is promoted and signaled by a variety of "mass management" practices, such as:

- A predominance of large group activities
- Grouping people for recreational and leisure activities on the basis of assumed "functioning level" rather than on the basis of individual interests
- Regimented practices such as walking in line, group bedtimes, group toileting, and so on
- Formal or informal "uniforms"

- A large number of rules, often justified by the fact that "many people live here"

Language   Dehumanization is created and signaled by spoken and written language that either fails to promote individuality or equates people with labels. For instance:

- A group of people, maybe even the place they live, is characterized by a label, such as "non-ambs," "behavior disorders," and so forth.
- An individual is characterized by a label such as "TMR," a "CP," a "schizophrenic."
- An individual or a group is referred to by an archaic term such as "mongoloid," "borderline," "high functioning," "low functioning."
- People are not called by name or are inappropriately called only by first or last name.
- Mealtime skill programs are referred to as "feeding program."

Program Checklist

		Yes	No
1.	Opportunities exist to make real choices.	—	—
2.	Staff train individuals to make choices.	—	—
3.	Programs, environments, and staffing patterns are designed to meet individual needs and maximize strengths.	—	—
4.	Staff serve as effective role models for individuals.	—	—
5.	Staff respect individual privacy.	—	—
6.	Individuals are not labeled or referred to by disability type.	—	—

Age Appropriateness

Conditions that Enhance Age Appropriateness

Many handicapped people have experienced near lifelong deprivation of age-appropriate opportunities and expectations. This may show up in a preference for age-inappropriate activity—as when as adult prefers to sing and listen to nursery rhyme songs—or in an attachment to an age-inappropriate possession such as a child's toy or a teddy bear.

In this situation, a tension between the need to support individual choice and self-expression and the stigmatizing effect of age inappropriateness must be recognized. The principle of normalization does not offer a simple answer like "take the teddy bear away." Instead, it directs attention to aspects of the situation that are under staff's immediate control, such as the number of more age-appropriate choices of activities and possessions the program offers the person, the effects over time of social reinforcement for more age-appropriate choices, and the effects over time of guidance, teaching, and interaction with valued peers.

Maintaining age appropriateness requires special effort. It must be a conscious focus in the design of program schedules and activities and an important factor in the development of individual program plans.

Program scheduling   Scheduling refers to the balance of activities that is potentially available to people in a program. An individual schedule of activities may be very different from the balance of available options, depending on individual need and choice. However, the program should be arranged so that age-appropriate choices are not limited by the scheduled activities and materials available, and so that:

- Young children have a balance of early education, small group, and individual play.
- School-aged children and adolescents have the option of 6 hours of school with appropriate vacations, opportunities for travel, and a variety of leisure activities.
- Adults have the option of an 8-hour productive workday with compensatory education and training available after work time. Adults have appropriate days off and annual vacation periods with opportunities for travel.
- Daily routines of waking, mealtimes, and bedtimes are not regulated to deny people age-appropriate ranges of choice (i.e., as people get older they have more choice of bedtime and, at least on days off from work or school, more choice of rising times and meal times).

Activity selection   Age appropriateness is a consciously applied criterion in the selection of teaching and living activities and materials. This poses challenges to programs serving adults with very limited abilities, because:

- Activities are designed to teach skills by age-appropriate processes and at appropriate times. For instance, a person receives training in self-care skills at appropriate times (on waking and before bed) in appropriate places (his or her own bedroom or bathroom), rather than in a classroom at midday.
- Materials are selected to reinforce an accurate perception of a person's chronological age. This often means shopping for adult materials in a hardware store or a grocery store rather than ordering them from a catalog of child-imaged developmental materials.
- A program that supplies residents with clothing, grooming aids, and perhaps gifts ensures that the range of selection is age appropriate.
- When an activity relies on behavior management techniques, age-appropriate cues and reinforcers are selected.

Individual program plans   A person's individual program plan (IPP), as it is written and, more importantly, as it is delivered, reflects a concern for age appropriateness. For example:

- IPPs identify age-inappropriate behaviors, appearances, and possessions as potential targets for change.
- IPPs systematically support age-appropriate appearances. When a person requires substantial assistance in dressing and grooming, the IPP should note the need for assistance and also specify that the person should be dressed and groomed in a fashion appropriate to chronological age.
- IPPs identify developmental challenges that will elicit increasingly age-appropriate behavior.
- IPPs balance work, formal education, and leisure time in a way that is age typical. If a person requires an age-inappropriate balance of activity, such as an adult who requires more education time, a plan is directed toward supporting or teaching the person skills that will eventually permit a more age-appropriate balance of activities.
- IPPs provide opportunities and support for a person to receive information and discuss feelings, responsibilities, and choice regarding the age-appropriate expression of sexuality.

Conditions that Contribute to Age Inappropriateness

For most people social expectations, opportunities, and experiences change as they age. Few people grow up all at once; the typical patterns of our culture wisely challenge us to develop a step at a time. The rhythms of our day, week, and year change as increasing age brings higher expectations for productive, responsible behavior and more choices of where, how, and to what extent those expectations will be met.

Age-inappropriate practices treat handicapped people as if they are, and always will be, children. It is not uncommon for people to explain another's continuing dependency by comparing him or her to a child. Thus, an elderly person who easily becomes confused is described as living in a "second childhood," and a person with mental retardation may be described as in a book titled *The Child Who Never Grew Up* (Buck, 1950). This comparison can become the basis for a vicious circle in which adults who are seen as children are treated like children and continue to behave in ways that reinforce that stereotype.

The conventions of intelligence testing contribute to age-inappropriate practices. A 25-year-old person who has not done well on such a set of tasks might be labeled as having a mental age of 2. From this it is easy to reach the erroneous conclusion that this person has the mind of a 2-year-old. This error leads many people to resist efforts to provide more age-appropriate activities and expectations because it seems unfair to treat someone who is really only 2 years old as if he or she were 25. However well intentioned, this mix-up of test scores and personal identity is damaging to people with developmental disabilities.

Space and settings   Age-inappropriate expectations can be communicated to people with disabilities and the public by building features. For example:

- Decorations that suggest childhood, such as cartoon murals or juvenile bedspreads and color schemes, are used in adult areas.
- The physical environment fails to make age-appropriate demands for good judgment, adaptation, and increasingly complex behavior.

Groupings and practices   Age-inappropriate groupings make it difficult for programs not to treat at least some participants age inappropriately. For example:

- Children of very different ages or children and adults are grouped together for major role-defining activities, such as work or education.
- Recreation and leisure activities happen at age-inappropriate times, as when adults spend weekday mornings or afternoons in recreational rather than work activities.
- Daytime activities are age inappropriate. Older children spend school time engaged in activities that would be appropriate for early education or primary grades. Adults do not have the option of meaningful, paid work and may be exposed to approaches to learning that are appropriate only to younger people.
- Adults use crayons and coloring books to develop eye-hand coordination.
- The future impact of the activity is of minimal concern. For instance, adults are taught to perform trivial jobs that have no utility for earning a living wage.

Language   Age-inappropriate perceptions are created and reinforced by language habits such as:

- Labeling people or programs in terms of mental age or developmental age
- Using program or location titles that suggest childhood, although adults are served
- Using paternalistic tones and patterns of speech

Program Checklist

	Yes	No
1. Staff make a deliberate effort to engage in age-appropriate, community-based activities.	___	___
2. Individual program plans are developed on chronological age rather than mental age.	___	___
3. The physical environment makes age-appropriate demands for good judgment and behavior.	___	___
4. Adults are provided opportunitites to work.	___	___

Participation

Conditions that Enhance Participation

If people with handicaps are to be accepted as participating citizens and offered the opportunity to lead culturally valued lives, a program must work systematically to overcome physical and social isolation. The ICF/MR must safeguard people from being isolated from their families, their relatives, and their home communities.

Physical presence Before people can participate in the social interactions of a natural community, they must be physically present and involved in it. For some facilities this is relatively easy. In other instances where locations are isolating, the ICF/MR must be particularly creative. Some positive efforts to improve physical presence are:

- The program is located so that it is easy for people to maintain contact with families and home communities.
- Imaginative efforts give people access to the community. For instance, extensive provision of transportation makes possible aggressive encouragement of home visits.
- The ICF/MR population is kept small to make frequent use of community resources practical.

Social participation Full community membership requires that people be active participants in a variety of individual and group relationships. Even people whose capacity for communication and mobility is very limited can and need to be part of a network of personal relationships with valued people. Some program supports for social participation include the following:

- Program time is arranged to allow people opportunities for individual and small (two to three persons) group participation in community events and activities such as church services, entertainment, civic meeting, and so forth.
- Individual program plans include specific objectives to increase social participation in valued settings, and skills are developed to make a person an appropriate participant.
- The program makes some social participation a reality for everyone, regardless of his or her current ability. Social participation in community life is not restricted to those who can earn their way to it.
- The program develops and maintains a person's active involvement with family and relatives. When a person appears cut off from family and relatives, the individual program plan includes a strategy for attempting to revitalize family contact or involve the person with valued community members who can, to some extent, stand in place of the family.

Conditions that Contribute to Isolation

Many service arrangements have moved people with handicaps out of the mainstream of their home communities, and some even isolate people from friends, relatives, and immediate family members. The goal of active habilitation is to meet individual needs in socially acceptable ways. If a person is to learn to function as independently as possible in the least restrictive community environment, he or she must experience that community as an essential part of habilitation. Good evidence indicates that the more severely handicapped a person is, the more necessary it is that teaching be done in the community. This means that an instructional goal cannot be considered met until a person is able to perform the task in an acceptable way in a natural community setting (Brown et al., 1976).

Space and settings   Many residential services for handicapped people originated when isolation was considered the treatment of choice. For a time isolation was justified by the belief that handicapped people need protection from the problems and dangers of community life. Isolation was later supported by the belief that the community needs protection from the costs or dangers posed by handicapped people. The effects of such isolation are especially severe in services where people spend 24 hours a day. Programs that are provided in isolated facilities must work against the influence of such physical features as:

- A location and pattern of travel that places many people a great distance from their families and communities (A program that, for example, serves people from an urban community is located in a small village miles away.)
- A location that makes it difficult to use community resources, including churches, shopping places, entertainment and eating places, public schools, community health care providers, and so on (This leads to the development of such resources within a facility, which further reduces opportunity to experience natural community settings.)
- A facility size that congregates more socially devalued people than can easily be absorbed within the surrounding community (It is not uncommon for several hundred handicapped people to live in or near a village with a population only a little larger.)
- Location of facilities for people with different handicapping or other socially devalued conditions near one another (This strains the ability of the community to assimilate individuals in the patterns of everyday life.)

Groupings and practices   People are isolated by practices that restrict their choice of relationships to other people with handicaps and the staff who serve them. Such practices deprive them of a wide variety of learning experiences, the support of valued peer models, the opportunity to exercise choice, the chance to become part of a natural social network, and the challenge of contributing to community life. Such isolation practices include:

- Scheduling time so that people never leave the grounds of a residential facility
- Designing activities so that people's only contact with natural community settings is in large groups (four or more people)
- Decreasing the contact between a person and his or her family and relatives (This occurs when a facility limits visiting hours and does not actively encourage home visits. The relationship between the program and family members makes a family feel unable to relate actively to its handicapped member.)

Program Checklist

		Yes	No
1.	The facility encourages contact with families and friends.	——	——
2.	All individuals are part of a network of socially valued nondisabled peers.	——	——
3.	Teaching takes place in natural community settings.	——	——
4.	Individuals participate in religious services in the community.	——	——
5.	Individuals interact in the community in very small groups of two to three people.	——	——

IMPLICATIONS

For Team Members

The implications for all interdisciplinary team members is that the normalization principle should extend across all training environments in the active treatment program. Whenever possible, training environments should extend into natural communities. Social integration and community participation are vital elements of active treatment.

The normalization principle should serve as a guide to team members as they design individual program plans. Team members should be able to identify how active treatment programs will increase the individual's performance rather than mere behavior. Team members should insist on opportunities for practice generalization of the goals and objectives in the individual program plan.

As the individual accomplishes goals and objectives, his or her programs, range of available choices, and surroundings should change.

The individual residing in the ICF/MR should be presented with new opportunities, choices, and challenges as old goals and objectives are accomplished.

For Qualified Mental Retardation Professionals

The qualified mental retardation professional (QMRP) must monitor the individualization of active treatment services. Different individuals in the facility should actually experience different schedules, activities, and supports based on individual needs. Different people should have different kinds of individualized adaptive equipment, communication devices, and other personal aids.

The QMRP is the individual's advocate who monitors the design and implementation of the individual program plan. Skill training, behavior shaping, and practice generalization should take place in community settings whenever possible. The QMRP should question the reason for certain goals and objectives if the opportunity to practice or use the skill in the present environment does not exist. The QMRP should determine if the active treatment program is sufficiently intense and specifically tailored to individual differences to yield meaningful behavioral and skill change.

For Specialized Service Staff

The specialized service staff have a responsibility to ensure that the "how" in the active treatment process is consistent with the normalization principle. The messages about people that active treatment programs transmit are often as important as what the program accomplishes. What a specialized service staff accomplishes in building skills and abilities will be offset if the process depicts the individual as devalued to the general public or other staff.

The specialized service staff often have access to the largest amount of knowledge and information that can be marshalled on behalf of the individuals in the facility. The specialized service staff have the opportunity to translate the latest technical and clinical innovations into teaching strategies on behalf of those individuals.

For Residential Staff

While many aspects of the ICF/MR environment are beyond the control of the residential staff, they can place special emphasis on grooming, dress, mealtimes, socialization, and the assurance of autonomy, privacy, individuality, and choice whenever possible. In many instances residential staff accompany individuals into the community. The staff must ensure that the behaviors, appearance, and interactions are as normative as possible.

The staff also serve as role models for the individuals residing in the ICF/MR. As such, they are, in part, responsible for the individual's sense of value and self-worth. The residential staff can influence greatly the individual's behavior by their consistency in responding to it.

For Management Staff

The management staff must recognize the tension between the normalization principle and the realities of residential facilities for persons with disabilities. They should be challenged by discrepancies and not become defensive. The challenge can lead to creativity and advocacy. By being sensitive to and aware of the implications of the normalization principle for residential programs, the staff will be better able to take advantage of opportunities for change when they arise.

The management staff of the ICF/MR have the responsibility for establishing the importance of the normalization principle for the facility. They can establish the importance of individuals spending time, whenever possible, outside the ICF/MR. What opportunities, for example, are provided for interacting with typical citizens in community settings? The management can also facilitate and encourage an open, supportive relationship with families that will foster interaction.

The management can also position the ICF/MR, large or small, as part of the larger community. At a minimum the ICF/MR is an open system that interacts with other providers of service, accepts individuals for active treatment, and discharges individuals to less restrictive settings when they have gained the necessary skills and behaviors.

CONCLUSION

The principle of normalization is a foundation in planning and providing services to people who are both different and devalued. The normalization principle can be applied to situations that involve a single individual, to small groupings of individuals, to large institutions, and to service delivery systems. The normalization concept will provide criteria for making decisions in these different situations.

The normalization principle will point to differences between what ought to be and what is. These differences can be particularly acute in large ICFs/MR that are both physically isolated and socially segregated from local communities. The same differences, however, can also be apparent in small ICFs/MR where individuals with developmental disabilities may live, but which are not a part of the local community. In both instances the normalization should not be rejected because it is nonapplicable. Rather, the skillful staff will use the concepts of normalization to plan how to change existing patterns of service and to apply the concepts to situations they can influence.

Many instances exist where staff do have considerable control over patterns of daily interaction between and among individuals. At this individual level the normalization principle offers important guidance in the provision of services. The principle is particularly effective in identifying and reversing vicious circles. Staff in the ICF/MR can incorporate the normalization principle to ensure dignity and individual respect, age appropriateness, and social integration with the local community.

REFERENCES

Aanes, D., & Haagenson, L. (1978). Normalization: Attention to a conceptual disaster. *Mental Retardation, 16*(1), 55–56.

Bank-Mikkelsen, N. E. (1969). A metropolitan area in Denmark: Copenhagen. In R. Kugel & W. Wolfensberger (Eds.), *Changing patterns in residential services for the mentally retarded.* Washington: President's Committee on Mental Retardation.

Brown, L., Hamre-Nietupski, J., & Hamre-Nietupski, S. (1976). Criterion of ultimate functioning. In M. A. Thomas (Ed.), *Hey don't forget about me!* Reston, VA: CEC.

Buck, P. S. (1950). *The child who never grew.* Day Co., New York.

ENCOR. (1979). *For we have promises to keep . . . and miles to go before we sleep.* Omaha, NE: ENCOR.

Gardner, J. F., & Chapman, M. S. (1985). *Staff development in mental retardation services: A practical handbook.* Baltimore: Paul H. Brookes Publishing Co.

Gilbert, T. F. (1978). *Human competence: Engineering worthy performance.* New York: McGraw-Hill.

McCord, W. T. (1982). From theory to reality: Obstacles to the implementation of the normalization principle in human services. *Mental Retardation, 20*(6), 247–253.

Minnesota State Planning Agency Developmental Disabilities Program. (1975). *Community alternatives and institutional reform.* St. Paul: Minnesota State Planning Agency Developmental Disabilities Program.

National Institute on Mental Retardation. (1974). *A plan for comprehensive community services for the developmentally handicapped.* Ontario: National Institute on Mental Retardation.

Nirje, B. (1969). The normalization principle and its human management implications. In R. Kugel & W. Wolfensberger (Eds.), *Changing patterns in residential services for the mentally retarded.* Washington: President's Committee on Mental Retardation.

O'Brien, John. (1980). The principle of normalization: A foundation for effective services. In J. F. Gardner, L. Long, R. Nicols, & D. M. Iagulli (Eds.), *Program issues in developmental disabilities: A resource manual for surveyors and reviewers* (pp. 11–32). Baltimore: Paul H. Brookes Publishing Co.

Throne, J. M. (1975). Normalization through the normalization principle. Right ends, wrong means. *Mental Retardation, 13*(5), 23–25.

Wolfensberger, W. (1983). Social role valorization: A proposed new term for the principle of normalization. *Mental Retardation, 21*(6), 234–239.

Wolfensberger, W. (1972). *The principle of normalization in human services* (p. 28). Toronto: National Institute on Mental Retardation.

Zigler, E. (1977). Twenty years of mental retardation research. *Mental Retardation, 15*(3), 51–53.

4
Positive Behavioral Programming
An Individualized, Functional Approach

Nancy R. Weiss

Severe behavior problems often present a challenge for the staff of intermediate care facilities for the mentally retarded (ICFs/MR). Often behavior problems, rather than lack of daily living skills, prevent full community integration.

During the past decade residential services for individuals with developmental disabilities have focused attention on methods for teaching new skills. Most ICFs/MR provide training in academic, vocational, and daily skills. Until recently refinements of methods to alter disruptive behaviors have lagged behind those that address teaching new skills.

The key to changing behavior is to understand its function and build new skills or provide motivation to change the behavior. This chapter describes a positive approach to changing behavior, which begins with identifying the function of that behavior. In addition, implementation strategies that reduce severe behavior problems are discussed.

BACKGROUND

Severe behavior problems are potentially dangerous to the individual with developmental disabilities or to others. These include physical aggression, property destruction, and self-injurious behavior. Behaviors such as verbal aggression, noncompliance, and self-stimulation can be severe depending on frequency and intensity. Severe behavior problems:

- Can be dangerous
- May limit an individual's ability to participate in activities
- Often interfere with the formation of relationships or with community acceptance
- Can place considerable demands on both staff and other residents

The definition and terms used in behavior programs often have varied meanings. Terms such as behavior, behavioral programming, positive reinforcement, positive reinforcers, aversive procedures, and positive programming need definition.

Behaviors are actions that can be observed and measured. They can be seen or heard and counted. Clear terminology is used to describe a behavior. Examples of behaviors include: laughing, running, hitting, hitting head on floor, following the verbal request to "come here," or sitting in seat for 5 minutes. Each of these actions can: 1) be observed and 2) be counted.

Behaviors are often confused with attitudes or feelings. Words like lazy, depressed, happy, confused, or uncooperative are descriptive of attitudes or feelings rather than behaviors. They can be inferred from behavior, but they cannot be observed or counted. For example, staff may infer that a person is happy because he or she was laughing. Laughing, not happy, is the behavior.

Behavioral programming or behavior management refers to methods to increase systematically positive behaviors or to decrease disruptive behaviors. A basic principle of behavioral programming is that behaviors are learned. If a behavior is followed by something pleasurable, the action is likely to be repeated. If an unpleasant consequence follows the behavior, the frequency of the behavior is likely to decrease. Behavior programs systematically apply this principle to increase or decrease behaviors.

Positive reinforcement refers to procedures that increase the frequency or strength of a behavior. These procedures involve the presentation of an object or event following a behavior and resulting in an increase in that behavior. For example, staff may tell an individual that after clearing the table, he or she can listen to music. The music is presented provided the individual has cleared the table. The presentation of the music would be considered positive reinforcement if there were an increase in the rate or frequency of table clearing.

A *positive reinforcer* is the object or stimulus used to strengthen a behavior. When positive reinforcers are used consistently, they increase the rate of the behavior they follow or the probability that the behavior will occur. Natural reinforcers, such as food, water, sleep, and companionship, are primary reinforcers. The value of other reinforcers is learned. Learned reinforcers, such as money, status, and praise, are called secondary reinforcers (Gardner & Chapman, 1985).

Aversive procedures involve the use of painful or uncomfortable stimuli following a behavior to decrease the frequency or intensity of the behavior. Examples of aversive procedures include water spray to the face, slaps or pinches, ammonia or other scents to the nose, electric shock, cold baths, or lemon juice or vinegar to the mouth. Other less severe aversive procedures involve limiting reinforcers, such as loss of privileges, fines in a token system, time-out, or verbal reprimands.

Positive programming is "a gradual educational process for behavior change that is based on a functional analysis of the presenting problems and involves systematic instruction in more effective ways of behaving" (Donnellan, LaVigna, Negri-Shoultz, & Fassbender, 1988). Positive programming uses a variety of approaches to teach systematically new skills that will reduce or substitute for the problem behavior. Teaching a person to use the sign language gesture for "help" rather than screaming is an example of positive programming. Positive programming techniques are usually paired with the use of positive reinforcement and effective instructional strategies.

Use of Aversive Versus Nonaversive Techniques

The use of aversive procedures to change behavior raises important questions. Debate among professionals centers on issues of value and efficacy. Many professionals believe that the use of aversive procedures is wrong. They argue that while aversive procedures may reduce disruptive behaviors, a substantial number of studies show that nonaversive strategies work as quickly and effectively (Repp & Deitz, 1974; Smith, 1985; Vukelich & Hake, 1971; Woods, 1982). They note that nonaversive techniques can eliminate very serious behavior problems.

The concerns regarding aversive techniques suggest exhausting the choices of positive approaches before resorting to the use of even mildly aversive procedures.

An Individualized Approach

Behavior programs, even those based only on positive techniques, can be implemented to assert control over "troublesome" individuals. Staff must ensure that behavior change strategies are not used to control others or to force individuals to meet an arbitrary expectation. Positive behavioral programming is appropriately employed to assure that people do not hurt themselves or others and to assist them to achieve their goals.

The Center on Human Policy, Syracuse University (Knoll, 1986) found that the most successful services for individuals with challenging behaviors had certain values and philosophies in common. The most effective services reviewed were characterized by:

- A completely individualized approach
- A commitment to the provision of behavior change techniques within the individual's natural environments
- An understanding of behavior as an attempt to respond to the demands of the individual's environment

An approach to behavior change built on these principles has the best probability of long-term success. In addition, this approach assists individuals to expand their repertoire of functional behaviors, ensures appropriate environments, and increases individuals' feelings of self-worth.

REVIEW OF THE STANDARDS

483.410(c)	*Client records*
483.410(d)	*Services provided under agreements with outside sources*
483.420(a)	*Protection of clients' rights*
483.420(d)	*Staff treatment of clients*
483.440(c)	*Individual program plan*
483.440(f)	*Program monitoring and change*
483.450(a)	*Facility practices—conduct toward clients*
483.450(b)	*Management of inappropriate client behavior*
483.450(c)	*Time-out rooms*
483.450(d)	*Physical restraints*
483.450(e)	*Drug usage*

The standards review the requirements for record keeping and written agreements with agencies providing contractual services. The sections under "Client Protections" cover the necessity for informed consent and the prohibitions against abuse, punishment, mistreatment, and the use of unnecessary drugs and physical restraints.

Standards also cover the requirements for the individual program plan process, assessment, team process, and documentation and monitoring of programs, including behavior programs.

The primary condition of participation related to behavior programs is "Client Behavior and Facility Practices." This condition covers standards of conduct toward clients, management of inappropriate client behavior, time-out rooms, physical restraints, and drug usage.

APPLICATION

Process of Positive Behavioral Programming

Positive programming for behavior change is a nine-step process. The steps can be visualized in a flow chart (Figure 1). The steps are:

1. Identify the behavior(s) to be changed.
2. Ensure that the identified behaviors are important to change.
3. Collect data on the frequency and severity of the behaviors.
4. Analyze the appropriateness of the environment.
5. Form a hypothesis regarding the function of the behavior for the individual.
6. Select an intervention strategy that tests the hypothesis.
7. Design and implement a written program.
8. Compare new frequency and severity data to those collected earlier.
9. If improvement is not demonstrated, check implementation reliability, review process, and return to step 4, if necessary.

Identify the Behavior

The behavior in need of change must be observable and measurable. Sufficient specificity will enable all staff to agree when the behavior is present. Statements such as "Jeffrey will not be so bossy" or "Rosemary will stop sulking" are not observable, measurable, or specific. Better statements would be: "Jeff will not tell others what to do. He will work with Linda on the plan for the garden" or "Rosemary will spend at least 1 hour each evening participating in a group activity of her choosing."

Staff should avoid statements like "Matthew has tantrums" or "Matthew had several outbursts over the weekend." Staff may interpret these statements differently. All members of the team working with the individual must share a clear and exact understanding of the behavior.

Ensure that the Identified Behaviors Are Important Enough to Require Change

Before writing a plan to change behavior, staff should consider the following questions:

• Is the behavior potentially dangerous?
• Does the behavior interfere with the individual's ability to learn new skills?
• Does the behavior interfere with the individual's ability to participate in activities?
• Does the behavior diminish potential for community integration?
• Does the behavior result in increased dependence on caregivers or other support?
• Do the actions of the individual create a need for medications to manage inappropriate behavior or other restrictive strategies (e.g., time-out, physical restraint, etc.)?
• Does the individual, or the individual's family or advocate when appropriate, *agree* that this is a problem behavior in need of change?

No single behavior is likely to meet all of the above criteria. However, these criteria will enable staff to identify behaviors that require change.

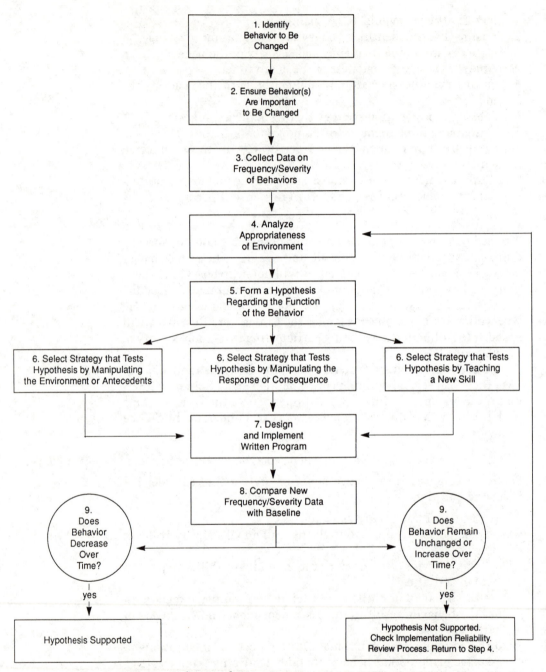

Figure 1. Behavior change strategy.

Sometimes behavior programs are designed and implemented to control unusual behaviors that are not disruptive or dangerous. These programs, however, can often result in the display of other difficult behaviors. This is likely to occur because the unusual behavior has functional utility or is reinforcing for the individual. For example, a complex reinforcement program was written to decrease an individual's behavior of snipping paper into tiny pieces. The behavior decreased, but the individual became withdrawn and agitated. In another program written to encourage an individual to eat with a fork rather than a spoon, conflicts over which utensil he used regularly escalated to full-scale incidents of aggression.

Staff should have considered whether these particular behaviors needed change. They should have considered the meaning and importance of these behaviors to the person performing them.

Collect Data on the Frequency and Severity of the Behaviors

Once the behavior to be changed is defined, staff should document the frequency and severity of the behavior. This documentation is referred to as "baseline data." Baseline data will enable staff to judge the success of intervention strategies. Instructions for recording baseline data must be clear so that all staff interpret and document behavior similarly. For example, unclear instructions may cause one staff member to count incidents of "kicking" each time the individual swings his lower leg from the knee, while another worker counts only those incidents in which the individual makes contact with something. These data would be confusing and unreliable.

Analyze the Appropriateness of the Environment

Before attempting to change the behavior, the appropriateness of the environment should be analyzed. Staff evaluate whether the behavior might be a rational response to the environment or expectations placed on the individual. Some behaviors may be a natural reaction to the services the individual is receiving. For example, programs can present too few or too many challenges and expectations. As a result, people can become disruptive or bored and withdrawn.

Frustration may be exhibited if the active treatment programs are not challenging, interesting, age appropriate, and functional. Before selecting an activity or teaching a skill, staff should ensure that the program will build on the individual's strengths and interests. The skill should:

- Have *immediate utility*. It should produce something useful for the individual or be part of a broader skill that does so.
- Have *desirability*. It should produce something the individual would likely choose if an appropriate choice situation were arranged.
- Be acquired in a *social context*. The acquisition should result from interactions with more than a single, caregiving person.
- Be acquired in the *actual, physical contexts* in which it will ultimately be used.
- Have *practicality* for the individual. It should be needed and practiced with some regularity.

- Be *age appropriate.* The behavior should facilitate social integration.
- Be *adaptable.* The skill should be generalizable to a number of settings and situations (Horner, Dunlap, & Koegel, 1988, pp. 68–69).

Staff must evaluate the environment for its appropriateness before attempting to change the indivdual's behavior.

Program Checklist

		Yes	No
1.	Behaviors to be changed are specifically identified.	—	—
2.	Data on the frequency and severity of the behavior are available.	—	—
3.	The appropriateness of the environment has been analyzed.	—	—

Form a Hypothesis Regarding the Function of the Behavior for the Individual

Forming a hypothesis regarding the function of the behavior enables staff to develop effective behavior programs. This process is often referred to as a functional analysis. A functional analysis identifies what the individual may be attempting to gain or communicate through the behavior. An ABC chart is used to identify the functions of a behavior.

"A" stands for antecedents. Antecedents are the events that precede a behavior. To understand the function of a behavior, staff record events that occur before the behavior. Not all of the events that precede a behavior affect the behavior. Analysis of antecedent behaviors enable staff to determine the influence of the specific events on the behavior. The analysis of antecedent behaviors must be detailed and must include an assessment of the environment. The antecedent event or behavior that influences the behavior might be as subtle as noise level, hunger level or the amount of light in the room. By analyzing antecedent data, staff may be able to identify the conditions that influence the behavior.

"B" stands for a description of the behavior. Describing the behavior that needs to be increased or decreased helps to ensure that all staff are targeting the same behavior for change.

"C" stands for consequences. Consequences are the events that follow a behavior and increase or decrease the likelihood that the behavior will occur again. Staff collect data on consequences before developing a behavior program to identify events that influence the occurrence of the behavior. These events may either support or inhibit the behavior. Figure 2 is a sample ABC data collection form.

ABC data are collected consistently over a reasonable period of time and then analyzed to determine:

Date	Time Incident Began and Ended	A: Antecedent Stimuli	B: Description of Behavior	C: Consequences	Individual's Response	Staff Initials

Antecedent Stimuli: Should include events or activities that preceded the behavior. Antecedents to consider include: what staff and other individuals were doing, environmental changes, etc.
Description of Behavior: Describe the exact behaviors exhibited.

Consequences: All the events or activities that followed the behaviors. Include response of staff and other individuals.
Individual's Response: Describe what the individual who performed the behavior did in response to the consequences.

Figure 2.   A sample ABC data collection form.

- What the person may be trying to communicate
- What he or she may be "buying" with this behavior
- When the behavior usually occurs
- What is happening just before or after the behavior occurs

By analyzing ABC data, staff may discover, for example, that an individual often displays a certain behavior when he is hungry, when he is bored, to avoid going to work, or when a lot of noise and activity are in the room. In other instances individuals may use behaviors to gain or "buy":

- Attention
- Permission to engage in an activity
- Relief from boredom or frustration
- Sensory stimulation
- Task avoidance
- Control
- Assistance with a task or skill

ABC relationships will be the key to designing a successful program. ABC charts are studied for patterns that identify approaches to behavior change. Staff design programs that manipulate the specific antecedents or consequences that are frequently associated with the behavior. For example, if an individual is often verbally aggressive just before dinner, staff may hypothesize that he or she is hungry and provide an afternoon snack. Staff will continue to collect data to determine whether receiving a snack leads to a decrease in verbal aggression.

Considerable creativity is sometimes required to discover the meaning of a behavior. Staff must attempt to view the experience from the perspective of the individual with whom they are working and consider the range of possible functions the behavior may serve.

Careful observation and good data collection techniques will assist staff to form a correct hypothesis regarding the meaning of the behavior for the individual. Once a correct hypothesis is established, staff will be able to design a behavior program that will change the behavior.

Program Checklist

		Yes	No
1.	ABC data are collected on behaviors to be changed.	—	—
2.	ABC data are analyzed for relevant patterns.	—	—
3.	Hypotheses regarding functions of the behaviors have been formed.	—	—

Select a Strategy that Tests the Hypothesis

After staff have formed a hypothesis about the function of the behavior, they select an intervention strategy that will:

• Manipulate the environment or antecedents
• Manipulate the response or consequence of the behavior
• Teach a new skill

Manipulate the environment or antecedents. In some instances the intervention strategy may require a modification of the environment or antecedents. For example, if staff suspect that an individual becomes aggressive when her work area becomes too noisy, the intervention strategy may require moving her to a smaller group or quieter room. If an individual eats cigarette butts and other objects from the floor, staff should maintain a clean floor.

Discovering the successful intervention strategy will sometimes be a matter of trial and error. For example, if a person becomes aggressive when staff stand close to him while teaching a vocational task, various interventions may be tested. Staff may try maintaining some distance by standing across the table. They may find the physical proximity was not the problem. Rather, the task may have been too difficult or of no interest. In this case a program strategy that allows the individual to select a different training task may be tried. Some behaviors recur because the individual has learned that a specific response will follow the behavior. If, for example, screaming results in immediate staff attention, staff must alter their response to change the behavior. In another example, when Bea refuses to help clean up after dinner, she is sent to her room. Bea may prefer to spend time in her room rather than to help clean. Staff encourage this behavior by inadvertently reinforcing Bea's task avoidance by sending her to her room.

Manipulate the response or consequences. Behaviors are repeated because they elicit a desired response. The challenge for staff is to discover the desired response and to provide it freely. If individuals exhibit difficult behaviors for attention, to participate in an activity, or for sensory stimulation, the program should provide those desired outcomes. Individuals should be assisted to obtain the desired object or sensation.

Successful behavior programs must identify the "right" reinforcer to motivate the individual. Reinforcers differ from person to person. Some people find affection reinforcing; others would rather not be touched. Some people will work hard for praise, while others seem unaffected by positive feedback. Behavior programs often require more than one reinforcer because the continued application of the same reinforcer decreases its appeal. A "menu" of different reinforcers ensures that the program will be effective over a longer period of time.

Reinforcers should be selected on an individual basis. Some individuals are able to learn that tokens, check marks, or stars can be converted into other desired reinforcers. Other individuals with more severe levels of mental retardation may not be able to understand the connection between the receipt and exchange of tokens for a delayed reinforcer. These individuals may need more immediate reinforcement, such as a pat on the back or an edible reinforcer.

The selected reinforcer must be available and convenient. For example, an individual may love to attend baseball games, and this might be one of the options on the menu of reinforcers. It would be a poor choice, however, as a sole reinforcer because it is not always possible to attend a baseball game within a reasonable period of time. Reinforcers should be selected only if they can be used readily in a variety of locations and over a range of times.

The reinforcers selected must be used consistently in accordance with the schedule described in the behavior program. Reinforcers may need to be given frequently at first to ensure that the individual can pair the reinforcer with his or her performance of the desired behavior. The success of the program hinges on teaching the individual that a certain behavior will consistently elicit a specific, desired response. The key to teaching this is the consistent delivery of reinforcement as per a schedule determined by the team.

Teach a new skill. Sometimes people with mental retardation lack the skills to make their needs known or to accomplish a task. In these cases the individual may use behaviors to express frustration or to accomplish a goal. For example, a woman who is deaf and blind learned to stop pulling down her slacks when she was taught a hand sign for "toilet." Once she learned the sign and found that staff consistently responded to her request, she no longer had to demonstrate her needs through inappropriate behaviors. People with mental retardation sometimes need to learn new skills that allow them to:

• Ask for help
• Communicate their feelings
• Say "No!"
• Deal with changes of schedule
• Reduce stress
• Assert control
• Initiate favorite activities and so forth

Behavior problems sometimes result from frustration over the inability to predict or control life events. In these instances augmentative communication systems and picture schedules assist individuals to increase control over their environments.

A wide range of augmentative communication devices can be made or are commercially available. These devices will range in complexity from simple cards with pictures, words, or symbols to computerized voice synthesizers that actually speak for the individual.

The ability to communicate can reduce frustration that often results in behavior problems.

Many individuals with developmental disabilities are unable to anticipate occurrences in their environment. Frustration and subsequent behavior problems may occur because of an inability to anticipate events or exert control over the environment. This is critical when there is an unexpected change of routine. For individuals who depend upon consistency, picture schedules are helpful. A picture schedule consists of photographs of an individual engaging in a range of daily activities. For example, there may be a series of photographs of the individual getting out of bed, putting on his or her slippers, brushing his or her teeth, taking a shower, and so forth. The schedule could be posted in the individual's room or carried in a small photo album. Staff can assist the individual to track the completed tasks and to plan for the next activity. The individual with developmental disabilities can use the schedule to request a change of routine, or staff can use it to explain upcoming changes. For example, staff can demonstrate that tomorrow an individual will not go to work in the van but will instead go by car to the dentist and then to work. People who frequently have behavior problems during periods of transition may benefit from picture schedules.

Program Checklist

	Yes	No
1. Intervention strategies relate to the hypotheses.	___	___
2. Reinforcers are specific to the individual.	___	___
3. Reinforcers are convenient and available.	___	___
4. Consistent use of reinforcers is documented.	___	___
5. Teaching new skills is considered when designing a program.	___	___

Design and Implement a Written Program

The agreed-upon strategy for changing a behavior is written as a detailed behavior program. Intervention strategies are a logical extension of the functional analysis. The program flows from the hypothesis regarding the function of the behavior.

All staff implementing the program should participate in its development. Direct care staff spend the most time with the individual and may have the best understanding of the functions of the behavior. In addition, the individuals implementing the program should understand it, believe that it will work, and support its implementation. Special clinical staff, residential and day program staff, and the individual may need to make compromises in designing the program so that all participants feel ownership.

The facility should ensure that all staff are aware of the program and respond to the identified behavior in a uniform and consistent manner. The behavior program should be written clearly, describing exact procedures to change the behavior. Specific instructions with regard to environmental modifications, responses to behavior, types of reinforcement, reinforcement schedules, and data collection should be included.

Training should be provided to all staff to ensure consistent implementation. In addition to reviewing the written document, the trainer may demonstrate appropriate staff responses to the behavior. Following staff training, reliability reviews should be initiated by first making a checklist of all of the steps in the program. Then an observer should record the number of steps that are performed accurately and determine the percentage of correctly performed steps. Observations of staff implementing the program should be made at different times during the day. Reliability of less than 85% indicates need for additional staff training. Reliability checks should be performed with regularity.

Compare New Frequency and Severity Data to Those Collected Earlier

The original hypothesis is tested by comparing current behavioral data to the baseline data collected before implementing the program. If the hypothesis regarding the function of the behavior was correct, and if the behavior program was well designed and consistently implemented, staff should observe a reduction in problem behaviors or an increase in positive behaviors. To expect that severe behavior problems will be completely eliminated may be unrealistic. The appropriate goal, in most cases, is to reduce severe behaviors to a manageable level and to teach a repertoire of alternate behaviors.

Under unusual conditions or in times of extreme stress individuals may revert to behaviors that served a past purpose. Staff should agree on the level of behaviors that will be tolerated and focus programming efforts on behaviors that exceed these levels.

Review Process

Programs that are not implemented accurately and consistently will not be successful. Before a great deal of effort is put into reanalyzing the behavior and revising the unsuccessful program, conduct a reliability check to determine if the program is being implemented correctly. If reliability data reveal that the program is being implemented properly, staff should return to step 4 of the process and examine the appropriateness of the environment and expectations for the individual. ABC data should be reviewed to formulate a second hypothesis regarding the function of the behavior. The involvement, in a brainstorming meeting, of a broad spectrum of people who know the individual is often helpful in identifying creative approaches to understanding difficult behavior. Finally, the new hypothesis will need to be tested with a second behavior program. The new behavior program should respond directly to the theory regarding the function of the behavior.

Choosing the Appropriate Strategy

Behavior is not arbitrary. Rather, it is a person's response to the demands of his or her environment. Therefore, to be successful, the selection of an intervention strategy cannot be arbitrary. Successful behavioral programming rests on the ability to identify accurately the message conveyed by the behavior.

A variety of criteria exist on which to base the selection of an intervention strategy. Experts in the field of behavior change often must try several different approaches before one is successful. The following are guidelines for the selection of a specific strategy:

- *Is the strategy a direct response to the hypothesized function of the behavior?* Successful behavior programs cannot be written until the behavior is analyzed and understood. The behavior was learned because it met a need for the individual. The behavior will not change until sufficient motivation is provided and alternate behaviors are learned.
- *Is the strategy likely to result in changed behavior?* Although this question can never be answered with absolute certainty prior to the implementation of a procedure, staff familiar with the individual should agree that the strategy appears to address the function of the behavior.
- *Is the strategy humane and socially valid?* The behavior program should affirm the rights of the individual, should not treat the person with disabilities in a stigmatizing manner, and should guard against the depersonalization of the individual.
- *Is the strategy practical?* Staff should design a strategy that can be understood and supported by the people who will be implementing it. The program should not be too complex or difficult to allow for continuous and consistent implementation.
- *Does the strategy contribute to an individual's positive self-image and society's image of individuals with disabilities?* The approach selected should enhance the individual's dignity and self-worth.

Program Checklist

	Yes	No
1. All staff implementing the program participate in its development.	___	___
2. Staff are trained for consistent implementation of the program.	___	___
3. Staff compare program data with baseline data to measure program effectiveness.	___	___
4. Reliability checks are performed.	___	___
5. Programs are modified based on data review.	___	___

IMPLICATIONS

For Qualified Mental Retardation Professionals

The qualified mental retardation professional (QMRP) is responsible for overseeing and coordinating all the services received by the individuals in the program. When individuals have severe behavior problems, the QMRP must ensure that effective behavior programs are implemented. The QMRP may need to involve different staff in this process. In addition, the QMRP ensures that the rights of the individual are protected.

The QMRP assists all staff to explore the link between the environment and the function of the behavior. Once a behavior program is developed, the QMRP and the psychologist assume responsibility for staff training, monitoring implementation, and reviewing documentation.

The QMRP and psychologist review the data collected on the behavior. Information regarding both the frequency and severity of the behavior should be readily available. Program data should document the accurate, consistent implementation of the program. If the program includes the delivery of reinforcers, data should indicate the time specific reinforcers were given.

The QMRP ensures that needed program revisions are based on collected data. Data should be formatted to allow program success to be determined. Records should reveal frequent reliability checks of the implementation of the program by a variety of staff, in all environments, and at different times during the day. Reliability checks revealing inconsistent implementation should lead to further staff training. Programs that do not result in improvement in the frequency or intensity of the behavior should not be continued. Revisions should be made by the interdisciplinary team. These should be based on a review of all data and include a further analysis of the function of the behavior.

For Specialized Service Staff

All specialized service staff contribute to the process of modifying challenging behaviors. Each staff member brings to the interdisciplinary team his or her own perceptions of the function and meaning of the difficult behaviors. Each assessment should contain a discussion of the meaning of the difficult behaviors for the individual. Each team member can contribute to a synthesized understanding of challenging behaviors.

The psychologist plays a particularly important role in analyzing and changing behavior by evaluating the information shared by team members. The psychologist generally supervises the development of the written behavior program based on the input of the team. Behavior programs can be developed by other team members. The psychologist in these cases may work with other staff to provide training in behavior change and to assist where needed. The psychologist is usually responsible for training team members, ensuring that staff understand the program, and overseeing the correct and consistent implementation of the program.

Finally, the psychologist is responsible for proper data and the analysis of the data to determine if the program is successful. When programs are successful, the psychologist considers methods to decrease the reinforcement or to substitute natural reinforcers for those provided by the program. When programs are not successful, the psychologist must take the lead in reanalyzing the behavior.

For Direct Care Staff

Direct care workers are generally most familiar with the individual. They can observe the behavior and identify when, where, and perhaps why the behavior occurs. As a result they provide critical input into an analysis of the function of the behavior. Direct care staff are equally responsible for implementing the program. Therefore, they must be certain that their understanding of the behavior is shared with the rest of the team and that the program is responsive. They need to seek clarification when they do not understand a program, when the approach does not make sense to them, or when the program seems too difficult or complex to implement consistently. With proper training direct care staff can also develop behavior programs in consultation with the team.

For Quality Assurance Coordinators

Quality assurance (QA) coordinators should note programs that respond to a careful analysis of the behavior. They should determine whether different staff contributed to the assessment and analysis of the behavior. The QA coordinator should be able to observe staff in all environments implementing the program consistently. Upon interview, direct care and specialized service staff should demonstrate familiarity with the behavior programs.

Behavior programs are individualized. Even in instances where more than one resident exhibits the same behavior, the programs must be individualized. Although two individuals may scream or throw objects, they are probably not exhibiting the behaviors for the same reasons. QA coordinators should look for written programs that are individualized and sufficiently detailed to allow consistent implementation.

Finally, QA coordinators should determine that positive strategies were exhausted before staff resorted to even mildly aversive procedures. In addition to records that reflect the creative and consistent application of positive programming, policies should be in place that support the use of nonaversive techniques. Training in positive approaches to behavior change should be provided to all staff.

CONCLUSION

Although behavior may appear to be unprovoked or unpredictable, all behavior has a function. A behavior that appears dysfunctional serves a purpose or function for the individual with developmental disabilities. Behaviors called "maladaptive" may be quite adaptive for the individual performing them. Individuals who have limited ability to communicate verbally may use behavior as a method of expression. This communication pattern may not always be realized or understood by the individual with developmental disabilities. Staff require good observation skills to discover the function of the behavior. The challenge for staff working with individuals with dangerous or disruptive behaviors is to refocus attention on the need for the behavior rather than on the behavior itself.

When staff analyze the functions of the behaviors of the individuals with whom they work, they will often uncover frustration or dissatisfaction with the environment or with the expectations of the program. Staff should examine the environment to determine if they would like to:

- Live there?
- Adhere to the schedule?
- Work in this environment?
- Follow these rules?
- Participate in these activities?
- Be allowed the same number of choices that are available to the individuals in this program?
- Be treated like individuals in this program?

If the answer to any of these questions is "no," staff need to change the environment and improve the places in which people work and live. Physical and program environments influence behaviors. Staff should examine whether they can make environments more pleasant and self-affirming.

Individuals with difficult behaviors offer a particular challenge to staff. Numerous programs throughout the country that serve individuals with severe behavior problems succeed through positive approaches to behavior change.

Staff must apply behavioral principles creatively to offer people opportunities to express needs, to make choices, and to control their environment without needing to resort to disruptive behaviors.

REFERENCES

Donnellan, A. M., LaVigna, G. W., Negri-Shoultz, N., & Fassbender, L. L. (1988). *Progress without punishment: Effective approaches for learners with behavior problems.* New York: Teachers College Press.

Gardner, J. F., & Chapman, M. S. (1985). *Staff development in mental retardation services: A practical handbook.* Baltimore: Paul H. Brookes Publishing Co.

Horner, R. H., Dunlap, G., & Koegel, R. L. (Eds.). (1988). *Generalization and maintenance: Life-style changes in applied settings.* Baltimore: Paul H. Brookes Publishing Co.

Knoll, J. (1986). Syracuse study shows integration works. *Journal of the Association for Persons with Severe Handicaps, 12*(6), 3–7.

Repp, A. C., & Deitz, S. M. (1974). Reducing aggressive and self-injurious behavior of institutionalized retarded children through reinforcement of other behaviors. *Journal of Applied Behavior Analysis, 7,* 313–325.

Smith, M. (1985). Managing the aggressive and self-injurious behavior of adults disabled by autism. *Journal of the Association for Persons with Severe Handicaps, 10*(4), 228–232.

Vukelich, R., & Hake, D. F., (1971). Reduction of dangerously aggressive behavior in a severely retarded resident through a combination of positive reinforcement procedures. *Journal of Applied Behavior Analysis, 4,* 215–225.

Woods, T. (1982). Reducing severe aggressive and self-injurious behavior: A non-intrusive, home-based approach. *Behavioral Disorders, 7*(3), 180–188.

5
The Team as a Small Group

James F. Gardner

Active treatment depends upon the interdisciplinary team process. The assessment, planning, and program implementation by professionals, clinical specialists, day and residential program staff, and other support personnel must be integrated and coordinated. A common uniform program is necessary so that staff behaviors are predictable to the individual with developmental disabilities.

Developing uniformity and predictability within any group of people is a difficult management task. The management of group process requires time and effort so that groups, through practice, can learn to work together. All teams must make extra efforts to take in new members and engage in new tasks.

Interdisciplinary teams in intermediate care facilities for the mentally retarded (ICF/MR) are no different. Team members must sacrifice individual and professional priorities at times to maximize the team effort. Effective teams also realize that the process for completing work is as important as the outcome of the meeting. Finally, the team process influences the content of the individual program plan. Effective team process that includes all team members, that encourages open questioning and feedback, and that is based on the individuals' strengths and desires will produce a superior program plan.

BACKGROUND: A MODEL FOR TEAM PROCESS

The interdisciplinary team in the ICF/MR program can be examined in the context of small group process and team building. R. M. Stogdill proposed a model that focused on the individuals in the group, their interrelationship, and joint action as a group (Stogdill, 1959).

Stogdill's theory of individual behavior and group achievement rested on four assumptions:

1. A team can be described in terms of the behaviors of its members.
2. People's past experience determines, to some extent, their behavior in the team context.
3. The behavior of the individuals and team is determined to some extent by the social order of the organization.
4. The behavior of the group will be determined by its membership and its social environment.

Team members bring their own attitudes and behaviors to the group process. The readiness to contribute to the group process and performance during team meetings are attributes of the individual group members and result in patterns of behavior and interaction. Over time these patterns and interactions result in a series of mediating variables such as status, norms, roles, and authority.

Stogdill's theory of group achievement provides insight into factors affecting group performance (Ivancevich, Szilagyi, & Wallace, 1977). For example:

- Successful group activities reinforce the expectation of further success. Group morale is related to group productivity.
- Productivity is increased when norms, roles, and status are clearly defined.
- Integration is facilitated when members of the group agree on the goals of the group.
- Group motivation is enhanced by setting attainable goals and reinforcing goal attainment.
- The norms, values, and status assignments of the larger social organization influence the behavior of teams.

Stages of Team Development

Groups and teams acquire behaviors and undergo change in a sequential process. Teams evolve through stages (Brill, 1976):

Stage 1: Orientation

Function: Exploration, learning, and evaluation
Member Tasks: Learn what is expected and deal with the unfamiliarity, anxiety, and stress of the new situation
Team Tasks: Define boundaries and provide support
Outcome: Acquaintance with fellow team members, understanding of the system, and early sense of security

Stage 2: Accommodation

Function: Movement and change of position during power struggles

Member Tasks: Find appropriate places both for the personal and professional self

Team Tasks: Provide a structure and climate to facilitate the adaptive process

Outcome: Beginning development of common values and norms as well as common language and communication

Stage 3: Mutual Understanding

Function: Establishment of boundaries and definition of the area of specialization

Member Tasks: Communicate, agree, and disagree

Team Tasks: Define boundaries of purpose and specialization Designate goals, tasks, and roles

Outcome: Establishment of dependency and differentiation Work rules are concluded

Stage 4: Achievement of Complementarity and Wholeness

Function: Achievement of complementarity and wholeness

Member Tasks: Relate to other members and the team

Team Tasks: Make decisions, plan and execute work

Outcome: Collaboration toward achievement of goals and realization of purpose

Stage 5: Finalization

Function: Team self-evaluation of the process and achievement in relation to purpose and goals

Member Tasks: Objective assessment of personal and team performance

Team Tasks: Provide support for the self-evaluation

Outcome: Personal and team change

Structural Dimensions of Teams

Within any team or small group, some structure for group activity develops over time. Stogdill's model for group achievement describes how that development takes place, and Brill outlines the stages of team development. The following variables influence team development (Ivancevich et al., 1977).

Group Composition

The characteristics of individuals who make up groups influence group performance. For example, groups with similar needs, motives, and personalities often display effective cooperation and communication. However, too much similarity among team members may result in excess group conformity.

In some instances diversity in individual characteristics may cause high performance levels as members stimulate the abilities of each other. Diversity among team members may allow for greater team problem-solving skills. Unfortunately, diversity also presents the potential for conflict.

Group composition and performance are also related to the nature of the group task. Teams composed of individuals with similar and compatible characteristics will perform more effectively on routine tasks. However, teams with diverse membership may outperform teams with similar members when faced with tasks that require a variety of problem-solving methods.

Status Systems

Status is defined as a social ranking within a group. Status is assigned to an individual on the basis of position in a group or because of individual characteristics. Status can be derived, for example, from the individual's title, salary level, or seniority. Status can have a positive consequence in providing clear definitions of responsibility and authority. An overemphasis on status, however, may reduce interaction among team members and the frequency of communication.

Disagreement over the level of status causes confusion, anxiety, and mixed communication. The team's energy is deflected from goal accomplishment to reaching agreement on the status system.

Roles

Members of small groups and teams expect other members to behave in certain ways. The expected roles of team members are usually derived from the job description, position title, licensure or certification, or professional training.

In addition to expected roles, individuals may also exhibit perceived roles. The perceived role represents a set of activities that an individual believes he or she should perform. The difference between expected role and perceived role is termed role ambiguity. Team members who don't know what they're doing often are suffering from role ambiguity, caused by the lack of a clear job description or by the nature of complex jobs.

Finally, a conflict in roles results when two or more individuals attempt to perform the role designed for only one person. Role conflict generally develops from multiple demands and conflicting directions and results in tension, stress, and anxiety.

Cohesiveness

Some groups display a closeness and share common attitudes and behaviors that are lacking in other groups. The following factors generally increase cohesiveness of groups:

• Agreement on group goal
• Frequency of interaction
• Personal attractiveness
• Intergroup competition
• Favorable evaluation

In a general manner the opposite factors decrease group cohesiveness. They include:

- Disagreement on group goals
- Increasing group size beyond four to six members
- Unpleasant experiences with the group
- Intragroup competition
- Domination by one individual

Norms

Norms are defined as any uniformity of attitude, opinion, feeling, or action shared by two or more people. Norms are the unwritten rules of small group behavior. The formation of group norms ensures that boundaries exist to maintain group performance. For example, cohesiveness does not lead automatically to increased team performance. Highly cohesive teams can perform at high or low levels depending upon the performance norms of the group.

Norms may not be the same for all group members. For example, all team members are expected to abide by the production norm, but only the supervisors can alter the production norm. In another setting all direct care workers begin work at 7 a.m., but professionals do not arrive at work until 8:30 a.m.

Norms represent a mediating variable in Stogdill's model. They develop over time from individual group member contributions. Once norms are established as mediating variables (interpersonal forces that influence individual behavior), social forces operate on each member of the group to ensure compliance with the norms. Because norms are unwritten rules at the informal level of the organization and because they serve group unity, they are almost impossible to change by ordinary supervisory methods.

Behavior and Group Process

All small groups depend upon certain behaviors to fulfill tasks and maintain the group. Another group of behaviors disrupts the group's interaction (Morris & Sashkin, 1976). Interdisciplinary teams, like other small groups, can identify members displaying harmonizing and disruptive behaviors.

Behaviors necessary for fulfillment of group tasks facilitate the group process. They include:

- *Initiation*—Providing new ideas and making suggestions for solving a problem.
- *Elaborating*—Expanding and clarifying the ideas of others, interpreting ideas for other team members, finding new possibilites in old ideas.
- *Summarizing*—Drawing separate ideas together, offering conclusions and recommendations.

- *Organizing*—Scheduling meetings, setting up the room, taking notes, mailing minutes of the meeting.

Behaviors that lead to team integration and cohesion are important for the group's maintenance. They include:

- *Encouraging*—All team members need support and positive feedback on contributions. Encouragement is provided by remarks, gestures, or facial expressions.
- *Harmonizing*—Differences need to be worked through. Part of this function is relieving tensions by humor or jokes so that the group can stay on task.
- *Gatekeeping*—Active participation of others should be encouraged and the discussion moved away from those team members who dominate it.
- *Processing/Observing*—Feedback should be provided to the team on its own group process.
- *Following*—All team members cannot lead at the same time. Following for a time is an acceptable role behavior.
- *Negotiating/Compromising*—No team member can or should be right all the time.

Certain behaviors are irrelevant to the problem-solving process. Sometimes they are negatively oriented and disrupt the team process. These negative behaviors include:

- *Aggression*—Attacking people or ideas without justification. Keeps the group off task.
- *Blocking*—Being in opposition to progress toward team goals.
- *Attention seeking*—Calling attention to oneself or pleading a special interest.
- *Dominating*—Attempting to take over and lead the group in an inappropriate direction; manipulating the team for his or her own purpose.
- *Agenda busting*—Diverting the group from its priorities. Moving off the agenda to new issues.

REVIEW OF THE STANDARDS

483.430(a)	*Qualified mental retardation professional*
483.430(b)	*Professional program services*
483.430(d)	*Direct care (residential living unit) staff*
483.440(a)	*Active treatment*
483.440(c)	*Individual program plan*
483.440(d)	*Program implementation*
483.450(b)	*Management of inappropriate client behavior*
483.450(e)	*Drug usage*
483.460(a)	*Physician services*

483.460(b) *Physician participation in the individual program plan*
483.460(c) *Nursing services*
483.460(e) *Dental services*
483.460 (i) *Drug regimen review*
483.480(a) *Food and nutrition services*
483.480(d) *Dining areas and service*

The standards discuss the qualified mental retardation professional's (QMRP) responsibilities for coordinating each individual's active treatment program. Appropriate facility professional and direct care residential living unit staff participate in the interdisciplinary team process. The purpose of the team process "is to provide team members with the opportunity to review and discuss information and recommendation relevent to the individuals' needs and to reach decisions as a team rather than individually (HCFA, 1988).

The active treatment standard covers the requirements for the interdisciplinary team in the development of the individual program plan. The requirements for comprehensive functional assessments, behavioral objectives, data collection, program implementation, and monitoring are stated.

The relationship between interdisciplinary team process and the development of behavior management programs is established. Team responsibilities and individual initiative are covered in standards on management of inappropriate client behaviors, drug usage, physician services, nursing services, dental services, and drug review requirements. Finally, team responsibilities for mealtime programs are established in the standards for food and nutrition services and dining areas and service.

APPLICATION

The interdisciplinary approach in the field of mental retardation and developmental disabilities evolved to focus attention on the whole person with a disability. It began in an effort to integrate and coordinate the increasingly specialized disciplines. Professional training programs recognized that the needs of persons with developmental disabilities extended beyond the skills and orientation of any single discipline. For example, the professional training of occupational and physical therapists required interaction with physicians, social workers, and special educators. The needs of people with cerebral palsy may require the coordinated efforts of a neurologist, physical therapist, nutritionist, and speech therapist.

Organizational Requirements for Effective Interdisciplinary Teams

The development and maintenance of good interdisciplinary team process require organization commitment. The management of the habilitation facility must structure the organization so that the inter-disciplinary teams can accomplish their purpose. The interdisciplinary team can be effective if the ICR/MR addresses six specific issues.

1. A clear mission statement for a habilitation facility must exist. The interdisciplinary team will not be able to identify its purpose and responsibility without one.
2. The administration must decide whether the facility is a closed or open system. An open system habilitation program is part of a larger community. People move into the facility for active treatment and flow to less restrictive settings for different programs and services. Movement within the facility might be present as people gain skills and abilities. In a closed system no movement is expected. The habilitation program is a segregated program.
3. The administration must establish an expectation for people residing in the facility. The facility can expect movement toward a less restrictive setting, or it can define the present program as the future program. In an open system with expectation for movement, interdisciplinary teams approach the planning process with the question, "What programs and services will provide skills and abilities necessary for the future environment?" In closed systems with few expectations, team members answer the question, "What services can my discipline provide in this setting?"
4. The administration must identify the scope and range within the facility for active treatment. Active treatment and the inter-disciplinary team process should extend across day and residental programs, cover all three shifts, and be carried out on week-ends and holidays.
5. Whenever possible, training should take place in real life environments rather than through simulations. Teach mobility skills on buses in local neighborhoods. Teach vocational skills in employment settings. Persons with mental retardation experience difficulty in generalizing experience from one setting to another. In addition, residents should have the opportunity to practice the skill or behavior in real environments. Interdisciplinary teams should question why a skill is being taught if no opportunity exists for practice.
6. The facility must identify the role of the clinical specialists. The traditional role of the clinical specialists was to provide treatment and therapy in the departmental office or clinic for a prescribed number of hours per week. A more contemporary program design defines clinical specialists as support for day and residential program staff. As such, they take part in the active treatment programs during bathing, mealtimes, leisure activities, and day habilitation programs.

Program Checklist

	Yes	No
1. The facility has a mission statement.	—	—
2. The facility is part of the community.	—	—
3. An expectation that individuals will be discharged from the facility is present.	—	—
4. Active treatment takes place in all program settings.	—	—
5. Training occurs in natural environments.	—	—
6. Clinical specialists support day and residential program staff.	—	—

Organizing as an Interdisciplinary Team

Professional teams practice. Theater companies, the symphony, and the ballet work hard at perfecting their performance. Professional teams recognize that the winning edge comes from team performance rather than individual performances. In fact, team performance is more important than any individual performance (Keidal, 1984). These same factors apply to interdisciplinary teams in the ICF/MR. Administrators should not expect good interdisciplinary team process without hard work, practice, and attention to the team process itself. In fact, administrators should recognize that teams will proceed through different stages of development and that they may need some extra assistance through the early stages.

Teams will need to decrease status differences between and among members. Despite different incomes, education, and prestige, membership on the interdisciplinary teams confers equal responsibility for decisions. In some instances clinical specialists will have to adjust status performance and expectations when they serve as members of interdisciplinary teams.

Day and residential staff will also have to accept new status definitions. When acting as team members, they assume a different status from that associated with their normal job. An increased responsibility is associated with team membership. In some instances day and residential staff will need special training to assume that responsibility and participate in the team process.

Most ICFs/MR employ staff to perform specific duties and responsibilities. Staff are seldom employed to serve only on the interdisciplinary team. Rather, they are hired as residential counselors or supported employment job coaches. One of the designated duties and responsibilities is to serve on the interdisciplinary team. ICF/MR staff must differentiate between their roles as unit staff and members of the interdisciplinary team. In an optimal program the difference between the two roles would be minimal. In most facilities, however, differences in responsibility between the team role and the service role will be evident. Within the context of the team meeting, individuals will exert more autonomy and independence. After returning to the service setting, however, staff have a responsiblity to a unit or department supervisor. ICF/MR staff need to appreciate the difference in autonomy between the team role and the service role.

Clinical and educational specialists also perform a different role in supporting program implementation by the day and residential program staff. In private practice or in acute care settings the clinical or educational specialist may provide direct service for a measured period of time. In the ICF/MR program, in contrast, the primary role of the specialist is to support the day and residential staff in providing active treatment programs. This support consists of training, supervising, and guiding staff through the provision of clinical, behavioral, or educational programs.

This support role for clinical and educational specialists is not an abandonment of professional or ethical responsibility. Rather, it is an acknowledgment that the ICF/MR is a 24-hour residential active treatment program. Clinical, educational, and behavioral specialists cannot provide individualized service to all residents across 3 shifts, 7 days a week. They are, by necessity, the support resource for day and residential staff in their provision of continuous active treatment services.

The interdisciplinary team must identify and make explicit the norms that govern the team's behavior. The team's norms will be different from the norms of the individual team members. Each team member will bring to the team process a set of norms from his or her primary employment affiliation. For example, staff from the cottage will bring the norms of the residential staff. The clinical specialists will adhere to a set of informal work rules that are derived from the clinical departments.

The challenge for the team, then, is to develop a set of norms that apply to its process and that supercede the other norms to which team members may adhere. Both newly formed and ongoing interdisciplinary teams should take an inventory of individual norms, existing team norms, and new norms that would maximize team performance.

In addition to clarifying roles and norms, teams can enhance effectiveness by adopting certain work rules. For example, team members might agree with the following rules for team meetings:

- All assessments and reports will be typed and distributed to team members 1 week prior to the meeting.
- All team meetings will begin on time, and no members will arrive late.
- All team members will read assessments and reports prior to the meeting.

- All team members will be more concerned with the needs of the resident that with the status or position of their own disciplines.
- All team members will be accorded equal responsibility in the design of the program plan.
- All team members will perform facilitative and maintenance tasks and minimize negative behaviors.

The attention to status, roles, and norms will increase team performance only if stability of team membership exists. Occasional attrition and turnover causes the team to devote time and energy to orientating new staff. The team does not, however, have to go through the developmental stages of orientation, accommodation, mutual understanding, operation, and self-evaluation.

In contrast, a substantial turnover of team members in a short period may cause a disappearance of mediated status decisions, roles, and norms. In this instance the interdisciplinary team must again journey through the stages of development. Repeating the process of team development can be minimized if a core of team members remains constant and influential. They become the custodians of the team culture and pass on the mediated status, roles, and norms to new members.

Program Checklist

		Yes	No
1.	The interdisciplinary team has the opportunity to practice team skills.	___	___
2.	Clinical staff conduct in-service training for direct care staff.	___	___
3.	Clear norms for team performance are evident.	___	___
4.	A stable core of team members pass on values and norms to new team members.	___	___

Structure and the Interdisciplinary Team

Structural issues that influence interdisciplinary team effectiveness include membership, leadership, pre-meeting activities, the format of the team meeting, and post-meeting follow-through.

Membership

The person with the disability is the most important member of the interdisciplinary team because his or her needs, interests, and concerns should guide the direction of the team's deliberation. To the extent possible, the individual should be made aware of the purpose of the interdisciplinary team and participate as an equal member. Other members of the team must support the individual's participation in the process. Most importantly, the individual must be provided the opportunity to make real choices from the options and alternatives considered by the team.

Teams may use several methods to prepare individuals for meaningful participation in the team process. First, individuals can be encouraged and taught to make choices. The commitment to assisting individuals to make informed choices, whenever possible, is a part of active treatment. Second, individuals should be counseled and supported as they participate in team planning. Finally, team members can involve individuals in simulated interdisciplinary team meetings.

The individual's participation in the team process should be encouraged, and residents should, whenever possible, attend the team meeting when the IPP is developed. Even in those instances where residents cannot participate in the planning, they may attend all or part of the meeting.

Because individuals will demonstrate varying capabilities as members of the team, team members should consider participation taking place along a continuum:

1. *Active participation*—The resident can participate as a full member of the team.
2. *Interpretive participation*—The resident is assisted in participating in the team process by a team member who explains issues (either verbally or through alternative communication modes) and assists the individual in making choices during the meeting. Many individuals with severe disabilities previously considered unable to contribute to the team meeting can participate at this level.
3. *Representative participation*—An advocate represents the resident who is unable to participate in the team meeting. The resident may attend all or part of the meeting.

In those instances where the individual is not of majority age or where a legal guardian has been appointed, the parents (or guardian) should be considered full members of the interdisciplinary team. They should participate in the team process and attend the whole interdisciplinary team meeting. Parents (or guardians) should not merely be asked to join the team at the end of the meeting.

Team meetings should be scheduled at times convenient for the parents. Frequent communication with the family, organization of parent groups, and invitations to join the team and residents in social and recreational activities all tend to increase family participation. Finally, parent involvement in the interdisciplinary team process is often enhanced by supporting visits home.

In those instances where individuals have reached majority age and have not been declared legally incompetent, the decision of whether or not to involve the family rests with that individual.

Staff participation on the team should be determined by the strengths, needs, and interests of the individual. No single discipline or interest group must participate in all team decisions or functions. Effective small groups can consist of five to seven people, although most teams will contain additional representatives. Teams should weigh the effectiveness of limited size with the need for comprehensive information and deliberation.

Program Checklist

		Yes	No
1.	The facility has policies and procedures for involving individuals with developmental disabilities in the team process.	—	—
2.	Team meetings are scheduled at times convenient for individuals and, when appropriate, their families.	—	—
3.	Team composition is determined by individual strengths, needs, and interests.	—	—

Team Leadership

The issues of interdisciplinary team leadership concern the role of the QMRP, the chairperson of the interdisciplinary team meetings, and the situational leadership exercised by the various team members.

The QMRP functions as the case manager or service coordinator for the individual and is also responsible for coordinating the delivery of services and for monitoring program plan implementation. The regulations do not identify the QMRP as the chairperson or facilitator of the interdisciplinary team.

The skills and abilities required for chairing and facilitating the interdisciplinary team process suggest that the QMRP would not chair the meeting but would serve as the individual's service coordinator during the team process. The chair of the team meeting would be concerned with the meeting process and leave the content to other team members. As such, the chair would ensure that all participants engaged in facilitative and maintenance behaviors, avoiding negative behaviors. The chairperson abides by and enforces the team norm, poses questions, redirects responses, clarifies, and summarizes the discussion.

Each of the participants in the team meeting assumes a leadership responsibility when the meeting shifts to his or her area of specialization. Leadership is a shared responsibility and will shift at different times in the group process. Residential and day program staff have a special leadership responsibility to ensure that active treatment programs extend through 3 shifts, 7 days a week.

The Individual Program Plan Meeting

The primary focus of the interdisciplinary team process is the development of the individual program plan. One of the most important parts of the IPP process is the development of the written program plan that outlines the habilitation services required by the individual and the manner in which they will be provided.

The IPP should contain goals for the individual as well as specific objectives. For each objective there should be a detailed teaching strategy that defines the manner in which staff will assist the individual to accomplish individual objectives. Finally, there must be evaluation procedures that will indicate whether the teaching strategy enables the individual to accomplish objectives.

The IPP is developed by the interdisciplinary team and used by all staff who plan, provide, or evaluate services for individuals. All staff need the IPP to ensure that active treatment services and activities provided are in accordance with the agreed-upon plan. Staff use the plan when they carry out the teaching strategies set forth in the plan. The individual program plan also provides a baseline for evaluation of program outcomes.

The chairperson of the team meeting assumes certain pre-meeting responsibilities. The schedule for the meeting should be circulated in advance so that the consumer, the parents or guardian, if appropriate, can attend. Assessments should be circulated to team members prior to the meeting to reduce the reading of documents during the meeting. Finally, the chairperson and the individual's QMRP should identify priority concerns for the team's consideration.

In developing the IPP, the interdisciplinary team should establish and follow basic guidelines. The meeting should be located in a meeting room convenient for the consumer. The meeting should generally last between 1 and 2 hours. The chairperson should run an orderly, but not overly rigid, meeting. Team members should focus on problem solving and avoid reading reports. They should stress the major goals and objectives for the individual. They should concentrate on defining the future for the individual and delegate the technical writing of teaching strategies to individual team members.

Implementation of the individual program planning process based on the requirements for active treatment can greatly enhance the quality of life for people living in the ICF/MR. For this reason the interdisciplinary team process greatly influences the quality of life for people residing in the facility. The team process and the resulting IPP are important to the individual because:

- The individual becomes involved actively in the planning and implementation of programs. The individual's strengths, needs, and interests become the primary considerations in the selection of program goals and objectives, and the person is given the opportunity to make meaningful choices.
- Expectations for the individual are made explicit.

In addition, the individual also benefits from the effect of the individual program planning process on staff because:

- The IPP provides a detailed outline of staff responsibilities. Through written records and documentation, the IPP strengthens communication among staff and increases consistency in staff behavior.
- The IPP process enables staff to document their success in assisting individuals to master new skills and behaviors.
- The IPP provides the detailed and organized process for linking the critical mass of professional knowledge with the needs of individuals in the facility.
- Staff approach the individual as a person with strengths, interests, and needs, rather than as a person whose identity becomes synonymous with a problems list.

Finally, the resident should benefit from the impact of the IPP on the residential facility because:

- The plan should ensure that residents are not merely fitted into existing programs; rather, the resident is at the center of purposeful planning and service delivery.
- IPPs function as action plans for the ICF/MR, and the facility can utilize the IPPs to document needed resources and services for residents.

Program Checklist

		Yes	No
1.	The QMRP functions as the service coordinator.	___	___
2.	The QMRP facilitates the team meeting.	___	___
3.	Assessments are circulated to team members prior to the IPP meeting.	___	___
4.	The IPP process stresses individual strengths and preferences.	___	___

IMPLICATIONS

For Team Members

When serving as a member of the interdisciplinary team, the effectiveness of the team is more important than the status of an individual or his or her profession or special interest. Professional and personal needs and interests are given a lower priority than team goals. In addition, all team members are responsible for team performance. Each team member must demonstrate facilitative and maintenance behaviors and avoid negative behaviors.

Teams go through developmental stages. Not all teams within a single ICF/MR will demonstrate the same level of maturity or effectiveness. Interdisciplinary teams need practice. Part of that practice should include on-the-job training. Teams should appoint a process observer who would chart the interactions between team members, citing instances of facilitative, maintenance, and negative behaviors. The process would be summarized at the end of the meeting. The utilization of a process observer can make each team meeting a training session.

For Qualified Mental Retardation Professionals

As a member of the interdisciplinary team the QMRP serves as the case manager or service coordinator. The QMRP's responsibility is to monitor the implementation of the individual program plan as established by the interdisciplinary team. The QMRP should be able to explain the active treatment program for any individual across all physical settings, at any time during the day, whether part of an informal or formal teaching program.

For Specialized Service Staff

Specialized service staff assist in the design of an individual program plan that addresses current and future needs of the individual. The role of the specialized service staff extends beyond the identification of the discipline-specific needs of the consumer and the provision of individualized therapy or service. The specialized service staff contributes to the active treatment program by participating in programs that are provided throughout the day in a variety of locations.

The primary role of the specialized service staff is to support the day and residential staff in providing active treatment programs to the individual residing in the facility. In this role the specialized service staff serves as an educator and trainer for other staff. In some instances specialized service staff will need to cross-train other specialized service staff.

The specialized service staff will also be responsible for the traditional functions of assessment, service provision, and monitoring. In addition, however, the specialized service staff will assume the role of a participant in the residential living unit program, providing input on when skills can be taught and where they can be used.

For the Team Facilitator

The team facilitator will need training and experience in managing small group meetings. The management and coordination of the team process is an important, and often overlooked, responsibility. The facilitator will need confidence and support in enforcing rules for team meetings and in reinforcing team members for facilitative and maintenance behaviors.

The team facilitator should focus the team meeting on the central issues of consumer needs in a less restrictive setting by attempting to move as many activities as possible from the team meeting to the pre-team and post-team periods, circulating assessment material to team members prior to the meeting, identifying key issues for team members before the meeting, and delegating the writing of the instructional or behavioral programs to the team members.

For Individuals in the Facility

The consumer should receive training and assistance to understand the purpose of the team process, the program plan meeting, and the resulting individual program plan. This training consists of two parts. The first is that the individual should receive training and assistance in making meaningful choices. Exercising rights and making choices is the purpose of active treatment.

The second part of the training is enabling the individual to make choices that are related to performance. The ability to make choices must be demonstrated within the context of the team process. The individual must display skills and behaviors that enhance participation in the team process.

For Residential Staff

The residential staff have a responsibility for participating as members of the team and for ensuring the provision of active treatment across all shifts 7 days a week. As such, they will be asked to make new contributions to the active treatment program. They will need clear instructions for providing program services. Residential and other direct care staff will need a mechanism to provide daily feedback and input for program modifications.

The direct care and residential staff will also need clear guidance on responsibilities for continuous active treatment programs in both formal and informal interactions. They will be responsible for translating formal programs and policy and procedure into informal interactions with individuals in a variety of settings.

Finally, residential staff will need training and support from the specialized clinical staff. The training should be specific to individuals in the facility and should cover the methods for teaching and/or managing behavior, methods of documentation, and the process for monitoring and evaluation.

For Management Staff

The management of the facility must ensure that a mission statement emphasizes the provision of active treatment through the interdisciplinary team process. The management must also provide the interdisciplinary teams with the time and resources to practice and develop as work teams.

The management of the facility must ensure that the inter-

disciplinary teams contain the number and variety of clinical specialists necessary to address the needs of the individuals residing in the
facility.

CONCLUSION

Individual team members bring their own norms, values, and behaviors to the interdisciplinary team process. These individual attributes result in the formation of mediating variables that, in turn,
influence all team members.

Status systems, roles, cohesiveness, norms, and group behavior
influence team performance. Each can be modified if the team is allowed to examine and enhance its own performance. All staff adhere
to different rules of behavior and perform differently as individuals
and as members of the team.

The individual with developmental disabilities is the most important member of the team. The ICF/MR can assist individuals to
participate in the team process through education, counseling, and
role-playing simulations. Individual participation can take the form
of active participation, interpretive participation, or representative
participation.

The QMRP serves as the case manager for the individual but is
not necessarily the facilitator of the team meeting. The facilitator requires specialized skills to move the meeting forward, allow all participants to contribute, provide feedback and clarification to team
members, and manage a consensus building process.

REFERENCES

Brill, N. (1976). *Team work*. New York: J. B. Lippincott.

Dyer, W. G. (1987). *Team building: Issues and alternatives* (2nd ed.). Reading,
MA: Addison-Wesley Publishing Co.

Health Care Financing Administration. (October 1988). *State operations
manual. Provider certification: Appendix J. Interpretive guidelines for
ICFs/MR*. W-168.

Ivancevich, J. M., Szilagyi, A. D., & Wallace, M. J. (1977). *Organizational behavior and performance*. Santa Monica, CA: Goodyear Publishing Co.

Keidal, R. W. (1984). Baseball, football, and basketball: Models for business.
Organizational Dynamics, Winter 1984.

Morris, W. C., & Sashkin, M. (1976). *Organizational behavior in action: Skill
building experiences*. New York: West Publishing Co.

Stogdill, R. M. (1959). *Individual behavior and group achievement*. New
York: Oxford Press.

II
THE ACTIVE
TREATMENT CYCLE

6
Active Treatment

Michael S. Chapman

Agencies providing services to individuals with mental retardation and licensed as an intermediate care facility for the mentally retarded (ICF/MR) are required by federal law and regulation to provide active treatment. Active treatment has been a part of the ICF/MR regulations since 1974. Prior to 1974 most agencies provided custodial care for individuals with mental retardation that stressed basic survival needs of the individual. Facilities attempted to ensure that individual health and medical needs were met. With the implementation of federal regulations mandating active treatment, however, the role of the agency shifted from meeting the health and medical needs of the individual to enabling individuals to achieve their maximum potential. Impoverished, nonstimulating settings providing custodial treatment were no longer acceptable. Facilities were required by the new federal regulation to provide enriched environments and to involve aggressively individuals with developmental disabilities in habilitation programs. The federal regulation provided minimum guidelines and required the agency to define how active treatment would be achieved within programs.

The 1988 regulation shifts the emphasis from paper compliance to aggressive action-oriented programs for individuals with developmental disabilities. As in the former regulations, the new regulation provides operational guidelines without specific guidance. The challenge for facility staff is to interpret the conditions of participation and to design programs that meet each person's needs.

This chapter explores active treatment. It begins by defining active treatment, then presents the six components of active treatment, and finally, offers issues for consideration by agencies as they implement active treatment.

BACKGROUND

Defining Active Treatment

The ICF/MR standards define active treatment by stating:

> Each client must receive a continuous active treatment program, which includes aggressive, consistent implementation of a program of specialized and generic training, treatment, health services, and related services described in this subpart, that is directed toward—(i) The acquisition of the behaviors necessary for the client to function with as much self determination and independence as possible; (ii) The prevention or deceleration of regression or loss of current optimal functional status.

Dianne Manfredini and Wayne Smith (1988), have described active treatment as:

> the consistent, aggressive, continuous, and accountable application of habilitative interventions by caregivers of persons with developmental disabilities.

This book presents a three-tier approach to active treatment, viewed within the individual, group, and organizational/system contexts.

Active treatment involves meeting the needs of individuals with developmental disabilities. The 1988 regulations focus on individual outcome measures. The design and evaluation of program plans focus on the individual. For most identified objectives, however, the implementation of program plans takes place within a group. The focus of instruction is on individual objectives within group settings and activities. Active treatment is measured by the effectiveness of the instructors' (mostly the direct care staff) ability to implement effectively individualized objectives in a group setting, as defined by the measurable outcomes in client growth and development.

The third tier views active treatment from a systems context where the major concern is agency effectiveness in the delivery of services to all residents in the program. Active treatment within this context means that the facility is responsive to the changing needs of the individual with developmental disabilities. The facility policy and procedures ensure responsiveness. Policy and procedures must address those processes the agencies put into place that govern the delivery of services to individuals with developmental disabilities.

This third definition enables the reader to view active treatment from a systems framework. The federal government provides a broad definition but requires the agency to operationalize the definition.

Six subsystems are included in the active treatment cycle: agency mission, assessment, the interdisciplinary team process, goals and objectives, intervention strategies, and monitoring and evaluation. Each subsystem is connected to the other. Good assessments influence an interdisciplinary team process which yields goals and objectives. The key to providing active treatment is to develop an in-depth understanding of each of these subsystems. The six components are applicable to the individual, group, and systems contexts of active treatment.

The active treatment process is visualized in Figure 1.

Mission Statements

The mission statement defines agency purpose. It establishes the agency's vision by defining for staff what the agency wants to achieve. The written mission statement creates a shared vision for staff and provides the basis for decision making. It also drives the active treatment process. With a clearly defined mission statement, staff are able to determine:

- What assessments are needed
- How to focus the discussions and decision-making process of the interdisciplinary team
- What goals and objectives need to be established
- How to structure learning opportunities
- How to accomplish the stated mission through identified monitoring and evaluations methods

The mission statement is set forth in clear, descriptive language. It provides a clear picture of the agency's desired state. For example, a mission statement that reads, "to provide active treatment through the integration of professional staff in day and residential environments in order to maximize training opportunities for the resident so that the resident is returned to the community," establishes clear expectations for staff. The remaining components of the active treatment process are focused on accomplishing the stated mission.

Assessment

The assessment process, the second step in the active treatment cycle, is critical to the active treatment process. The assessment proc-

Figure 1. The active treatment process.

ess provides a clear understanding of the individual with developmental disabilities. Staff learn what the individual can and cannot do, likes and does not like, and desires for his or her life. The assessment process is dynamic, and ongoing. It is comprehensive in nature, requiring the contribution of many different specialized service staff and the direct care worker. Assessment is a focused process. For example, an assessment by a physical therapist or other staff member focuses on an individual's ambulation skills and gross motor development, and the residential staff assessment focuses on dressing, eating, toileting, leisure, and socialization skills. Chapter 8 provides an overview of the assessment process.

The Interdisciplinary Team Meeting

The third step in the active treatment process is the interdisciplinary team meeting. Facility staff need an opportunity to share and discuss openly assessment information, and the interdisciplinary team meeting provides this forum. During the team meeting assessment results are shared. Together, the team develops strengths, interests, and needs that provide the basis of the individual program plan. Chapter 5 discusses the interdisciplinary team process in detail.

Goals and Objectives

Establishing goals and objectives, the products of the interdisciplinary team meeting, is the fourth step in the active treatment process. Goals and objectives are written by the team and detail the intervention priorities of the team. They are an extension of the individual's strengths and interests and are written in behavioral terms. Goals and objectives serve to focus the staff's integration with the individual. Chapter 9 discusses developing the individual program plan (IPP), including formulating goals and objectives.

Intervention Strategies

Intervention strategies, the fifth step in the active treatment process, detail how staff will assist the individual with developmental disabilities to acquire new skills or maintain existing skills. Intervention strategies describe what staff will do for each objective established by the team. Intervention strategies usually include error-free learning methods, sequence of fading procedures, reinforcers to use, materials that are needed, opportunities for practice/generalization of the skill, and the data collection procedures to track the individual's progress. Each of these areas is defined in more detail in Chapter 10.

Monitoring, Evaluation, and Documentation

The final step in the active treatment cycle is monitoring, evaluation, and documentation. Monitoring and evaluation refer to two processes. A larger, systemic view of monitoring and evaluation refers to the process of determining how responsive the facility is to the needs of the individual. From a systemic viewpoint the facility evaluates the systems or processes put into place, such as those within the active treatment cycle, to determine if in fact they are responsive to the needs of each person. The facility must show that it is truly responsive as demonstrated in written policy and procedure and ultimately in day-to-day practice. Demonstrated responsiveness to the needs of the individual may include, for example, written policies and procedures involving incident/injury reporting and follow-up, and the provision of health services and transportation services.

The more focused view of monitoring, evaluation, and documentation involves the role of the qualified mental retardation professional (QMRP) in the active treatment cycle. The QMRP tracks each person's progression through the active treatment cycle and ensures that the facility is responsive to the needs of each individual. Once the IPP is written, the QMRP monitors its implementation and provides documentation of the person's progress. These roles are further discussed in Chapter 11.

The active treatment cycle is a dynamic process. The data collected during the year on the various intervention programs provide assessment information for the next interdisciplinary team meeting. Any team member at any time and for any reason can request a meeting of the team. The reason for requesting a meeting may include changes in the medical status of the person, lack of progress in programs, accomplishment of objectives, and so on. The facility's quality assurance (QA) coordinator will want to document the facility's responsiveness in meeting the person's changing needs.

REVIEW OF THE STANDARDS

483.410(d)	*Services provided under agreements with outside sources*
483.420(a)	*Protection of clients' rights*
483.420(b)	*Client finances*
483.430(a)	*Qualified mental retardation professional*
483.430(b)	*Professional program services*
483.430(e)	*Staff training program*
483.440(a)	*Active treatment*
483.440(b)	*Admissions, transfers, and discharge*
483.440(c)	*Individual program plan*

483.440(d) *Program implementation*
483.440(e) *Program documentation*
483.440(f) *Program monitoring and change*
483.450(a) *Facility practices—conduct toward clients*

The requirements for active treatment are set forth in the standards that cover services provided by an outside program, protection of client rights, instruction in management of financial affairs, and facility practices and conduct toward clients.

The requirements for active treatment are also covered in the section on the duties and responsibilities of the qualified mental retardation professional, professional program services, and the direct care staff. The standards stress the need for initial and continuing training that enables employees to perform duties effectively, efficiently, and competently. The standards (483.430(e)(4)) indicate that "staff must be able to demonstrate the skills and techniques necessary to implement the individual program plans for each client for whom they are responsible."

The standards define active treatment and discuss the components in the active treatment cycle: admission, assessment, the individual program plan, program implementation, documentation, monitoring, and change. The active treatment standards integrate the roles and responsibilities of professional and direct care staff with the sequence of requirements in the active treatment cycle.

APPLICATION

Active treatment focuses on each individual with developmental disabilities who resides in a facility. The application of active treatment depends upon staff's understanding of services required by an ICF/MR.

The ICF/MR program is a residential program for individuals with developmental disabilities. The facility generates federal financial participation based on the number of certified beds and the census of the facility. Facility staff must evaluate services and determine if they are designed and provided with the individual's needs in mind. Active treatment is a 24-hour requirement. Surveyors determine compliance without regard to the time of day. The facility must ensure that services are available throughout the waking hours of the individual with developmental disabilities. Resources must be available throughout the day. The facility cannot operate as if it were a 9:00 a.m. to 5:00 p.m. business.

Staff identify the many different opportunities or treatment environments where learning takes place throughout the individual's day. Clearly defining these opportunities will assist team members in planning and structuring the individual program plan. For example, in the larger institutions, most individuals with developmental disabilities awaken at 6:00 a.m. to begin their day and go to a day program around 9:00 a.m. The time in between represents one treatment environment. Staff then determine the focus of intervention during this treatment environment. For most people the focus will be on activities of daily living: learning to dress, feed, and toilet themselves. Additional focus may be placed on socialization skills. Planning total treatment opportunities for each individual involves developing schedules for Monday through Friday activities, as well as developing a weekend schedule. Completed schedules may look like the following:

Active Treatment—Opportunities for Intervention for Adults
Focus on Activities
Monday through Friday

Time of Day	Focus of Intervention
6:00 a.m. until 9:00 a.m.	Activities of daily living Socialization
9:00 a.m. until 4:00 p.m.	Work—Productivity Socialization
4:00 a.m. until 10:00 p.m.	Activities of daily living Recreation Leisure Socialization

Active Treatment—Opportunities for Intervention for Adults
Focus on Activities
Saturday, Sunday, and Holidays

Time of Day	Focus of Intervention
6:00 a.m. until 9:00 a.m.	Activities of daily living Socialization
9:00 a.m. until 4:00 p.m.	Leisure and Socialization
4:00 p.m. until 6:30 p.m.	Activities of daily living
6:30 p.m. until 10:00 p.m.	Recreation

The ICF/MR must clearly define treatment opportunities that exist within the facility. Once treatment opportunities are identified, staff can allocate staff to ensure needed services are provided to each individual in each environment.

Program Checklist

	Yes	No
1. Services are available, as needed, 24 hours per day, 7 days per week.	___	___
2. Opportunities for learning on Monday through Friday are clearly defined.	___	___
3. Learning opportunities are clearly defined for weekends and holidays.	___	___

The allocation of staff resources presents dilemmas. Many agencies have difficulty locating specialized service staff, such as psychologists, and occupational, physical, and speech therapists to work in residential settings. In addition, many specialized service staff are accustomed to providing services within the confines of an office or a clinical setting. In an active treatment setting the deployment of specialized service staff shifts. Specialized service staff expertise is needed across all treatment environments or opportunities. Due to the scarcity of specialized service staff and the need for the deployment of their services 7 days per week, 24 hours per day, the focus of their work changes from direct clinical interventions to the training of direct service workers within the different treatment environments. This shift in roles has disadvantages and advantages.

The major disadvantage to the deployment of specialized service staff across treatment environments is the resulting resistance. Specialized service staff working in residential settings are required to provide services in a manner that is inconsistent with their professional training and different from their peers in other conventional settings. In addition, the deployment of staff across treatment environments will complicate scheduling and monitoring.

The ability to spread specialized clinical skills across more treatment environments is the greatest advantage to this approach. Specialized service staff acting as trainers have a positive impact on a greater number of individuals in a variety of settings. In addition, the specialized service staff are able to model appropriate intervention strategies, assess the direct service workers' ability to implement programs, and observe firsthand the effectiveness of those programs.

Some specialized services may require high levels of training and professional expertise. Some of these services may best be provided through a clinic. However, many specialized clinical techniques can be provided by ICF/MR staff throughout the day.

"When do I know if active treatment exists in my facility?" is a question frequently asked by facility staff. Facility staff can readily look at the operational systems or processes and determine if they are designed to teach skills and behaviors to individuals. The manner in which the facility operates ensures the responsiveness of policy and procedures to the needs of the individual. This requires that:

1. Assessments are functional.
2. Interdisciplinary teams are driven by the needs of the individuals with developmental disabilities.
3. Goals and objectives are developed by the team and reflect the team's best evaluation of how to maximize the facility's resources.
4. Intervention strategies are integrated throughout the individual's day.
5. Monitoring and evaluation systems are in place to ensure the individual's continued growth and development.

Active treatment is based on the premise that all people, regardless of the severity of their disability, grow and develop throughout their lives. Whether a facility is a large state institution or a small community-based program, staff values will determine to a large degree the success of active treatment.

Management staff can mandate policy and procedures around the active treatment cycle. They cannot mandate how staff feel about people with disabilities. They must, therefore, maintain a constant presence to ensure that the values behind the federal regulation are present at all times. For example, do staff:

- Dress people in clothing too large, use pins to take in the excess material, use torn or out-of-style clothing **OR** dress people in age-appropriate clothing, fitted to the individual?
- Speak to people using age-inappropriate nicknames, talk about the person to others in the presence of the person, scream or yell at the person, or only engage with the person when the person does something "bad" **OR** speak to people showing respect for their age, engage the person in conversation outside structured learning times, tell the person what is about to happen prior to an event, speak in soft even tones, and actively encourage the person throughout the day?
- Use age-inappropriate materials such as crayons and coloring books, engage the individual in activities that are meaningless or unmotivating, employ activity schedules that do not encourage individual choices, or allow the individual to spend hours doing nothing **OR** use materials that are age-appropriate, engage in activities that have purpose and enhance the person's self-esteem, employ schedules that encourage and support individual choices, and plan a day that is filled with interesting, challenging, and productive activities?

Program Checklist

	Yes	No
1. Specialized service staff focus on training direct care workers in the different treatment environments.	—	—
2. Specialized service staff model intervention strategies for direct care workers.	—	—
3. Specialized service staff observe direct care workers implementing programs.	—	—
4. Services are based on the premise that all people, regardless of the severity of their disability, grow and develop.	—	—
5. Individuals with developmental disabilities are dressed in appropriate clothing.	—	—
6. Staff interact demonstrating respect for the individual.	—	—

Facility staff must consider strategies to ensure that all staff understand both the procedural issues and the values in active treatment. Two strategies enable staff to monitor programs: performance indicators and facility surveys.

Performance indicators are not commercially available. Facilities create their own. Performance indicators are based on areas that the facility staff wish to monitor. Performance indicators can cover a variety of areas, including, but not limited to:

External environment (the area outside a building)
Internal environment (the area inside a building)
Interdisciplinary team meetings
Assessments
Implementation strategies
Services provided by specialized service staff
Integration of services in the community
Resident-to-resident interactions
Staff-to-resident interactions
Staff-to-staff interactions
Facility management
Facility policy and procedures
Supervisory staff
Day programs
Age-appropriate materials and activities

The number of topics included will vary from agency to agency. Facility staff determine the critical success factors for performance in each area. These critical success factors are written in behavioral terms and as such are observable and measurable. For example, performance indicators written for the external environment may include the following statements:

1. The area around the building is free of litter. ____ yes ____ no
2. The area around the building is free of fallen trees or branches. ____ yes ____ no
3. The outside of the building is free of chipped or cracked paint. ____ yes ____ no
4. The area around the building is well lighted at night. ____ yes ____ no
5. Sitting areas exist outside the building appropriate for individuals living in the building. ____ yes ____ no

Performance indicators can be written for nonprogramming areas. The exterior of a building is important to the provision of active treatment. The appearance of the building, the way in which it is kept, communicates attitudes toward individuals with developmental disabilities. Building appearance suggests staff expectations and the programs being implemented inside the building.

Performance indicators for assessments may include:

1. Assessments are written based on staff's direct observation of the individual. ____ yes ____ no
2. Assessments are written free of professional jargon. ____ yes ____ no
3. Assessments are easily read by direct care workers. ____ yes ____ no
4. Assessments are turned in to the QMRP 1 week prior to the interdisciplinary team meeting. ____ yes ____ no
5. The assessment includes recommendations for programming. ____ yes ____ no

Once written, the performance indicators have a variety of uses, ranging from staff development to scheduled monitoring of the facility.

A second strategy for ensuring the provision of active treatment is to conduct facility surveys. These surveys are shortened versions of the performance indicators, the length of which would prohibit their use on a routine basis. Facility surveys are conducted around the most relevant performance indicators. The frequency of reviews is defined by the facility's management staff. Experience indicates, however, that more frequent reviews enable the facility to monitor better the implementation of active treatment. Management staff are able to target problem areas and allocate resources to address these areas. Facility surveys are used at least daily in each treatment environment and more frequently if staff are available. Sample questions on the facility survey may include:

1. Program environment _____
2. Number of residents present ____
3. Number of staff present ____
4. Ratio: ____ staff to ____ residents
5. Staffing ratio is sufficient to meet the needs of residents. ____ yes ____ no
6. Activity schedules are present. ____ yes ____ no
7. Activity schedules reflect resident goals and objectives. ____ yes ____ no
8. Staff are observed interacting with residents. ____ yes ____ no
9. Staff are observed reinforcing appropriate behaviors. ____ yes ____ no
10. Staff are able to state the objectives for each assigned resident. ____ yes ____ no
11. Staff are able to demonstrate program. ____ yes ____ no
12. The environment is free of:
    obnoxious odors ____ yes ____ no
    health/safety violations ____ yes ____ no
    rodents ____ yes ____ no
    insects ____ yes ____ no
13. Behavior management programs are present in the records for each person on psychotropic medications. ____ yes ____ no

14. Data are kept on each program. ___ yes ___ no
15. Ninety-day reviews are present in the record. ___ yes ___ no

As with the performance indicators, the facility survey will vary in length from facility to facility. The primary thrust behind the survey is to conduct regular on-site audits of each treatment environment. Data collected are compiled and summarized. The results provide an excellent management tool for identifying and correcting problems before staff habits and routines become established. Surveys enable management staff to determine at a glance the status of each treatment environment.

Program Checklist

	Yes	No
1. The facility monitors staff's understanding of active treatment.	—	—
2. The facility employs procedures to monitor its compliance with active treatment.	—	—
3. The facility is surveyed on a scheduled basis.	—	—
4. Management decisions to add, delete, or change agency/policy procedures are data based.	—	—

IMPLICATIONS

For Qualified Mental Retardation Professionals

The QMRP has the most extensive range of duties in the active treatment cycle. As required by federal regulation, the QMRP monitors the individual with developmental disabilities throughout the various steps of the active treatment cycle. The QMRP monitors the active treatment system for each person, flagging breakdowns in the system and ensuring the agency's responsiveness in correcting the situation. The QMRP must ensure that the systems or processes put into place by the facility management staff are responsive to the individual needs of each person. Programs must be designed to meet the specific needs of each developmentally disabled individual—the individual must not be placed into a preexisting, generic program. Breakdowns in the system can occur at any step in the cycle. Therefore, the QMRP must know where each assignee is in the active treatment cycle. Some individuals on the QMRP's case load may be involved in the assessment process, while others are in program implementation.

The most critical active treatment responsibility for the QMRP relates to documentation. The QMRP serves as a historian, providing documentation of each person's progress. Documentation usually takes place around the time of the 90-day-review when staff responsible for the implementation of each identified objective on the IPP summarize what has occurred during this time for the individual objective.

The QMRP, however, is the only person who must look at all the identified objectives and draw conclusions about the person's overall progress. This process is important because the QMRP looks at all the available data, identifies inconsistencies, and documents all findings. This procedure is critical because it demonstrates the facility's efforts toward meeting the needs of each individual. In addition, the facility proves to QA coordinators that the system of active treatment is responsive to individual needs.

The 90-day review is not the only time for documentation which can, and should, occur regularly. It is the responsibility of the QMRP to ensure that each individual makes progress. If the data do not demonstrate consistent progress, the QMRP must intervene. For example, the review of a data sheet on a program for hand washing indicates that for the past 30 days the individual has performed the skill at the same level. The QMRP asks why progress has not been made. He or she may request changes in the implementation strategies or reinforcement procedures. These changes are then documented in the individual's record. This approach demonstrates responsiveness of the facility and a genuine concern for program effectiveness for the individual. Another example might be helpful. Data from a hand washing program show that the person performs the task independently in the morning but needs physical assistance in the evening. The QMRP observes these data and calls a meeting of staff from both shifts to determine the reason for the difference.

Finally, the QMRP must ensure that the delivery of services meets the needs of individuals with developmental disabilities. Services must be integrated throughout the individual's day. Specialized service staff must work with the direct service staff in the transfer of appropriate skills and knowledge. All staff must submit required paper documentation in a timely manner. And the leadership of the facility must be responsive to needed changes in policy and procedures.

For Specialized Service Staff

The role of the specialized service staff, such as occupational and physical therapist, speech pathologist, psychologist, and so on, changes in the ICF/MR program where most people reside because of their complex needs. In considering the best strategy for the utilization of specialized service staff skills and abilities, the transdisciplinary model of training direct care staff emerges.

Traditional assessments conducted by the specialized service staff change in this model. Assessments written by specialized service staff are based on their direct observation of the individual within the different treatment environments. Assessments completed in this manner stress the functional abilities of the individual and result in interdisciplinary team discussions of the direct application of intervention strategies. The goal of functional assessments is to encourage team participation in the development of the IPP. This can only occur when all staff have an understanding of specialized assessments that are free of jargon and conducted in actual program settings.

In the ICF/MR program direct service staff have the most contact with each individual. Therefore, the efforts of the specialized service staff should be directed toward training the direct care worker to incorporate each discipline's skills into the daily routines and rhythms of the individual's day. The specialized service staff shift from the provision of one-to-one intervention to providing training, technical assistance, and consultation to the direct care worker. Specialized service staff are able to model program techniques and observe first-hand the direct service worker's ability to implement programs.

With the shift of focus specialized service staff observe persons throughout their day and provide training to all direct care workers who work different shifts. ICF/MR programs are not 9 a.m. to 5 p.m., Monday through Friday operations. They are 24-hour programs, 365 days per year. Weekend and/or holiday workers should have access to specialized service staff in order to implement programs. The specialized service staff will need flexible hours and work days to ensure that all staff benefit from the expertise they offer.

For Quality Assurance Coordinators

The quality assurance (QA) coordinator determines a facility's compliance with the federal regulation that provides the framework from which the facility develops systems or processes for the delivery of services. The QA coordinator reviews the application of these systems, usually written in the form of facility policy and procedures, and determines if the needs of individuals with developmental disabilities are being met. A variety of ways exist to evaluate the facility. The best evidence is direct observation of program implementation. Through observations, the QA coordinator determines:

• What is the objective to be taught?
• Why and how was the objective selected?
• What is the next step in the program?
• Where is this objective leading?
• Where is the progress documented?

Staff able to answer these questions have a good grasp of programs. The QA coordinator generally finds correct responses to be an indication of active treatment.

In addition to direct observation, the QA coordinator conducts an audit of the individual's record and determines:

- All required components of the IPP are present.
- Documentation of progress is evident.
- Behavior management programs are present for all individuals on psychotropic medication written to decrease dependence on medications.
- The QMRP conducts routine audits of the individual's total program.
- The facility is responsive to the changing needs of each individual.
- There is evidence of integrated services throughout the day.

Finally, the QA coordinator conducts audits of the environment. These audits ensure that the environment is free of current or potential health/safety violations.

CONCLUSIONS

Active treatment is required by federal regulation. Active treatment is individually based. The identified needs of each individual with developmental disabilities are met through the application of systems or processes designed by the facility staff to enhance the skill level of the individual. This requires the agency to review critically the application of its policy/procedures and to plan strategies for their refinement. Central to active treatment, as defined in the new standards, is the shift from paper compliance to the aggressive application of intervention programs.

REFERENCE

Manfredini, D., & Smith, W. (1988). The concept and implementation of active treatment. In M. Janicki, M. W. Krauss, & M. M. Seltzer (Eds.), *Community residences for persons with developmental disabilities: Here to stay* (pp. 123–131). Baltimore: Paul H. Brookes Publishing Co.

7
Mission Statement

Michael S. Chapman

Lewis Carroll understood the importance of missions. He wrote in *Alice in Wonderland:*

> "Cheshire Puss, . . . would you tell me, please, which way I ought to go from here?"
> "That depends a good deal on where you want to get to," said the Cat.
> "I don't much care where," said Alice.
> "Then it doesn't matter which way you go," said the Cat.

The focus of this chapter is on agency missions. Effective mission statements provide a direction for facility staff in adopting and initiating change. No facility is free of change, whether coming from internal or external sources. Mission statements and the subsequent planning process help an agency gain mastery over change, rather than being victimized by it (Tregoe & Zimmerman, 1980). Furthermore, a mission statement enables facility staff to set program priorities, provides the foundation for defining tasks to meet established objectives, and aids in the allocation of the facility's resources.

This chapter focuses on the beginning steps required for successful planning and for developing mission statements. Developing a facility mission statement is part of a larger planning process referred to as strategic planning. The chapter discusses strategies for developing effective mission statements.

BACKGROUND

The world is ever changing. Profit and nonprofit organizations alike have direction and momentum. Without a clear mission statement and a defined planning process, management runs the risk of having company direction established by external forces (Tregoe & Zimmerman, 1980).

Successful businesses engage in a two-step planning process to ensure that their services or products are responsive to the needs of consumers—strategic and long-range planning.

Strategic Planning

The planning process for determining what an organization should be is often referred to as strategic planning. Strategic planning in business became popular in the United States around 1950. Many of the terms used in strategic planning—strategy, tactics, and obstacles— have military origins. Strategic planning is considered a senior management responsibility (Marrus, 1984; McFarland, 1979; Tregoe & Zimmerman, 1980). Through strategic planning, management defines two critical components for success in the organization: mission and goals. How an organization views its purpose and where it wants to go are addressed by these two components. Through this process the organization is able to see the big picture (Marrus, 1984).

Mission statements provide a shared vision of the organization's future and are developed from agency values, expectations, and direction. As such, the mission statement conveys the organization's primary goals and values.

Following the formation of the mission statement, goals are established that describe the future status of the organization. Much like the goals of the individual program plan (IPP), organizational goals are written using behavioral terminology. Goals make it clear to all staff what the organization wants to achieve.

Strategic planning enables an organization to take charge of its future. Without such a plan, business decisions are made by reacting to whatever external forces, threats, or opportunities management is avoiding or pursuing at any given time. Strategic planning enables top management to break this reactive cycle and become proactive in determining the organization's future. Proactive planning prepares staff for change and provides a process for meeting the demands of the future.

Long-Range Planning

The strategic plan defines what a facility should become; the long-range plan defines how the facility will get there. The strategic planning process is a top-level management responsibility, while the long-range planning process involves all staff. The purpose of long-range planning is to develop, implement, and evaluate methods to achieve the future vision of the facility as defined in the strategic plan.

The long-range plan begins where the strategic plan ends and is the first step in translating the strategic plan into operational reality.

Five critical steps make up the development of long-range plans. These include: stating the objective, assigning responsibilities, identifying steps needed to attain the objective, establishing a time frame, and identifying obstacles (Gardner, Chapman, Donaldson, & Jacobson, 1988).

Stating the objective in clear concise language enables staff to understand the basis of the long-range plan. The strategic plan will affect many aspects of the facility's operation. Each area will need detailed objectives that describe the desired future state of the overall operation of the facility.

Once clear objectives are identified, management staff are able to delegate or assign to personnel the responsiblity of implementing and accomplishing each objective. This person or group of people is held accountable for the success or failure of the objective. In addition, this person monitors the implementation of strategies to accomplish the objective within a given period.

Identifying the steps needed to attain the objective is much like writing a task analysis on a complex behavior. The responsible staff, knowing the desired future state of the facility, list those changes that must take place in the order they must occur to accomplish the objective successfully. In this approach the staff are better able to monitor the facility and more accurately identify areas of difficulty in the change process.

For each objective and subsequent listing of steps a time frame is assigned that identifies expected completion dates. Assigning time frames is necessary in order to establish clearly expectations of staff in the change process. Also important are those instances where one step in the change process must be completed before another step can begin.

Finally, for each objective identified, staff should consider potential obstacles that may interfere with their ability to accomplish the objective successfully. Failure to do so may result in unnecessary delays in the implementation stage of this process.

The Health Care Financing Administration is changing the way it will evaluate the provision of services to individuals with developmental disabilities. The new federal regulations will present a challenge to top management staff of agencies across the country. Top management in each facility will need to engage in a planning process to determine if their facility complies with the minimum requirements set forth in the new regulations. Among the many issues they will need to consider are:

- Does the facility mission statement provide the vision of the future required for staff to meet the new regulations?
- What new capabilities and resources will be required?
- Does the current organizational structure need changing?
- Are staff deployed in the right manner?
- What agency policy and procedures need to be written or modified?

- Are the appropriate internal tracking systems in place to ensure outcome measures?
- What changes or modifications are needed in the facility's long-range plans?
- What new facility goals and objectives need to be developed?
- How can top management best communicate to staff the changes in the regulations?

These issues and many others will need to be addressed by top management. Long-range plans will need to be developed that provide staff with information regarding the agency's changing business practices. Long-range plans can only be effective if the agency has first developed a mission statement that provides a vision of the future, clearly identifying for all staff the facility's purpose.

REVIEW OF THE STANDARDS

The 1988 ICF/MR conditions of participation focus on outcome measures for individuals with developmental disabilities. They focus on what the individual must receive rather than those services the facility must provide. This fundamental shift in emphasis requires that the facility prove its effectiveness, not on paper but through competent interactions between staff and the individual that result in increased skill abilities in the person.

The new conditions of participation do not mention the need for a facility strategic planning process that results in a well-defined mission statement. They do not mention values, agency goals, and objectives, or even long-range facility planning, because the conditions focus more on the outcome and less on the process of service delivery systems. The conditions leave to management the "how to." Contemporary practice, however, suggests that a facility cannot plan programs with individuals with developmental disabilities without first knowing its own direction, values, mission, and priorities. Organizations must clearly know:

- Their own value base for services provided
- The direction or mission of the facility
- The desired goals and objectives of the facility
- The long-range plan for accomplishing each objective

APPLICATION

Three components are required to develop a mission statement: values, expectations, and direction.

The first step in the planning process is to identify the philosophical basis for the services provided. Active treatment regulations are based on values. They assume that all people, regardless of the severity of their disability:

- Are capable of growth in their skills and abilities
- Live in the least restrictive environment possible
- Engage in daily routines and rhythms similar to those experienced by the general public
- Benefit from the use of age-appropriate materials and activities

Staff in facilities participating in the ICF/MR program should discuss openly their values that consciously and/or unconsciously motivate each individual within an organization and direct staff behaviors. Staff values can also unite or divide an agency, aid in the staff's ability to work as a team, or contribute to a dysfunctional team process. For example, staff divided on the issue of age-appropriate materials and activities will not agree on whether toys are appropriate for instructional purposes for a 35-year-old man.

Values are the beliefs held by people about what is worthwhile in life. They describe what is desirable and provide guiding principles for living. Mink, Shultz, and Mink (1979) describe two different but related types of values: process values and outcome values.

Process values describe what is the desirable conduct of staff within an organization while dealing with others. Honesty, respect, and dignity are examples of process values. Outcome values describe what is worth striving for in life. A sense of accomplishment, productivity, and improved self-worth are examples of outcome values.

Every profession operates from a set of process and outcome values. For example, the medical profession believes in health and well-being, the educational profession believes in learning and knowledge, the legal profession believes in truth and justice, and so forth.

These values may or may not be verbalized within a particular organization. However, the underlying beliefs held by the staff in an organization or the manner in which staff achieve a desired outcome provide the basis for staff cohesion—working together toward accomplishing the organization's stated purpose or mission.

Most people enter a profession with some understanding of its underlying value system. A student becomes a teacher out of desire to help others learn or becomes a doctor to help others maintain their health. In a human services profession or in working in an ICF/MR program, however, the underlying values may not be clear. Values may change over time. The custodial model has evolved to the provision of active treatment. Staff may be unclear as to agency's value base for service delivery.

Management must establish written value or philosophy statements to ensure that all staff understand expected behaviors within the facility. Written philosophy statements may assist in preventing unnecessary discussion regarding expected values.

Most people live their lives with a set of rules that are based on values. In a study (Dalkey, Rourke, Lewis, & Snyder, 1972) that asked students at the University of California at Los Angeles to identify and rank those values that contributed to the quality of life, the following values were identified in the order of importance (Rubinstein, 1975):

1. Love
2. Self-respect
3. Peace of mind
4. Sex
5. Challenge
6. Social acceptance
7. Accomplishment
8. Individuality
9. Involvement
10. Well-being (economic, health)
11. Change
12. Power (control)
13. Privacy

A group study of the American Academy of Arts and Sciences identified and ranked those values expected to be important in the year 2000. Their list included:

1. Privacy
2. Equality
3. Personal integrity
4. Freedom
5. Law and order
6. Pleasantness of environment
7. Social adjustment
8. Efficiency and effectiveness of organizations
9. Rationality
10. Education
11. Ability and talent

Program Checklist

		Yes	No
1.	Programs are based on the value that all people with developmental disabilities are capable of growth.	__	__
2.	Individuals with developmental disabilities engage in the same daily routines and rhythms as the general public.	__	__
3.	Values are openly discussed at the facility.	__	__

Management, clinical staff, and direct care workers must decide whether a different value base exists for people with developmental disabilities just because they are retarded, have epilepsy, are blind, have challenging behaviors, or are autistic. The systems developed for the implementation of active treatment programs will demonstrate staff values. Staff behaviors reflect values. For example, a staff member silently pushing an individual in a wheelchair to breakfast is not demonstrating the values that underlie active treatment. A more appropriate response consistent with the values of active treatment would be to engage the individual in conversation while walking to the breakfast table.

As a part of the planning process, written philosophy statements identify the values and assumptions of staff concerning the delivery of services to individuals with developmental disabilities. The values statement should clearly provide the guiding and operating principles of the facility.

Staff should write out their philosophy statement beginning with, "We believe. . . . " Writing the statement in this manner will prevent staff from confusing the values with the long-range objective. For example, a facility committed to the provision of active treatment may have a philosophical statement that reads:

- We believe in an individual's right to privacy.
- We believe all people are treated with respect.
- We believe that learning situations should be challenging for the individual.
- We believe in treating each person as an individual, with individual likes, dislikes, and/or preferences.
- We believe in providing services that enhance the individual's self-worth and self-respect.
- We believe in providing services that encourage the individual's freedom to choose from an array of available options.
- We believe all individuals continually grow and develop.
- We believe in providing services in the least restrictive setting possible.
- We believe all individuals have the right to work.
- We believe all individuals are productive workers.
- We believe work enhances self-esteem.
- We believe planned activities for individuals with developmental disabilities should be integrated with the normal population.
- We believe that learning opportunities should be meaningful to the individual and provide purpose to the individual's life.
- We believe in treating individuals with developmental disabilities with dignity and respect, as demonstrated through the use of age-appropriate materials and activities.

Most agencies will spend large amounts of time and energy defining their value base for services. In addition, considerable time will be spent integrating these values into the day-to-day behaviors of staff. The role of the facility leadership is critical in ensuring the continued presence of the agency's values in every aspect of its operation. Staff will respond to the expectations set by the facility leadership. Therefore, the facility leadership must continually strive to demonstrate how values are used to direct the decision-making process. This is especially true in agencies that experience high staff turnover.

Without continually addressing the values, the guiding principles behind the agency mission statement may get lost in the day-to-day operation of the facility. Staff will lack the unity provided by values. They often begin to pursue areas of interest to themselves or departments rather than to the beneficiary of services, the individual with developmental disabilities.

Expectations

The second step in the development of a mission statement is to identify staff expectations. Expectations are an extension of basic values and define staff belief about the individual's future. For example, staff may value work and the associated values of productivity and accomplishment. Therefore, staff expect all individuals with developmental disabilities, regardless of the severity of their disabilities, to be productive. This expectation is directly observable in the activities planned for the individual.

Discussing staff expectations prevents vicious cycles. The vicious cycle begins with a prejudice about a person that results in low performance expectations. Because of low expectations, staff present limited opportunities for development. Without enhanced learning environments the person performs accordingly, thus reinforcing the belief. Without a planned system for managing staff expectation, facilities may continue the vicious cycles in the provision of services.

Discussion of staff expectations can reverse these cycles. Administrative and professional staff can provide leadership in establishing expectations for persons with developmental disabilities. The leadership can define expectations and establish policy and procedures to support them.

Program Checklist

	Yes	No
1. The facility has a written value or philosophy statement.	—	—
2. Values are used in making program decisions.	—	—
3. Staff have identified expectations of resident behaviors and skill development.	—	—

Direction

The third step in writing mission statements is to define future direction of the facility. The management staff of the facility should consider three critical questions in developing the facility's direction (Drucker, 1974):

1. What is our business?
2. What will the business be?
3. What should the business be? (Drucker, 1974)

Each of these three questions should be considered as a separate issue without regard to the other two.

These questions challenge most facilities. No formulas or software programs exist that can answer these questions for facility staff. These difficult questions require staff's critical thinking, imagination, and personal judgment.

Without a clear sense of direction, most facilities will develop long-range plans that are future projections of current service programs. The limitation in this type of planning lies in the assumption that today's services will be priority services in the future. This practice forces agencies to defend the current structure of organizational life. Rather than adapting and growing to meet the challenges of tomorrow, the facility becomes inflexible and unable to react to the change in the environment.

Values, expectations, and direction provide the foundation for a mission statement that identifies a shared vision for all staff, from the maintenance personnel, to the direct care worker, to specialized service staff. The written mission statement is clear, simple, and direct. It is easily communicated to all staff. The mission statement focuses on the "big picture." Mission statements provide the basis for decision making. Decisions to add, delete, or change existing services can be evaluated against the facility's mission to determine if a proposed program fits with the purpose of the facility. For example, the mission statement "to provide services that enable the individual with developmental disabilities to return to the community" enables staff to determine if a new services or program will better enable the person to return to the community.

The process of establishing an agency mission statement is visualized in Figure 1.

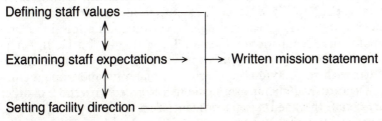

Figure 1. *The process of establishing an agency mission statement.*

Examples of mission statements that contain these elements include:

> The XYZ Center provides residential and habilitation services to persons with mental retardation when no appropriate less restrictive setting is available currently or within a reasonable time. The center provides an environment where active treatment is used to meet the social, psychological, health, developmental, educational, and vocational needs of each individual. Services are provided to assist each individual to achieve increasing autonomy. The center continually strives to return persons to the community. The center works cooperatively with other agencies to ensure that persons with mental retardation receive appropriate services in the proper setting.

> The mission of the ABC Company is to act as a change agent in increasing the capacity of local communities to meet the needs of persons with developmental disabilities by accessing the knowledge, skills, and resources of the (parent) institute and by communicating and coordinating community services and outreach activities at the institute. The ABC Company will assist community service agencies to incorporate the most recent advances in clinical services, education, and training so that persons with developmental disabilities can continue to live and work in their community.

> To rehabilitate persons with disabilities by offering services and opportunities to promote economic and social independence.

Facility mission statements facilitate the active treatment process. Decisions about the future direction of the facility and individuals with developmental disabilities have a clear organizational context. A well-defined mission statement at the center of the active treatment cycle provides the cohesion for the active treatment cycle. All other steps in the active treatment cycle flow from the facility mission statement. For example, staff in a facility with a strong mission statement such as, "to provide those services that enable the individual to return to the community" are better able to choose those assessments that focus on community participation and integration. Assessment reports would then focus on functional skills and support systems required for community participation. The mission statement provides the interdisciplinary team with guidance and direction for decision making that ensures movement toward accomplishing a desired future state for the individual. Established program goals and objectives are evaluated against the mission statement.

Once the facility's mission statement is written, each department within the facility should develop corresponding mission statements that describe how the department services assist the facility in achieving its mission. For example, a corresponding mission statement for the Occupational Therapy Department of a facility may read, "to provide active treatment services through a transdisciplinary approach to individualized program planning and implementation. Occupational therapy services are integrated with those of other educational, therapeutic, and residential services to provide a supportive environment that enables the individual to return to his or her community." This process of developing departmental mission statements enables senior management to assess the understanding of staff in the delivery of active treatment services. In addition, mission statements enable all staff to understand clearly how they fit into the overall operation of the facility and their importance in accomplishing the facility's mission.

Good mission statements are sometimes difficult to develop. For many facilities the process takes several months to complete. During this time staff look critically at every aspect of the facility. It is reviewed not only on the basis of the facility's current purpose but also its future direction.

Mission statements should not be viewed as "etched in stone." They need to be responsive to the changing needs of the individual and the services provided to meet those needs. Establishing a system for the periodic review of the current mission statement ensures the agency's responsiveness to the future.

Program Checklist

		Yes	No
1.	The facility has a written mission statement.	___	___
2.	The mission statement contains the three critical elements: values, expectations, and direction.	___	___
3.	All staff can state or paraphrase the facility mission statement.	___	___
4.	All departments within the facility have mission statements that support the overall mission statement.	___	___
5.	The mission statement is used in making decisions about the active treatment cycle.	___	___

IMPLICATIONS

For Top Management Staff

The role of top management staff in the formation and dissemination of the facility mission statement is critical. All staff need:

• A clear understanding of the facility's purpose
• A sense of future
• To understand how the services they provide fit into the organization and the provision of active treatment services to individuals with developmental disabilities

Management leadership will determine whether the organization's future is defined by internal direction or external demands. The leadership requires an understanding of the values that underlie service delivery to individuals with developmental disabilities. The leadership must also clearly define expectations for growth and change for all people regardless of the extent of their disability. These values and expectations provide the foundations for the facility mission statement.

For Qualified Mental Retardation Professionals

In their role, qualified mental retardation professionals (QMRP) must ensure that the active treatment cycle is implemented and evaluated based on the facility's mission statement. This includes determining that:

1. The mission is reflected in the assessment process. For example, when the facility mission is to return individuals to their communities, staff choose assessments that focus on community participation and integration. In addition, the QMRP reviews assessments completed by outside agencies to ensure their appropriateness. An agency providing a work environment assesses for productivity, socialization, and work habits.
2. The discussion at the interdisciplinary team meeting is focused around the desired state the staff envision for individuals with developmental disabilities.
3. Goals and objectives are developed that result in clear expectations for the individual's movement.
4. Implementation strategies are written and carried out in such a way as to produce client outcome measures in a defined direction.
5. Monitoring and evaluation strategies ensure the continued responsiveness of the facility and result in staff's ability to demonstrate clearly progress of the individual. They also ensure that the day and residential programs are integrated.

For Specialized Service Staff

Specialized service staff must ensure that their service delivery models are consistent with the facility mission statement. Standard operating procedures that specialized service staff are accustomed to providing in a clinical setting may not apply in the ICF/MR program. The facility mission statement may require the specialized service staff to view their role in a different manner. Rather than scheduling clinic appointments for individuals with developmental disabilities, staff may schedule service appointments in a living unit to provide training to staff on teaching a person to hold a spoon. It is important for specialized service staff to have a clear understanding of the facility mission, to determine strategies for the implementation of their services that emphasize the integration of their programs across the different treatment environments, and to establish delivery services that enhance the abilities of the direct care worker to carry out programs independently.

For Quality Assurance Coordinators

While the 1988 federal regulations do not require the agency to write facility mission statements or operating procedures that include agency philosophy or goals and objectives, facilities would have difficulty demonstrating consistent, predictable outcome measures for individuals with developmental disabilities without a coherent mission statement. Mission statements provide direction and create a sense of future within the facility. This sense of future is evident in the programs developed for individuals with developmental disabilities. It is evident in the staff interactions with the individual and in the team discussions with the person. Quality assurance (QA) coordinators, through their observation of programs, should be able to identify future directions for all individuals with developmental disabilities in the facility. Clearly evident to the QA coordinator during his or her observations are answers to questions:

- "Where is this program leading?"
- "Why is this objective important to the future development of the person?"
- "What is the next step after the accomplishment of this objective?"

Without the clearly defined sense of purpose provided by the mission statement, QA coordinators may find unrelated assessments, dysfunctional team process, randomly assigned goals and objectives, implementation strategies that are not integrated, and little or no monitoring of the overall program.

CONCLUSION

Clearly defined and written, mission statements provide direction and a sense of future for facility staff. Through mission statements staff are able to evaluate new or old program options and determine program priorities for the facility. The facility mission statement is at the center of the active treatment cycle. Staff are better able to make decisions regarding the allocation of resources and the use of their time. In addition, mission statements enable facility staff to establish monitoring and evaluation systems that ensure agency responsiveness in meeting the needs of individuals with developmental disabilities.

The facility mission statement should be shared with and understood by all staff working at the facility. All staff should be able to state, in their own words, the mission of the facility. Staff able to do this will have a better understanding of their roles and responsibilities in the provision of active treatment services and in meeting the needs of individuals with developmental disabilities.

REFERENCES

Dalkey, N., Rourke, D., Lewis, R., & Snyder, D. (1972). *Studies is the quality of life: Delphi and decision making.* Lexington, MA: D.C. Health and Co.

Drucker, P. (1974). *Management.* New York: Harper & Row.

Gardner, J. F., Chapman, M. S., Donaldson, G., & Jacobson, S. G. (1988). *Toward supported employment: A process guide for planned change.* Baltimore: Paul H. Brookes Publishing Co.

Marrus, S. (1984). *Building the strategic plan.* New York: John Wiley & Sons.

McFarland, D. (1979). *Management foundations and practice.* New York: MacMillan Publishing Co.

Mink, O. G., Shultz, J. M., & Mink, B. P. (1979). *Developing and managing open organizations: A model and methods for maximizing organizational potential.* San Diego, CA: University Associates.

Rubinstein, M. F. (1975). *Patterns of problem solving.* Englewood Cliffs, NJ: Prentice-Hall.

Tregoe, B., & Zimmerman, J. (1980). *Top management strategy.* New York: Simon & Schuster.

8
Assessments

Michael S. Chapman

INTRODUCTION

The active treatment cycle begins with the assessment process. Functional assessment provides the basis for team discussion that results in the formulation of the individual program plan. Assessments enable facility staff to understand clearly the person's strengths, weaknesses, likes, dislikes, and interests. Good assessment data enable staff to provide optimal habilitation and training programs.

This chapter discusses the assessment process. It provides information on the importance of assessments, strategies for conducting assessments, and use of assessment data.

BACKGROUND

Accreditation and certification protocols have required comprehensive assessments of the individual for approximately 15 years. During this time the nature of assessment strategies has changed. Traditional assessment approaches focused on the use of norm-referenced and criterion-referenced tests. Contemporary practice suggests that functional assessment data are required in program design.

Because norm-referenced and criterion-referenced tests continue to be widely used, understanding both their limitations and strengths is important. Norm-referenced (or standardized) tests are used to evaluate one individual's performance against other individuals who have also taken the test. Designers of the test administer it to thousands of individuals. An individual's performance can then be compared with the norm or average score. As the word standardized implies, this type of testing follows strict guidelines in the administration of the test. The staff administrating these tests are usually highly trained. Special procedures are used to score the test. The resulting score is usually expressed in the form of an intelligence quotient (IQ) or social quotient (SQ). The score obtained from the IQ test provides diagnostic information about the person. This is helpful in obtaining funding or determining eligibility for programs.

The IQ score is not particularly helpful in implementing active treatment. IQ scores do not provide information that is helpful in the development of goals and objectives. Knowing that a person has an IQ of 30 does not provide information about what the person can or cannot do. In addition, this type of information is subject to misuse, especially when the score is used to limit an individual's opportunity for growth. For example, the day program supervisor in an intermediate care facility for the mentally retarded (ICF/MR), noting an individual's IQ of 30, may assume that the individual cannot work. Therefore, work opportunities are not provided. As a result of low expectations and diminished opportunities, the individual performs at a lower level than that of which he or she may be capable. The initial belief held by the staff is reinforced, and future growth opportunities are also denied the individual.

Using norm-referenced tests to group individuals is another potential misuse of the IQ score. Staff often equate IQ scores with ability. However, two individuals with the same IQ scores may have very different abilities and interests. To state that an individual with developmental disabilities has an IQ of 30 tells staff little about the person.

Criterion-referenced tests assess the skills and abilities of an individual without comparison to others. Criterion-referenced tests are designed to identify what a person can and cannot do. This type of information is used by the team in the development of goals and objectives. Criterion-referenced tests serve three general purposes:

1. Assessment of the person in real or simulated settings
2. Assessment of a specific area of development
3. Determination of how a person learns a new concept.

Criterion-referenced tests are developmental in nature. Before an individual learns to walk, he or she usually learns to crawl, stand, and cruise. The assessment determines where along the developmental continuum the individual is functioning. This information provides staff with knowledge of what the individual can and cannot do in specific developmental areas. This is the strength of the criterion-referenced test. Criterion-referenced tests exist in many different developmental areas such as fine motor, gross motor, receptive language, expressive language, social/emotional, and practical activities such as handling money or doing laundry. In fact, criterion-referenced tests are available in just about every skill area. The problem with criterion-referenced tests is that no one test provides sufficiently detailed information in all skill areas that need to be assessed. This means that agency staff will need knowledge of several criterion-referenced tests and use bits and pieces of each in order to assess an individual effectively.

In addition, criterion-referenced tests usually contain a limited number of test items at any given developmental level. For example, a gross motor test may only have two or three test items at any age level. In reality, there are many different skills being developed at each age level. To list them all would be impractical.

An additional limitation of criterion-referenced tests involves staff's understanding of test design. Most test items are activities used to measure underlying skill development. For example, the ability to stack blocks is used on many tests to assess the underlying skills of reaching, grasping, positioning in space, and releasing an item. These skills, performed in a coordinated manner, are assessed by stacking blocks. To assume that the person needs to learn stacking blocks when this activity is failed on an assessment may be an erroneous conclusion. Staff need to understand clearly the underlying skill(s) being assessed by the test item in order to prevent training in inappropriate areas. Further assessment of the person will determine if stacking blocks was failed due to his or her inability to reach, grasp, position an object in space, or to release the object. Instruction can then focus on the appropriate skill.

A final limitation appears in the development of the strengths and needs lists. Many staff believe that items passed on criterion-referenced tests are listed as strengths, and failed items become needs. To use test results in this manner is a misuse of the data. Staff need to understand clearly why the individual failed the test item in order to identify the person's needs appropriately. Using the example above, to list stacking blocks as a need does not indicate if the appropriate need is in the area of reaching, grasping, positioning in space, or releasing an object.

In addition to norm-referenced and criterion-referenced assessments, those completed by specialized service staff traditionally focus on specific areas of interest to the examiner. For example, the occupational therapist uses assessment instruments to evaluate areas such as fine motor development or activities of daily living. This information is usually supplemented by standardized tests available for commercial use.

Contemporary practice suggests that no one assessment will capture all the information about the person that is sufficient for program planning (Meyers, Nihira, & Zetlin, 1979; Simeonsson, Huntington, & Parse, 1980). Staff will need to use a variety of assessment tools.

The nature of assessments has changed in recent years to focus on the individual within a current or planned environment. In this context the individual's skills and abilities are assessed using criterion-referenced, performance-based measures and/or functional assessments (Manfredini & Smith, 1988). In addition, assessments focus not only on the individual but also on the environment in which the individual is functioning (Wilcox & Bellamy, 1987).

The goal of the functional and environmental assessment phase is to obtain information about the person's abilities throughout the day and in environments where the person is expected to perform. What the person can do is the focus of the assessment process. This approach to assessment does not imply that evaluations from specialized service staff are no longer needed. Assessments completed by specialized service staff will focus on what the individual can do and also the specific environments in which these skills occur. The emphasis is on the specialized service staff's direct observation of the individual in the different program areas and on assisting staff in understanding what they should do.

REVIEW OF THE STANDARDS

483.410 (d) *Services provided under agreements with outside sources*

483.430(b) *Professional program services*

483.440 (c) *Individual program plan*

483.440 (f) *Program monitoring and change*

Requirements for assessment extend to programs not provided directly by the ICF/MR. The requirements for assessment are covered in sections that discuss admission decisions and preliminary evaluation, the individual program plan (IPP), interdisciplinary assessments, and reassessments within 30 days after admission.

The standards state the need for comprehensive and functional assessment. Facilities are required to "identify the client's needs for services without regard to the actual availability of the services needed" (483.440(c)(3).

Finally, the standards discuss the process of assessment within the context of the interdisciplinary team process and individual program planning. The need for at least an annual functional assessment of each person is discussed in program monitoring and change.

APPLICATION

Assessment is a three-phase process within the active treatment cycle. The first assessment phase begins when the individual with developmental disabilities enters the active treatment cycle. The second phase relates to assessments needed for developing the individual program plan. The third phase provides assessment information related to exit from the active treatment cycle. Figure 1 provides a visual representation of the three phases.

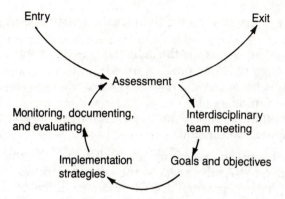

Entry

Exit

Assessment

Monitoring, documenting, and evaluating

Interdisciplinary team meeting

Implementation strategies

Goals and objectives

Figure 1.   The three-phase assessment process in the active treatment cycle.

Phase 1: Assessments Related to Entry into the Active Treatment Cycle

In this phase comprehensive assessments are completed in order to obtain baseline data prior to any intervention strategies. Assessments are completed by day and residential staff using a variety of commercially available assessment tools. In addition, specialized service staff conduct comprehensive evaluations related to their areas of specialty.

Assessments upon entry into the active treatment cycle are clinical in nature. They provide measures against which future clinical assessments can be compared in order to prove the effectiveness of designated intervention strategies. Conducting clinical assessments yearly is neither necessary, nor desirable. Facility management staff and specialized service staff will need to develop policy and procedures around time frames for conducting formal clinical assessments. Some professions will consider formal assessments every third year, others every fifth.

Phase 2: Assessments Related to the Development of Individual Program Plans

Assessments in this phase are not clinical in nature; rather, they are more functional. Clinical assessments provide little utility in the development of individual program plans. Here, the clinical data are translated to everyday experiences and expectations of the individual with developmental disabilities. For example, the occupational therapist's clinical evaluation of one individual reveals, among other things, that the person is only able to extend his elbow 45 degrees. While important as baseline data for the therapist, assessment in this phase relates this information to the application of the day-to-day needs of the individual. How does this skill relate to:

- Mealtime behaviors and the individual's ability to use a fork, knife, and/or spoon?
- Dressing behaviors and the individual's ability to put on his or her shirt and socks, or button his or her shirt?

- Self-care behaviors and the individual's ability to brush his or her teeth?
- Vocational behaviors and the individual's ability to operate machinery, sweep the floor, or stack wood?
- Recreation behaviors and the individual's ability to play basketball, go swimming, or play cards?
- Leisure behaviors and the individual's ability to look at a magazine, paint, or use a camera?

Functional assessments require the staff, especially the specialized service staff, to base their data on their direct observation of the individual with developmental disabilities in the different treatment environments. How the individual performs in the day-to-day demands of each setting is the focus of functional assessments.

Assessments completed in this manner offer several advantages. They enable the team to pinpoint clearly goals and objectives for the individual. Second, they enable the direct service worker to participate actively in the assessment process. Third, the assessment enables specialized service staff to base program recommendations and subsequent intervention strategies on their direct observation of the person in a variety of settings. Finally, the resulting data aid in the development of goals and objectives that are directly applicable and meaningful to the individual with developmental disabilities.

Program Checklist

	Yes	No
1. Functional assessments are used at the facility.	——	——
2. Assessments are based on the therapist's direct observation of the individual in different environments.	——	——
3. The observations of the direct care staff is an integral part of the assessment process.	——	——

At the center of the active treatment cycle is the agency mission statement. Assessments in phase 2 are based on the agency's mission statement. For example, if any agency's mission statement is to provide active treatment services that enable the person to return to the community, then the team employs those assessment tools that identify needed skills and services that will ensure the successful placement of the individual in a less restrictive environment.

A variety of commercially designed criterion-referenced, performance-based, or functional assessments are available for use in determining the strengths, interests, and needs of individuals with developmental disabilities (Table 1) (Holman & Bruininks, 1985). No one assessment will address all areas of interest to the agency staff. Additionally, there may be a particular area of concern to the staff for which the chosen assessment tool contains too few items to measure the person's ability accurately. Staff may have to "cut and paste" different assessment tools in order to capture needed data.

Table 1. Content areas assessed by selected adaptive behavior scales

	Adaptive Behavior Inventory for Children (Mercer & Lewis, 1977)	AAMD Adaptive Behavior Scale (Nihira et al., 1974)	AAMD Adaptive Behavior Scale—School Edition (Lambert & Windmiller, 1981)	Balthazar Scales of Adaptive Behavior (Balthazar, 1976)	Inventory for Client and Agency Planning (Bruininks, Hill, Woodcock, & Weatherman, 1985)	Scales of Independent Behavior (Bruininks, Woodcock, Weatherman, & Hill, 1984)	Social and Prevocational Information Battery (Halpern et al., 1975)	Social and Prevocational Information Battery, Form T (Irvin et al., 1979)	The TARC Assessment System (Sailor & Mix, 1975)	Tests for Everyday Living (Halpern et al., 1979)	Vineland Adaptive Behavior Scales (Sparrow et al., 1984)	Weller-Strawser Scales of Adaptive Behavior (Weller & Strawser, 1981)	Number of scales, including content area
Self-help, personal appearance													
Feeding, eating, drinking	x	x	x	x	x	x			x		x		8
Dressing	x	x	x	x	x	x	x		x		x	x	10
Toileting		x	x	x	x	x			x		x		7
Grooming, hygiene	x	x	x		x	x	x	x	x		x		9
Physical development													
Gross motor skills		x	x		x	x			x		x		6
Fine motor skills		x	x		x	x			x		x		6
Communication													
Receptive language		x	x	x	x	x			x		x	x	8
Expressive language	x	x	x	x	x	x			x		x	x	9
Personal, social skills													
Play skills	x		x	x	x				x		x	x	7
Interaction skills	x	x	x		x	x			x		x	x	8
Group participation	x	x	x		x	x			x		x	x	8
Social amenities		x	x		x	x			x		x	x	7
Sexual behavior											x		1
Self-direction, responsibility	x	x	x	x		x					x	x	7
Leisure activities	x	x	x	x		x					x	x	7
Expression of emotions			x							x	x	x	4
Cognitive functioning													
Preacademics (e.g., colors)	x					x				x	x		4
Reading	x	x	x		x	x	x	x	x		x		7
Writing	x	x	x		x	x			x		x		5
Numeric functions		x	x		x	x					x		5
Time		x	x		x	x					x		6
Money	x	x	x		x	x					x		3
Measurement						x					x		4

(continued)

Table 1. *(continued)*

	Adaptive Behavior Inventory for Children (Mercer & Lewis, 1977)	AAMD Adaptive Behavior Scale (Nihira et al., 1974)	AAMD Adaptive Behavior Scale—School Edition (Lambert & Windmiller, 1981)	Balthazar Scales of Adaptive Behavior (Balthazar, 1976)	Inventory for Client and Agency Planning (Bruininks, Hill, Woodcock, & Weatherman, 1985)	Scales of Independent Behavior (Bruininks, Woodcock, Weatherman, & Hill, 1984)	Social and Prevocational Information Battery (Halpern et al., 1975)	Social and Prevocational Information Battery, Form T (Irvin et al., 1979)	The TARC Assessment System (Sailor & Mix, 1975)	Tests for Everyday Living (Halpern et al., 1979)	Vineland Adaptive Behavior Scales (Sparrow et al., 1984)	Weller-Strawser Scales of Adaptive Behavior (Weller & Strawser, 1981)	Number of scales, including content area
Health care, personal welfare													
Treatment of injuries, health problems	x	x	x			x	x	x		x	x		8
Prevention of health problems		x	x			x	x	x		x	x		7
Personal safety	x						x	x		x	x		5
Child-care practices							x	x		x			3
Consumer skills													
Money handling	x	x	x		x	x	x	x		x	x		9
Purchasing	x	x	x		x	x	x	x		x	x		8
Banking		x	x		x	x	x	x		x	x		8
Budgeting		x	x		x	x	x	x		x	x		9
Domestic skills													
Household cleaning	x	x			x	x	x	x		x	x		8
Property maintenance, repair	x					x	x	x		x	x		6
Clothing care	x	x	x		x	x	x	x		x	x		9
Kitchen skills	x	x			x	x	x	x		x	x		8
Household safety	x				x	x	x	x		x	x		6
Community orientation													
Travel skills	x	x	x		x	x					x	x	7
Utilization of community resources	x	x	x			x							4
Telephone usage	x	x	x		x	x					x		6
Community safety	x					x					x		3
Vocational skills													
Work habits and attitudes	x	x	x		x	x	x	x		x	x	x	10
Job search skills	x		x			x	x	x		x			6
Work performance	x	x	x	x	x	x	x	x		x	x	x	11
Social vocational behavior						x	x	x		x	x		5
Work safety		x	x			x	x	x		x			6

Note: Many scales also assess problem behaviors.

Reproduced with permission from Holman, J. G., & Bruininks, R. H. (1985). Assessing and training adaptive behaviors. In K. C. Lakin & R. H. Bruininks (Eds.), *Strategies for achieving community integration of developmentally disabled citizens* (pp. 73–104). Baltimore: Paul H. Brookes Publishing Co.

Many agencies have developed their own assessments in those instances where supplemental information is needed or where assessment tools do not exist. These homemade tools usually follow a specific developmental sequence and are designed to:

1. Identify the specific area to be assessed
2. Sequentially list the behaviors that are to be assessed
3. Identify other factors of importance to the staff such as completion of the task with assistance, without assistance, with reinforcers, without reinforcers, and so forth
4. Identify a procedure for collecting data and analyzing the results

Table 2 provides an example of a staff-designed assessment tool to determine a person's ability to use a telephone.

The direct observations of staff are very important in the assessment process. A structured interview with key staff in day-to-day direct contact with the individual with developmental disabilities will provide the team with pertinent data about the person. Questions to consider in constructing a staff interview may include:

1. Is the person left or right-handed?
2. Does the person appear to look at objects with the left or right eye?

Table 2. Instructor-designed assessment in independent use of the telephone

Task: To telephone community residence—532-6410	With assistance	Without assistance
The individual:		
1. Picks up telephone		
2. Puts telephone to ear		
3. Listens for dial tone		
4. Identifies the number 5		
5. Dials the number 5		
6. Identifies the number 3		
7. Dials the number 3		
8. Identifies the number 2		
9. Dials the number 2		
10. Identifies the number 6		
11. Dials the number 6		
12. Identifies the number 4		
13. Dials the number 4		
14. Identifies the number 1		
15. Dials the number 1		
16. Identifies the number 0		
17. Dials the number 0		
18. Says "hello"		
19. Carries on conversation		
20. Says "good-bye" to end conversation		

Reproduced with permission from Gardner, J. F., & Chapman, M. S. (1985). *Staff development in mental retardation services: A practical handbook* (p. 76). Baltimore: Paul H. Brookes Publishing Co.

3. Does the person prefer to have work task presented:
   - to the left side?
   - to the right side?
   - from the top of the work space?
   - from the bottom of the work space?
4. Does the person show a preference for reinforcers? If yes, name.
5. Does the person work better in a group setting or individually?
6. Does the person prefer physical assistance or gesturing?

Many agencies view the assessment process in phase 2 with a beginning and an end. The individual's team meeting is scheduled promptly, and staff undertake assessments. The process, however, is an ongoing one. Assessments and programs developed in the previous year, implementation strategies, and data collected provide invaluable assessment information. Using this information, staff are able to identify areas where additional or supplemental assessment information is needed. Assessments are scheduled and completed only where needed and are used to build upon an ongoing individual program plan.

Program Checklist

	Yes	No
1. Staff use multiple assessment tools.	—	—
2. Assessments are supplemented with instructor-designed tests.	—	—
3. The assessment process includes direct observations of the individual.	—	—
4. The assessment process is viewed as an ongoing process where the previous year's data are used as assessment information.	—	—

A new assessment process that relates directly to phase 2 and the development of individual program plans has emerged. This process involves assessing not only the person but also the environment in which the acquisition of skills will take place (Manfredini & Smith, 1988; Wilcox & Bellamy, 1987). The environment is assessed to determine the effects on the individual's skill performance. Through an analysis of the environment, staff are able to identify environmental variables that may have an influence on the person. An assessment of the environment may also include:

1. Lighting—bright or low; direct or indirect
2. Noise—loud or soft; background noise such as music; no noise
3. Work space—large room or small room; large work space or small work space; bright-colored walls or soft-colored walls; work cubical or table
4. Room temperature—summer/winter temperatures 68 or 78 degrees
5. Group size—one to two people or three to five people in group

6. Time of day—a.m. or p.m. for maximum attention to task
7. Recent changes in the person's life—increased/decreased medications; increased/decreased visits from family or advocate; new direct care worker assigned to living unit; new resident assigned to the living unit

Environmental factors have a large influence on all people. Understanding these factors and how they affect the performance of individuals with developmental disabilities will increase the effectiveness of the team in developing program plans.

The purpose of assessment in phase 2 is to obtain a comprehensive understanding of the person with developmental disabilities. Criterion-referenced, performance-based, and/or functional assessments coupled with staff-designed assessments, staff observations, data from the previous year's work, and an assessment of the environment provide the needed data for teams to revise, change, or create the individual program plan. Individual program plans developed as a result of this process increase the effectiveness of the team to plan meaningful and purposeful goals and objectives for the individual.

Phase 3: Assessments Related to Exit from the Active Treatment Cycle

With the emphasis on deinstitutionalization and living in the least restrictive environment possible, many individuals with developmental disabilities are returning to the community or moving to less restrictive environments within the community. Exiting from the active treatment cycle requires an assessment that combines clinical and functional data. Initial and subsequent clinical assessments completed by the specialized service staff are compiled and summarized. Special emphasis is placed on proven techniques that resulted in gains during the active treatment process. Criterion-referenced, performance-based, and/or functional assessments are summarized with the emphasis placed on the acquisition of new skills and on emerging skill development. Pertinent staff observations are reported with an emphasis on individual preferences, such as reinforcers, error-free learning strategies, staffing ratios, and so on. Finally, environmental factors that increase the probability of successful implementation of the program plan are identified.

Program Checklist

		Yes	No
1.	The facility assesses environmental factors that may affect the individual's performance.	——	——
2.	Assessments that combine clinical and functional information are completed before exiting the facility.	——	——
3.	Assessments are used as the foundation for IPP development.	——	——

The purpose of the assessment in phase 3 is to provide information from a historical perspective for the staff/caregivers in the next living and/or working environment. This process aids in the successful transition of the person from one environment to another. It also provides the basis for staff in the new environment to make decisions regarding needed assessments that will assist them in writing a new individual program plan.

IMPLICATIONS

For Qualified Mental Retardation Professionals

Contemporary practices suggest that the qualified mental retardation professional (QMRP) or team chairperson receives assessments at least 1 week prior to the interdisciplinary team meeting because:

1. The QMRP is able to review the assessment data in advance of the meeting and identify discrepancies in reports. For example, the psychologist identifies the person as profoundly retarded, and the speech pathologist identifies the person as severely retarded. The QMRP is able to return the assessments and request clarity and consistency in reporting information.

2. The QMRP is able to review assessment data for requirements of each phase. For example, assessments completed by specialized service staff in phase 2 are based on their direct observation of the individual with developmental disabilities across the different treatment environments. If not, the QMRP returns the assessment prior to the team meeting and requests assessment data based on the therapist's direct environmental observations.

3. The QMRP reviews assessments looking for professional jargon that may not be understood by all team members. The QMRP is able to return the assessment report and request clarity on these points.

4. With the critical shortage of specialized support staff and the demands placed on them, the QMRP is able to review all reports and make decisions regarding attendance at the team meeting. This process will aid in freeing specialized service staff so that their time may be spent in direct contact with the person with developmental disabilities.

For Specialized Service Staff

Many specialized service staff may experience difficulty making the transition to a three-phase assessment process. Their professional training and/or previous experience in clinical settings often leave them unaccustomed to such a process. Within the active treatment cycle the expertise of the specialized service staff is needed not only to obtain clinical baseline data on the person but also to translate their findings into meaningful day-to-day experiences for the individual with developmental disabilities and the direct care staff directly responsible for the implementation of program plans. Their training focuses on writing detailed assessments, including usage of words specific to their profession. In this model the emphasis is placed on assessment reports written in a manner that could be understood by all staff. Specialized service staff focus on sharing their knowledge and skills with all staff who come in contact with the individual.

For Direct Care Staff

The role of the direct care worker is vital in the assessment process. The direct care worker is in contact with the individual with developmental disabilities more than any other staff. The direct care worker needs the lead role in the assessment and subsequent team process. Observations of the person's rhythms and routines in his or her day-to-day life cannot be adequately measured on an assessment tool.

For Quality Assurance Coordinators

The issue for the quality assurance (QA) coordinator centers around the assessment process and the goals and objectives identified on the individual program plan. A comprehensive assessment process as described in this chapter yields program plans that focus on outcome measures for the individual with developmental disabilities. Good assessments will yield good program plans; poor assessment, poor plans. The QA coordinator will need to look for those systems employed by the facility to assess individuals and determine if they are in fact comprehensive in nature. The process needs to address critical areas such as clinical baseline data, functional assessments based on direct observation of the individual, and environmental factors that influence the acquisition of skills. The facility staff need to demonstrate clearly that they understand the importance of assessments and the relationship between the assessment and program planning processes.

CONCLUSION

The active treatment cycle begins with the development of the facility mission statement followed by the assessment process. The assessment process is critical. With a well-defined assessment process, the remaining steps in the active treatment process have a greater likelihood of success for the individual. Staff need to have a clear, comprehensive understanding of each person in the facility if they are to develop meaningful individual program plans. Assessment within the active treatment cycle is a three-phase process.

Upon entry to the facility, and on a defined schedule thereafter, each individual needs comprehensive clinical assessments completed. These assessments focus on obtaining clinical baseline data and provide measures against which intervention strategies can be evaluated.

Functional assessments are required for the development of individual program plans. Criterion-referenced, performance-based measures, functional assessments, staff-designed assessments, and direct staff observations are used to collect data related to the day-to-day performance of the individual in different treatment environments. Environmental factors that affect the performance of the individual are also assessed. The focus of this phase is on obtaining assessment data that promote the development of program plans by teams that stress outcome measures for the individual as a result of the intervention strategies employed by staff.

Leaving the active treatment cycle requires assessment that summarizes clinical and functional assessment data. The report stresses successful intervention techniques that resulted in skill acquisition. The focus of this assessment process is to facilitate the transition of the person into a new environment through the sharing of information about the person's experiences in the current placement.

All staff have a role in the assessment process. Direct care staff assume a lead role. Their daily contact with the individual and their responsibilities for the implementation of program plans make their observations invaluable. The specialized service staff base assessments on direct observations of the individual. The sharing of their observations with other staff in easy-to-understand terms aids in all staff understanding the person better.

Finally, facility management staff need to develop policy and procedures related to the assessment process. They need to ensure that all staff understand the importance of the assessment process.

REFERENCES

Balthazar, E. E. (1976). *Balthazar Scales of Adaptive Behavior for the Profoundly and Severely Mentally Retarded.* Palo Alto, CA: Consulting Psychologists Press.

Bruininks, R. H., Hill, B. K., Woodcock, R. W., & Weatherson, R. F. (1985). *Inventory for Client and Agency Planning.* Allen, TX: Developmental Learning Materials/Teaching Resources.

Bruininks, R. H., Woodcock, R. W., Weatherman, R. F., & Hill, B. K. (1984). *Scales of Independent Behavior.* Allen, TX: Developmental Learning Materials/Teaching Resources.

Gardner, J. F., & Chapman, M. S. (1985). *Staff development in mental retardation services: A practical handbook.* Baltimore: Paul H. Brookes Publishing Co.

Halpern, A. S., Irvin, L. K., & Landman, J. T. (1979). *Tests for Everyday Living.* Monterey, CA: Publishers Test Service.

Halpern, A., Raffeld, P., Irvin, L. K., & Link, R. (1975). *Social and Prevocational Information Battery.* Monterey, CA: Publishers Test Service.

Holman, J. G., & Bruininks, R. H. (1985). Assessing and training adaptive behaviors. In K. C. Lakin & R. H. Bruininks (Eds.), *Strategies for achieving community integration of developmentally disabled citizens* (pp. 73–104). Baltimore: Paul H. Brookes Publishing Co.

Irvin, L. K., Halpern, A. S., Reynolds, W. M. (1979). *Social and Prevocational Information Battery, Form T.* Monterey, CA: Publishers Test Service.

Lambert, N. M., & Windmiller, M. (1981). *AAMD Adaptive Behavior Scale—School Edition.* Monterey, CA: Publishers Test Service.

Landesman, S., & Vietz, P. (Eds.). (1987). *Living environments and mental retardation.* Washington, DC: American Association on Mental Retardation.

Manfredini, D., & Smith, W. (1988). The concept and implementation of active treatment. In M. Janicki, M. W. Krauss, & M. M. Seltzer (Eds.), *Community residences for persons with developmental disabilities: Here to stay* (pp. 123–131). Baltimore: Paul H. Brookes Publishing Co.

Mercer, J. R., & Lewis, J. F. (1977). *Adaptive Behavior Inventory for Children.* New York: Psychological Corp.

Meyers, C. E., Nihira, K., & Zetlin, A. (1979). The measurement of adaptive behavior. In N. R. Ellis (Ed.), *Handbook of mental deficiency: Psychological theory and research* (ed. 2). Hillsdale, NJ: Lawrence Erlbaum Associates.

Nihira, K., Foster, R., Shellhaas, M., & Leland, H. (1974). *AAMD Adaptive Behavior Scale.* Washington, DC: American Association on Mental Deficiency.

Sailor, W., & Mix, B. J. (1975). *The TARC Assessment System.* Lawrence, KS: H & H Enterprises.

Simeonsson, R. J., Huntington, G. S., & Parse, S. A. (1980). Assessment of children with severe handicaps: Multiple problems—Multivariate goals. *Journal of the Association for the Severely Handicapped, 5*(1), 55–72.

Sparrow, S. S., Balla, D. A., & Cicchetti, D. V. (1984). *Vineland Adaptive Behavior Scales.* Circle Pines, MN: American Guidance Service.

Tjosvold, D., & Tjosvold, M. (1981). *Working with mentally handicapped persons in their residences.* New York: The Free Press.

Weller, C., & Strawser, S. (1981). *Weller-Strawser Scales of Adaptive Behavior.* Novato, CA: Academic Therapy Publications.

Wilcox, B., & Bellamy, G. T. (1987). *A comprehensive guide to the activity catalog: An alternative curriculum for youth and adults with severe disabilities.* Baltimore: Paul H. Brookes Publishing Co.

9
Developing the
Individual Program Plan

Chaya M. Kaplan and Cynthia Shima Kauffman

This chapter focuses on the individual program plan (IPP)—the substance and outcome of interdisciplinary team planning. The chapter builds directly on chapter 8 on assessments. Functional, comprehensive assessments are the foundation for effective planning. In addition, this chapter should be viewed as the complement of chapter 5, "The Team as a Small Group," that discusses how a team collaborates in planning. This chapter describes the plan that is the product of the collaboration.

The IPP is the unifying element of the active treatment process; it shapes the process and holds it together. The IPP may be viewed as a road map for the individual's future. In clearly stating who will do what and when, it establishes responsibility and accountability. It is the basis for reviewing progress and is a record of achievement. To be effective the IPP must be positively focused and have the maximum possible participation of the individual with developmental disabilities.

The specific topics that are discussed in the development of the IPP are:

- Developing goals and objectives from assessments utilizing strengths, interests, and needs
- Formulating goals and reviewing them for functionality
- Writing goal and objective statements
- Setting priorities among goals
- Developing the service record
- The IPP as a written document

BACKGROUND

The use of goals and objectives in educational settings occurred as early as the 1940s (Mager, 1962). The development of prescriptive teaching in education, a practice of teaching by goals along a developmental continuum, in the 1960s and early 70s provided the strongest direct influence on the use of planning in the field of mental retardation. Although goals and objectives were being used in many facilities serving people with mental retardation, not until 1974 did federal regulations mandate individualized plans of care. The purpose of the plan of care was, and continues to be, to enhance the quality of services and to ensure active treatment for individuals living in intermediate care facilities for the mentally retarded (ICFs/MR). Since 1974 court litigation, state regulations and licensing requirements, and accreditation standards have mandated individualized planning.

In addition to educational settings, goal and objective planning has been extensively utilized by management in business and industry for a number of decades. A brief review of management literature and research gives strong indication as to why goal setting has become widely practiced. Robbins (1984, p. 144) defines planning as "the process of determining objectives and assessing the way these objectives can best be achieved." This indicates that planning is concerned with means as well as ends. He points out that even when ends or anticipated achievements are not reached, planning is still of great value in setting direction and purpose and focusing energy. He further differentiates between formal and informal planning. Formal planning requires a written plan with specific objectives, which is disseminated to members of the organization. Robbins reports that companies and organizations that engage in formal planning show markedly improved performance and outperform comparable companies that do not.

The literature on goal setting is also strongly positive. E. A. Locke (1968) reported that the setting of specific, challenging goals led to improved performance. To determine the practical relevance of Locke's research, Latham and Yukl (1975) later reviewed 27 field-based studies in a range of employment settings. They found that goal setting led to improved performance in diverse organizations. This was also true over extended periods of time and at management and nonmanagement levels of performance. To be useful, goals had to be specific as opposed to "do your best." They also found that difficult goals, if accepted by the worker, were more effective than easy goals. Finally, David McClelland et al. (1976), in the now classic work on the need to achieve, found that high achievers are persistent in the setting of realistic yet challenging goals for themselves.

While the use of goals and objectives in human services holds as great a promise as in business and industry, Blake and Mouton (1983) express the need for caution. They contend that if goals are expressed in abstract terms or are remote from the activities in which people are engaged, they may exert little or no influence on people's lives.

483.440(c)   *Individual program plan*

The standards for individual program plan development are found in 483.440(c). These standards cover both the roles and responsibilities of the interdisciplinary team and the components of the individual program plan: comprehensive functional assessment, strengths, needs, specific behavioral objectives, training programs, schedules, responsible persons, data, and location of the program.

The presentation of assessment information occurs at the beginning of the planning process. The assessments, to be most useful, focus on the individual's functioning in his or her current natural environments (e.g., in the morning while preparing to leave the residence for the day or during his or her daytime program, etc.). Contemporary practice suggests that assessments should be based on direct observation of the individual in real life situations and, whenever possible, include direct input from the individual.

To make optimal use of the time team members spend in the planning meeting, each assessment should be made available to all team members prior to the planning meeting. This enables team members to become familiar with each other's assessments prior to the meeting. The assessments should focus on the skills, strengths, and interests the individual demonstrates each day. Early and continued emphasis on strengths and interests promotes development of a positive, individualized plan.

Strengths are statements about an individual that give a positive picture of the person. They reflect abilities that the individual currently possesses. Any part of a task or skill that a person can do should be seen as a strength. Strengths may exist in areas of personal care, communication, education, work, relationships, recreation, as well as others. Strengths identify successes of the individual. Each assessment should list strengths. Examples of strengths are: eats independently, makes eye contact, dresses with verbal reminders, and so on.

In addition to strengths, assessments should indicate interests of the individual—areas of preference or value to the individual. Interests vary from simple preferences, as in food, to complex activities such as photography. An interest may be the basis of a goal, or it may be utilized as a reinforcer in an instructional program.

Prior to the actual interdisciplinary planning meeting, the chairperson, qualified mental retardation professional (QMRP), and/or designated others should utilize the assessments to begin to develop lists of the strengths and interests of the individual. These lists should be made available to all team members at the beginning of the planning meeting. Their purpose is to highlight areas of promise upon which to build to meet developmental needs. For example, a strength of being able to pull on pants could be the basis of a goal involving greater independence in dressing. An interest in food might lead to a goal around cooking skills. As team members present their assessments, they can then augment and integrate the strengths and interests lists.

The presentation of assessments can affect the team's planning effectiveness. The order of presentation should reflect which team members implemented the previous year's programs and spent the most time in direct contact with the individual. For this reason, the direct service workers in residential and day programs should present their assessments first. The medical, psychological, and social work assessments and other specialty assessments, such as nutrition and physical therapy appropriate to the individual, would follow. During presentations team members should be encouraged to ask clarifying questions. The team should also maintain flexible boundaries among members. For example, the residential counselor or parent may comment on the individual's manual coordination while shaving. These comments assist in forming a more cohesive, integrated view of the individual. A review of progress on the prior year's goals is an important part of assessment data. If a goal has not been met, the team should consider the reason. Relating progress on goals to the strengths and interests lists may provide valuable insights.

Team members must understand that strengths and interests are the primary basis for the development of objectives. Just as non-disabled people choose careers, household chores, and hobbies based on their strengths and interests, so must the objectives of individuals with developmental disabilities be tied to their strengths and interests. College students do not major in their weakest areas. Neither should people with disabilities be expected to work on programs based only on their weaknesses. Everyone learns best by building on success.

Houts and Scott (1975) suggest that strengths and interests can serve as a "pool of choices" to be utilized in the three steps of: 1) writing goals, 2) writing objectives, and 3) developing instructional strategies. For example, if Carol likes to go shopping and can count and follow directions, a goal for her might be to learn to use money. When setting objectives for this goal, the team, after a second review of the strengths and interests lists, may find that Carol likes soft drinks. An objective for her might be to select two quarters for the soda machine. The teaching design may be aided by a third review of the strengths and interests lists. Since Carol responds well to praise, praise as well as the soft drink may be used to reinforce her appropriate use of coins.

Level of functioning influences the process of creating strengths and interests lists. Of primary importance is the person's ability to contribute to the list. For a person with many competencies, interests will become increasingly important. For example, if a person is able to ride a bicycle but has little interest in doing so, training as a bicycle messenger or recreational cycling would not be appropriate to that individual.

When an individual is severely handicapped with multiple disabilities, the team may literally need to go on a hunt for strengths. In the case of a young woman with profound multiple disabilities who gave almost no indication of awareness of her surroundings and showed no preferences, even in foods, her mother's observation that she appeared to attend to the patterns and colors of a lap blanket was valuable. It gave the team a strength on which to address the need of the woman to attend to the activities in her environment.

In planning with individuals having very challenging behaviors, development of the strengths and interests lists becomes especially important. Listing an individual's strengths and interests calls attention to positive behaviors. Successful planning requires strengths on which to build.

Identifying strengths may require staff to shift their perceptions of people with disabilities. Wolfensberger (1988) calls attention to frequently overlooked assets of people who are retarded. He notes that some individuals with disabilities are more emotionally available for open, caring relationships than more sophisticated people. While acknowledging individual differences, he also mentions an ability to enjoy many things, the capacity for honesty, and the successful engagement in repetitive tasks. Noting attributes of this kind is important in developing the strengths list.

Program Checklist

	Yes	No
1. Team members are familiar with each other's assessments prior to the meeting.	___	___
2. The team identifies strengths and interests of each individual.	___	___
3. Direct service workers are the first to present at the team meeting.	___	___
4. The individual with developmental disabilities participates with team members in the development of the individual program plan.	___	___

Developing the Needs List

The team uses the strengths and interests lists to identify needs. The strengths indicate areas in which potential exists for further learning. The interests highlight areas in which the individual may be most motivated. Needs that identify skills that the person with disabilities will learn or refine through participating in instructional programs are called programmatic needs. They lead to the development of goals, objectives, and instructional strategies. When successfully addressed, these needs result in positive, behavioral change in the individual.

Programmatic needs should be identified by considering both skills and partial skills that the individual can demonstrate (i.e., strengths and skill deficits that impact on the individual's quality of life). For example, if an individual has demonstrated enough verbal skill to interact briefly with others, increasing skills in holding a conversation may be a useful, practical need of the person.

Interests may be the primary source for identifying a programmatic need. For example, an individual may be interested in watching baseball on television. A need might be learning to turn on the television or learning to tell time to know when to turn on the baseball game. These needs would be based on the person's interest. The need chosen should make the most sense when the team considers the individual and his or her life as a whole.

Another example of how strengths and interests assist in identifying needs and objectives follows. Ted likes music and can follow multistep instructions. He is apt to hit or kick others when no activity is happening in the house. Ted could be taught how to turn on the radio, use a tape recorder, or ask someone to turn on the stereo. Ted would be learning to initiate an activity he enjoys when he wants it.

Emphasizing strengths and interests instead of deficits in identifying needs may represent a significant change for some teams. Another critical shift for some teams to make is from focusing on the individual's skills by domain (e.g., gross motor, communication, etc.) to a more integrated view of the person. This change emphasizes the whole person. The team can best do this by considering the person in his or her home, work, leisure, and social environments. Looking at all aspects of a person's life provides greater opportunities for teaching. Staff will benefit from approaching a total person who participates in varied activities in different settings throughout the day. Valuable suggestions to promote success in planning and implementation will be gleaned through this approach.

Strengths, interests, and needs lists are a means to integrate multiple specialized assessments, with input from the individual who is developmentally disabled. Throughout the process the team should give special attention to involving the individual. In many cases the individual may be able to contribute to the lists directly. Since it is not possible in many circumstances to be sure how much the individual understands, the team should presume some understanding. This position treats the individual with the greatest respect and dignity. At the very least, even if the individual's understanding of the discussion is minimal, positive attention will be directed toward him.

Formulating Goals and Reviewing for Functionality

After the team identifies programmatic needs, goal statements are formulated. Goals are behavioral statements of change that the individual with developmental disabilities is expected to accomplish within a 1-year period. The definition of goals and objectives, particularly in terms of time frames, varies from state to state and agency to agency. The time frame per se is less important than that each agency is consistent within itself in its use of terms.

While team members may come to the planning meeting with suggestions for goals, formal statements should be generated after full team discussion of the individual's strengths, interests, and needs. During the process of building the strengths, interests, and needs lists, team members will be shifting from individual decision making about their specialized assessments to a collaborative, consensual mode of planning. This group collaboration should continue in developing the goal statements. Formalized goals should reflect team decisions. The selection of goals should also enhance each team member's commitment to assist in the achievement of those goals. While the goals are developed for and with the individual with disabilities, they are also owned by the team. Full team discussion and participation in decision making helps build member commitment.

A key element in goal development is ensuring that goals are relevant to the individual's life situation. Accomplishing a goal must help the individual to function more independently in his or her real life. For example, learning a pincer grasp may help a person to turn on his radio, but the skill will be irrelevant if the radio has push button controls.

Lou Brown et al. (1979) provide three criteria to determine if a goal is functional:

1. Does it involve the use of age-appropriate materials?
2. Does the instruction take place in the actual setting where the skill will be used when learned? For example, is the individual learning to shave in the bathroom, in the morning, using a razor?
3. Will accomplishing the goal increase the individual's independence or improve his or her quality of life in a very practical way? For example, learning to turn on the radio will be useful if the person likes to listen to it. Learning to name body parts may be of questionable use.

Ensuring that goals are functional requires continual review. Studies in educational settings have documented how often this is overlooked. For example, in a recent review of individualized education plans (IEPs) of transition-age students, over 60% of the goals were found not functional (Weisenfeld, 1987).

The traditional use of developmental checklists, which emphasizes a specific sequence in skill acquisition, has drawn team attention away from concern for functionality. This occurs when failed items on checklists become the basis for identifying needs. For example, does it matter that a person does not walk with an alternating gait, if she walks successfully? Does it matter if an individual grasps a fork by wrapping all his fingers around it, if he feeds himself successfully? It may be more important to develop goals in other areas of his life, if the person functions independently at mealtimes.

In general, if an activity can be successfully carried out by the person, the precise form of approach may be of less consequence. The important question that the team must ask is, "Will accomplishing this goal make a difference in this individual's everyday life?" The concept of functionality requires putting a priority on whether a person can successfully perform an activity. The precise way or form in which the task is performed is of less importance. Developing an IPP that is functional and may have a practical impact on an individual's life should be the central focus of the team's attention.

Program Checklist

	Yes	No
1. The individual's strengths/interests are reflected in the identified goals and objectives.	___	___
2. Goals and objectives are developed at the team meeting.	___	___
3. Identified goals are relevant to the individual's life.	___	___
4. Identified goals and objectives are functional.	___	___

Written Goal and Objective Statements

Goals look at the big picture of what may be accomplished over a 1-year period. They state in positive behavioral terms the specific outcome that is expected.

Examples of goal statements are:

1. John will dress himself.
2. Ann will launder her own clothes.
3. Tom will follow two-step directions.

Stating goals in a positive manner makes clear what behavior will be taught and assessed. "Peter will not kick the person who sits next to him" does not indicate what Peter should do. "Peter will keep his feet to himself when sitting next to others" does give that information. In addition, stating, "Pam will understand safety rules when crossing the street," does not specify the desired behavioral change, and, therefore, is not a goal statement. The word "understand" is not a behavior because it is not observable. An alternative goal of "Pam will cross the street when the light is green" does tell staff what behavior Pam will demonstrate in meeting the goal.

Goal statements only have one behavioral outcome. For example, stating, "Ann will launder and put away her clothes," is not an optimal goal statement. Multibehavior goal statements are problematic because of difficulties evaluating a program in which only one behavior has been achieved. Can one say that the goal has been met if

Ann has learned to put her clothes away but is still not doing the laundry by herself? Finally, with regard to goal statements, they should identify the individual by name, and they should indicate the anticipated completion date, if it is other than 1 year.

Like goals, objectives indicate the individual's expected achievements. Objectives, however, target more discrete behaviors that are steps toward the accomplishment of the goal. Usually objectives are achieved in a 3- to 6-month period. Agency policy often indicates the time frame. An objective statement has three critical elements:

1. The behavior to be learned
2. The conditions under which the behavior will occur
3. The standard or criterion that indicates how well the behavior must be performed

The behavior to be learned must be observable and measurable as in the goal statements above. Observable means that the behavior can be seen or heard, and that agreement exists among observers about what constitutes the behavior. For example, does kicking occur when a person puts his foot out or only when bodily contact has been made. Kicking is generally defined by bodily contact. Thus, kicking is a clear, agreed upon, observable behavior.

Measurable means that there is at least one way to measure the behavior. Behavior is measured by counting how often it occurs or for how long it lasts. In the case of kicking, "how often" would be the appropriate measure. In the case of doing laundry, "how long" would be the appropriate measure. At times when measuring "how often," clearly specifying what represents an occurrence of the behavior is necessary. For example, a rapid succession of many kicks can count as 20 kicks or one episode of kicking.

The condition addresses questions of where, when, with whom, and with what assistance the behavior will occur. For example, "Given the verbal command 'put on your pants, John,' John will pull on his pants with physical guidance" is an objective statement. Two conditions are in this statement. "Given the verbal command, 'put on your pants, John'" tells when the behavior is expected to occur. "With physical guidance" notes what assistance will be given.

The criterion is an essential part of the objective statement because it defines when a behavior has been learned successfully. Criterion may reflect accuracy, speed, quantity, or duration. Accuracy is the most common criterion and is usually reflected in the form of a percentage. For example, "Ann will correctly sort her colored and white clothes 80% of the time when doing laundry." An occasional error would be acceptable in doing laundry. On the other hand, in dangerous or critical situations 100% accuracy will be required. Crossing the street on the green signal or using safety glasses while operating power machinery requires a 100% criterion.

When an individual can accomplish a task but takes so long to do it that it is not practical, an objective to increase speed might be appropriate. For example, "Given the verbal command, 'put on your pants, John,' John will pull on his pants with physical guidance within 5 minutes."

In some instances a criterion of quantity would be most appropriate. For example, "Steve will count the three city blocks he must walk to the grocery store." When a person must know or use a specific count to do an activity, quantity is the most useful criterion. Finally, duration of response would be a useful criterion. Finally, duration of response would be a useful criterion if the time spent on a behavior needs to be increased. For example, "When given materials, Larry works on constructing a three-piece hose nozzle for at least 10 minutes."

In order to demonstrate the consistency of the learned behavior over time, the criterion might include a statement such as "on 3 consecutive days." For example, "Janet crosses the street on the green signal with 100% accuracy on 3 consecutive days." In determining the most appropriate criterion to set for a given objective, the team should be practical. The team will be asking at what level of performance will accomplishing this objective contribute to the individual's increased independence in everyday life. Mager (1962) points out that the criterion is not a barely tolerable minimum but the desired level of proficiency needed in a specific situation. For example, Mager states that while it might be acceptable for a shipping clerk to tie an occasional knot that slips, this could not be tolerated from a surgeon. The level of performance needs to be appropriate to the situation.

The number of goals to a plan is another practical consideration for the team that must also be consistent with agency policy. Consideration of such factors as the individual's energy level, health, interest in programs, and age, particularly of children and persons over 55, will affect the number of goals. While the practical question of adequate staffing ratios to carry out teaching programs may legitimately be raised, it should not become an excuse for inadequate or underprogramming with too few goals for an individual.

Program Checklist

	Yes	No
1. All goals are stated positively.	___	___
2. All goals and objectives include only one behavioral outcome.	___	___
3. Sequential objectives are identified that lead to accomplishing the goal.	___	___

Setting Priorities

Once the team has determined that attainment of functional goals will have a practical impact on the person's life, it must establish priorities among the goals. Setting priorities indicates the order in which the team will implement the goals. The goals selected as priorities should reflect the individual's strengths, interests, and needs and not the agency's priorities. Mobility training must be important for an individual. The team should not select mobility training as a goal because the agency has a staff person with an opening to teach mobility. Listed below in order of importance are questions the team should ask when setting goal priorities. Many of these questions are drawn from the work of Houts and Scott (1975):

- Is the individual at risk of causing harm to himself/herself or others? A goal to address a life, health, or safety need must be given top priority.
- Is the individual at risk of losing his or her current placement and moving to a more restricted environment?
- What preferences or priorities has the individual with developmental disabilities expressed as goals? Even if the staff does not agree with the individual's choices, these goals should be given high priority because of their influence on motivation and success.
- Will achieving a goal enhance the individual's opportunities to move to a less restrictive environment?
- Does a goal address a legal mandate? For example, 1988 federal ICF/MR regulations require that agencies take aggressive actions to improve self-care of persons with severe multiple disabilities.
- Is accomplishment of one goal necessary for the achievement of others? For example, a person must learn to hold a spoon before he or she can learn to scoop with it.
- Does a greater chance of success exist due to high team interest and available resources? Caution should be exercised here to ensure that: 1) the individual's wishes are not made second to the team's preferences and 2) higher priority goals are not given less weight because of lack of resources.
- Have the family or interested others recommended a goal in order to spend more time with the individual who is developmentally disabled?

By utilizing the above questions to set priorities among goals, the team individualizes the plan and promotes success. Those goals that do not become priorities still remain part of the written plan. They should be reviewed in the process of developing subsequent IPPs.

Developing the Service Record

In addition to goals and objectives, the IPP should identify the services to be provided to the individual. Services may be offered on a one-time, occasional, or ongoing basis. They include further evaluations and assessments, acquisition of material articles such as adaptive devices, and activities such as community trips. Services might be specific to the needs of the individual, such as a wheelchair, or of general use by anyone, such as a step stool in the kitchen. Services may be provided by agency staff directly or by an outside source, such as optometrist, behavioral consultant, or volunteer.

The need for some services will become apparent in the course of the team discussion of strengths, interests, and needs. To ensure careful consideration of services, however, the following checklist is offered:

Type of Service	Examples
Medical	Examinations and treatments by physicians and nurses Primary health care (e.g., treatment for dry skin) and specialty health care (e.g., seizure disorders, orthopedic problems, etc.) Medication reviews
Clinical	Consultation and treatment by speech pathologists, physical therapists, occupational therapists
Behavioral	Collection of baseline data Consultation by nonagency psychologist
Residential	Services that support living in the most appropriate setting and foster independence An in-home aide for an individual who becomes ill frequently Textured landmarks for a person who is blind
Day program	Adaptive devices that will promote participation in work or work-related activities
Mobility	Arranging for taxi vouchers or bus tokens
Recreation and leisure	Arranging for a magazine subscription Enrollment in a recreation program Community trips
Personal needs	Concrete items to enhance self-esteem Obtaining a wig for someone losing her hair Providing opportunities to decorate personal living space
Emotional support	Services to support adjustment Counseling or group discussion if housemate becomes ill, dies, or is transferred to another setting or for other reasons
Family-related	Supports that promote family relationships Transportation for a family visit Activities to involve family at ICF/MR
Promoting community integration	Opportunities to participate in the same settings as people without disabilities Trips to church that respect the individual's religious preferences Providing opportunities to form friendships with others in the community
Financial	Locating and documenting sources of funds and structures for the use of funds SSI, personal income, other

Sometimes service provision is necessary before a goal can be developed. For example, baseline information is necessary before a behavioral program can be designed. At other times providing a service leads to a new strength around which to build a goal. For example, an optimetric consultation and new eye glasses may lead to improved vision and greater ability to follow written instructions.

The IPP as a Written Document

By looking at the content and form of the written IPP, one can review the main components of the planning process. While each agency will develop its own format for the IPP document, the breakdown of specific sections may include the following:

- *Identifying Page*—Provides basic information about the individual with developmental disabilities, such as name, date of birth, diagnosis, names of concerned others, and so forth. Signatures and identifying information about all team members who participated at the planning meeting are also included.
- *Strengths, Interests, and Needs Lists*—Provide the foundation for goal setting.
- *Annual Goals Sheet*—A list of goals organized or listed in order of priority with regard to the settings or environment in which they will be addressed.
- *Objectives Sheets*—For each priority goal, an objective sheet will be completed. At least three objectives should be written as steps to the goal. During the year the team will need to review, revise, and/or add objectives, depending on the individual's progress. For each objective the estimated start and completion dates are given. The actual completion date will be filled in as the objective is achieved. The name of the person responsible for developing and monitoring the instructional program should also be listed. In addition the location of instructional strategies should be given here. While the instructional strategies are not part of the IPP, federal regulations require that their location be cited in the IPP.
- *The Service Record*—Lists all services to be provided or arranged by staff. The service record should list the service, responsible person, and initiation and completion dates.
- *Comment Sheet*—Will provide a place for team members to address their specific concerns or lack of agreement with sections of the plan. It can also provide the place where the person responsible for finalizing the document indicates explicitly how the plan provides opportunities for client choice and increasing self-management.

Program Checklist

	Yes	No
1. Goals/objectives identified for each individual are given priorities by the team.	—	—

Program Checklist—*continued*

	Yes	No
2. The individual program plan includes a service record.	___	___
3. The facility utilizes a consistent format from individual to individual in developing the IPP.	___	___

IMPLICATIONS

For Management Staff

Three major implications are present for management staff. The first is that they must set clear expectations for staff through the development of policies and procedures. The policies and procedures provide the structure to ensure positive, functional, individualized planning. Management must support staff in carrying out substantive planning and implementation, rather than a paper process to comply with regulations.

Second, management must provide adequate resources to carry out an effective planning process. Sufficient personnel who are effectively organized must conduct timely assessments, prepare for the planning meeting, attend the full meeting, and carry out and monitor the plan. Adequate clerical staff, appropriate meeting space, and so on are also important resources.

The third major task of management is to ensure team competency. This involves assessment of team functioning, positive feedback on appropriate behaviors and outcomes, provision of training as needed, and monitoring of team effectiveness.

For Qualified Mental Retardation Professionals

The QMRP is responsible for the IPP process. Some of the specific activities listed below may be delegated to others, but coordination rests with the QMRP.

The QMRP prepares the individual with disabilities for his or her meeting; monitors early submission of assessments; reviews assessment information; assists or provides leadership in the development of strengths, interests, and needs lists; ensures the maximum participation of the individual with disabilities in the planning meeting; and, with other team members, works to develop a plan that is individualized, functional, and enhances the person's real life.

For the Chairperson

The chairperson's role may be assigned to the QMRP or another team member. The chairperson facilitates the meeting to ensure that the team remains on task, while supporting participation of the individual with disabilities, the family, and nonagency team members. Through the use of clarifying questions, review, and summation, the chairperson integrates divergent data and information about the individual with disabilities. Finally, the chairperson encourages active participation and flexible role boundaries by all members of the team.

While the QMRP is responsible for the development, implementation, and monitoring of the IPP, the chairperson focuses on the process and content of the planning meeting. The chairperson must possess good communication and leadership skills to complete the planning task in a timely manner with the utmost respect for the individual with whom planning is done.

For Team Members

All team members provide input based on their relationship with the individual with disabilities, their direct observations of the person, and areas of expertise. Though the chairperson and QMRP are expected to facilitate full team participation, each team member needs to take responsibility for contributing to the development of the IPP. Team participation is a learned process. Most people can function as effective team members if the value of membership and participation is supported by all.

Team members are responsible for preparing assessments and relevant information for submission to the chairperson or QMRP prior to the planning meeting. Each member of the team also reviews assessments of other team members prior to the meeting, identifying and focusing on the strengths and interests of the individual. Finally, all members participate throughout the planning process to promote practical and functional goal planning.

Team members from specialized disciplines such as physical therapy or nursing should model a transdisciplinary approach as they serve as consultants rather than direct service providers. This requires increased role flexibility in the planning and implementation processes.

Direct care staff, as those most involved with the individual with developmental disabilities, play an increasingly central role in the planning meeting and in implementing programs. Direct care staff will need to work toward integration of assessments and consistent programming across shifts.

CONCLUSION

A well-structured, values-based planning process enhances the development of a practical, growth-oriented, individualized plan. The individual's strengths, interests, and needs are the foundation for planning. The plan must be tailored to the individual with developmental disabilities.

Goal attainment should have practical impact on the person's ability to function. This involves considering the activities and routines of the person's life as he or she works, relaxes, and maintains himself/herself throughout the day. In this sense the plan is developed to create practical, positive change in the quality of the person's life. Implementation of the plan can increase the ability of the person with disabilities to make choices and have greater control in shaping his or her life.

Finally, the IPP should be future oriented. The goals and objectives need to focus on what the person will do over a period of time and, as such, become steps toward the future. This is true whether the future holds a move to independent living, employment, or a greater degree of self-determination and choice within the individual's current setting.

REFERENCES

Blake, R. R., & Mouton, J. S. (1983). *Consultation* (2nd ed.). Reading, MA: Addison-Wesley.

Brown, L., et al. (1979). A strategy for developing chronological-age appropriate and functional curricular content for severely handicapped adolescents and young adults. *Journal of Special Education, 13*(1), 82–90.

Houts, S., & Scott, R. A. (1975). *Goal planning with developmentally disabled persons: Procedures for developing an individualized client plan.* Lebanon, PA: Boyer Printing and Binding Co.

Latham, G. P., & Yukl, G. A. (1975, Dec.). A review of research on the application of goalsetting in organizations. *Academy of Management Journal, 18*(4), 824–843.

Locke, E. A. (1968). Toward a theory of task motivation and incentives. *Organizational Behavior and Human Performance, 3*, 157–189.

Mager, R. F. (1962). Preparing instructional objectives. Belmont, CA: Fearon-Pitman.

McClelland, D. C., et al. (1976). *The achievement motive* (2nd ed.). New York: Irvington Publishers.

Robbins, S. P. (1984). *Management: Concepts and practices.* Englewood Cliffs, NJ: Prentice-Hall.

Weisenfeld, R. B. (1987, Oct.). Functionality in the IEPs of children with Down syndrome. *Mental Retardation, 25*(5): 281–286.

Wolfensberger, W. (1988, April). Common assets of mentally retarded people that are commonly not acknowledged. *Mental Retardation, 26*(2): 63–70.

10
Implementation Strategies
Michael S. Chapman

Interdisciplinary team process begins with the sharing of assessment data and results in the development of goals and objectives for each individual with developmental disabilities. Each individual has his or her own set of goals and objectives. Staff attending the interdisciplinary team meeting are assigned responsibilities for developing strategies for the acquisition of new skills specified in the objective. Implementation strategies are written documents that describe in detail what staff are expected to do when, in order to assist the individual with developmental disabilities acquire skills. This chapter focuses on the development of implementation strategies. It defines the steps required in the development of good strategies. Strategies for providing instruction to the individual as well as the group process are discussed. Finally, documentation strategies are presented.

The development of implementation strategies is a relatively new process. The change from providing custodial care to active treatment in the early 1970s reflected the changing beliefs held by society about people with developmental disabilities. Active treatment is grounded in the belief that all people, regardless of how severe the disabilities, are capable of growth and development throughout their lives. In order to facilitate the individual's growth, strategies are needed that maximize the individual's abilities and support the achievement of new skills and/or abilities. This process, referred to as "instructional strategies," focuses on the psychology of learning. It requires the staff's understanding of the individual and what supports are needed by the individual with developmental disabilities in order to acquire new skills.

The process is evolving. As professionals in the field gain more experience in assessing individuals with developmental disabilities and in developing instructional strategies, the process will continue to be refined.

Instructional strategies involve utilizing error-free learning strategies: verbal cues, gestures, arranging the environment, modeling, and physical assistance. Earlier designs of instructional programs focused on teaching new skills by moving from one error-free strategy to another throughout the instructional period. Error-free strategies were believed to have existed on a continuum from least intrusive to most (e.g., from verbal cues to physical assistance, respectively). Implementing instructional strategies involved developing a task analysis and presenting a different error-free strategy for each step of the task analysis depending upon the response of the individual. The same error-free strategy may or may not have been repeated at the next instructional period. This process is visualized in Figure 1.

Designing instructional strategies has evolved beyond the use of error-free learning strategies in this way. Today, the best approach to developing instructional strategies is to choose one error-free strategy for use and to develop a sequence of fading around the chosen strategy. Instructional strategies developed in this manner are believed to enable the individual with developmental disabilities to acquire skills more easily.

REVIEW OF THE STANDARDS

483.410(c) Client records
483.410(d) Services provided under agreements with outside sources
483.430(a) Qualified mental retardation professional
483.430(b) Professional program services
483.430(d) Direct care (residential living unit) staff
483.430(e) Staff training program
483.440(b) Admissions, transfers, and discharge
483.440(c) Individual program plan
483.440(d) Program implementation
483.440(e) Program documentation
483.440(f) Program monitoring and change

The standards concerning implementation strategies are found in sections on client records and services provided under agreement with outside sources. The responsibilities of the qualified mental retardation professional (QMRP), professional program service staff,

Name: _John Smith_

Program: _handwashing_

CODE:
- I — independent
- G — gesture
- M — model
- V — verbal cue
- PP— physical prompt

Task analysis

	1/4	1/5	1/6	1/7	1/8	1/9	1/10
1. Turn on water	G	M	M				
2. Pick up soap	M	I	I				
3. Rub soap on hands	V	V	I				
4. Put soap down	I	I	M				
5. Rub hands together	PP	PP	G				
6. Rinse hands	I	M	M				
7. Turn off water	PP	G	PP				
8. Dry hands	PP	G	M				

Figure 1. *Example of the inappropriate use of error-free strategies in program implementation.*

and direct care residential living unit staff cover program implementation. The requirements for staff training directly impact on the facility's ability to implement the individual program plan.

Implementation requirements are also found in the component parts of the active treatment cycle: admission, assessment, individual program plan, implementation, documentation, and monitoring and change. The standards cover both the process of implementation as well as the content requirements.

Finally, implementation requirements should be considered within the context of active treatment and the interdisciplinary team process. Program implementation extends across service areas throughout the day in both formal and informal settings.

APPLICATION

Active treatment evolves around good teaching/interacting practices in both formal and informal settings. Developing effective implementation strategies is a planned process. It involves analyzing information and deciding in advance of the instructional period the expected behaviors of the staff in the teaching situation. The primary thrust of instructional planning is for staff behaviors to be predictable to the individual with developmental disabilities. Finally, instructional planning greatly reduces the inconsistency encountered when more than one staff member is responsible for the implementation of an objective (Gardner & Chapman, 1985).

Figure 2 provides an overview of the planning required for effective instructional programs. Requirements include the determination of:

- Person's name
- Program implementor
- Program area
- Date started
- Date completed
- Instructional objective
- Instructional command statement
- Task analysis
- Sequence for fading cues
- Consequences for correct responses
- Consequences for incorrect responses
- Criterion level of acceptable behavior for movement between program steps
- Materials
- Settings
- Opportunities for practice/generalization

Person's Name

While the appropriate response may seem obvious, instructional programs are written for individuals. To list "clients in cottage A" on the line for person's name would be inappropriate. The individual with developmental disabilities for whom the instructional program is written is identified by name.

Program Implementor

This information identifies the staff member who is responsible for the implementation of the program. It identifies, by name, the staff member who has the ultimate responsibility for overall coordination and evaluation and the authority for making changes in the program. Other secondary staff are also identified in those situations where there are relief staff or other shift staff responsible for program imple-

Person's name: _____   Date started: _____

Program implementor: _____   Date completed: _____

Program area: _____

Instructional objective: _____

Instructional command statement: _____

Task analysis: _____   Sequence for fading cues:

_____   _____

_____   _____

_____   _____

_____   _____

Consequences: A. Correct response — _____

               B. Incorrect response — _____

Criterion level of acceptable behavior for movement between program steps: _____

Materials: _____

Setting: _____

Opportunities for practice/generalization: _____

Figure 2. *Form for organizing an instructional strategy. Reprinted from Gardner, J. F., & Chapman, M. S. (1985). Staff development in mental retardation services: A practical handbook [p. 111]. Baltimore: Paul H. Brookes Publishing Co.*

mentation in the absence of the primary staff. Remember, the goal of effective instructional strategies is for staff behaviors to be predictable to the individual with developmental disabilities. For this reason it is important to identify all staff responsible for program implementation.

Many agencies employ staff who write instructional programs for direct care workers to implement. Contemporary practice suggests that direct care workers should be trained in the design of instructional strategies. This practice enhances the skills and abilities of the direct care worker and generalizes the instructional strategies by the direct care worker to informal teaching situations.

Program Area

The program area is determined by the focus of instruction provided by an agency. Some agencies operate programs for children with developmental disabilities. For them, program areas may include: fine motor development, gross motor development, cognitive development, receptive language, expressive language, or social/emotional development. For agencies serving adults, program area may refer to activities of daily living, money management, productivity, and so forth. Staff need to review agency policy and procedures to determine appropriate responses specific to the agency.

Start and Completion Dates

The actual dates that the instructional program began and ended are identified. The identification of actual dates provides additional assessment data for program staff to consider in the development of future programs. For example, in developing an instructional strategy on hand washing, staff could determine from previous programs appropriate error-free strategies, staff resources, and time required for learning the new skill.

Program Checklist		
	Yes	No
1. The facility employs strategies for developing instructional programs.	—	—
2. Developed instructional strategies stress predictable staff behaviors.	—	—
3. All instructional strategies are individualized.	—	—

Instructional Objective

The instructional objective identifies the expected outcome of the instructional strategy. It answers the question, "What do I expect the person to do as a result of the planned intervention?" While the intermediate care facility for the mentally retarded (ICF/MR) regulation does not require goal statements, many state regulations do. A goal is written to provide program direction, usually 6 months to 1 year in duration. Goals are usually broadly stated. Objectives are written to identify a discrete behavior of the goal statement. They are usually narrowly stated. The definitions of goals and objectives vary from state to state. For this reason, staff need to consult agency policy and procedures to determine appropriate operating procedures.

Three elements are necessary for an instructional objective: 1) stating the behavior to be learned, 2) stating the conditions under which the behavior will occur, 3) stating the criteria for accomplishing the objective. Stating the behavior to be learned requires that staff understand the difference between behavior and attitudes. Behavior refers to anything a person does that is observable and measurable. For example, making a bed, opening a can of soup, hitting a nail with a hammer, and attending to a task are all behaviors. They are observable and measurable. In contrast, "tolerates," "cooperates," "lazy," "cheerful" are not behaviors. These are attitudes or projections of an individual's feelings. Goals and objectives only identify behaviors. Statements such as "John will tolerate range-of-motion exercises" or "John will cooperate in training sessions" do not identify behaviors. Tolerate and cooperate are not behaviors. Objectives list observable and measurable behaviors. Examples of behaviors include:

John will brush his teeth.
Mary will make her bed.
Susan will run 50 meters.
Derrick will stack boxes.

Behaviors are stated in positive terms. In addition, only one behavior is listed for each objective. For example, to state, "John will pick up the toothbrush, apply toothpaste, and brush his teeth," is inappropriate.

Condition statements identify the circumstances under which the behavior will occur. They clarify whether staff expect the behavior to occur with verbal instruction or physical assistance. These statements describe the performance of the behavior. For example, if the desired behavior is to brush teeth, the condition statement is used to provide additional information related to the performance of the behavior:

Given a verbal command, Jack will brush his teeth.
Given a verbal command and a toothbrush with a built-up handle, Jack will brush his teeth.
Jack will brush his teeth with physical assistance.
Jack will brush his teeth within 5 minutes following each meal.

In each of these examples the behavior, "will brush teeth," does not change. Rather, the conditions under which the behavior is performed change. Changing the condition statements radically changes the desired outcome, ranging from self-initiated behavior to requiring assistance from staff.

Criteria statements identify when the objective is considered accomplished. While many different ways exist to write criteria statements, three formats are most frequently used: accuracy, duration, and quantity. Accuracy statements are the most commonly used criteria statements and describe how well a behavior will be performed. For example, "4 out of 5 correct responses" and "80% correct responses" are accuracy statements that describe how well a behavior will be performed.

Duration statements are used to describe behaviors that either increased, decreased, or remained constant in the time required to perform the behavior. For example, a heat-sealing process requires that a lever is held down for a 12- to 17-second interval. Depending on the skill level of the individual, training will focus on either increasing or decreasing the amount of time the lever is held down.

Quantity statements identify exact numbers required to perform the behavior. Counting 25 nails per bag, walking 30 steps, and stacking 15 trays are examples of quantity statements.

Combining the elements of the behavior, the conditions under which the behavior will occur, and the criteria for determining when the objective is accomplished results in instructional objectives. Instructional objectives identify for staff the focus of their intervention activities. They provide direction and aid in the allocation of staff and material resources.

Instructional Command Statements

Instructional command statements identify what staff say to initiate the behavior. While they may seem irrelevant, they are a very important aspect of the instructional strategy. This is especially true when more than one instructor is training the same instructional program. Using the same command to initiate the behavior results in consistency across instructors. In choosing the appropriate instructional command statement, one must consider the individual's cognitive abilities. The length of the command statement should correspond to the individual's functioning level. A statement longer than what the person is able to comprehend may confuse the individual and will interfere with progress on the program.

Program Checklist

	Yes	No
1. All behavior/instructional objectives are written with behavioral terminology.	—	—
2. All objectives include: The behavior to be learned	—	—

Program Checklist—*continued*

	Yes	No
The conditions under which it will occur		
A criteria statement		
3. Staff use instructional command statements appropriate to the individual's functioning level.	___	___

Task Analysis

Task analysis involves the process of studying the behavior to be learned and breaking it down into smaller steps. During the instructional period the presentation of complex behaviors in smaller steps makes the learning of the skill easier for the person and therefore more likely to occur. For example, if the instructional objective identified toothbrushing as the terminal behavior, the task analysis may include the following steps:

1. Pick up toothpaste.
2. Unscrew cap.
3. Put cap down.
4. Pick up toothbrush.
5. Squeeze toothpaste onto end of toothbrush.
6. Put toothpaste down.
7. Turn on cold water.
8. Wet toothbrush under water.
9. Brush right side of upper outside teeth.
10. Brush left side of upper outside teeth.
11. Brush right side of upper inside teeth.
12. Brush left side of upper inside teeth.
13. Brush right side of lower outside teeth.
14. Brush left side of lower outside teeth.
15. Brush right side of lower inside teeth.
16. Brush left side of lower inside teeth.
17. Pick up cup.
18. Fill cup with water.
19. Rinse mouth.
20. Spit water into sink.
21. Rinse toothbrush under water.
22. Return toothbrush to holder.
23. Turn off water.
24. Pick up toothpaste.
25. Pick up cap.
26. Screw cap back onto toothpaste.
27. Put toothpaste down.

In this task analysis, there are 27 steps required to teach toothbrushing. The number of steps in the task analysis is determined by the individual with developmental disabilities. For some individuals, a fewer number of steps may be required. For others, many more may be necessary. Task analyses are listed in the order in which the behavior occurs. They are listed in logical, sequential order.

Sequence of Fading Cues

Good teaching involves pairing task analysis with one of five error-free learning techniques and fading assistance provided until it is no longer needed. The purpose of error-free strategies is to increase the probability of skill acquisition through ensuring successful completion of the desired skill. The instructor "gives away" the correct response, thus increasing the probability that the individual will complete the task. Then the instructor employs a planned strategy for eliminating the error-free strategy in order to prevent the individual's dependency on the instructor for assistance. The process of eliminating the error-free strategy in a planned, systematic manner is referred to as fading. The five error-free strategies include: verbal cues, modeling, arranging the environment, gestures, and physical assistance.

Verbal cues involve the use of verbal instruction or feedback as a teaching method. The instructor tells the desired behavior to the individual. The person responds appropriately and is reinforced. For example, in teaching the complex behavior of preparing a can of soup, staff may say:

"Open the can with the can opener."
"Throw the lid away."
"Pour the soup into the pan."
"Turn on the cold water."
"Fill the can with water."
"Pour the water into the pan."
"Throw the can away."
"Stir the soup with a spoon."
"Turn on the burner."
"Continue stirring the soup until steam is rising from the mixture."
"Turn off burner."
"Pour soup into bowl."

In this example the desired behavior is verbally described to the person. Each step is reinforced.

The limitation with error-free strategies is that they create a dependency on the instructor for the completion of the skill. For this reason, fading procedures are employed to reduce gradually the assistance provided. Fading involves making the selected error-free strategy less and less complete until it is no longer necessary. In the above example the instructor could begin by leaving off the last verbal cue, then the next, and so on until the person is able to perform the skill without the use of verbal cues.

Modeling involves showing or demonstrating the behavior to be learned. In modeling the instructor completes the desired behavior alongside the individual. Using the example above, the instructor and the individual prepare a can of soup side by side. The instructor models the correct behavior for the person, who in turn imitates each step. Fading procedures require the instructor to make the modeling less and less complete. As in fading the verbal cue, the instructor could begin by leaving off the last step, then the next, and so on until the modeling is no longer needed. Another example may be useful. Teaching a person to hit a nail with a hammer by using modeling requires the staff to:

1. Pick up the hammer, raise the hammer over head, lower hammer, strike nail, and put the hammer down.

This is the error-free strategy of modeling. Fading this procedure involves gradually and sequentially making the modeling less and less complete. The fading procedure may include:

2. Pick up the hammer, raise the hammer over head, lower hammer, strike nail.
3. Pick up the hammer, raise the hammer over head, lower hammer.
4. Pick up the hammer, raise the hammer over head.
5. Pick up the hammer.
6. Give instructional command only.

In this example the behavior of the instructor is gradually reduced. The individual with developmental disabilities is required to perform more and more of the behavior without the added assistance provided by the instructor before being reinforced for the behavior.

Program Checklist

	Yes	No
1. Task analyses are used to break down complex behaviors.	—	—
2. Task analyses for the same behavior vary in length and complexity from individual to individual.	—	—
3. Error-free learning techniques are used by the staff in planning instructional strategies.	—	—
4. Fading procedures are written for each error-free strategy.	—	—

Arranging the environment involves analyzing the environment rather than the person and determining how the environment can change to make the performance of the behavior easier. Using oversized clothing for teaching dressing, built-up eating utensils for teaching eating, and color coded storage cabinets are examples of arranging the environment. Arranging the environment is particularly helpful for teaching a skill where the individual understands the concepts behind the desired skill but experiences difficulty completing the task. For example, teaching a person to put a folded letter into a 4-inch × 9-inch envelope may require first teaching the person to:

1. Use a 13-inch × 18-inch envelope

Using the larger sized envelope, the instructor has arranged the environment to make the behavior easier for the person. Fading the assistance may include:

2. Using a 10-inch × 15-inch envelope
3. Using a 7-inch × 12-inch envelope
4. Using a 4-inch × 9-inch envelope

The size of the envelope is gradually reduced over time until the person can use a regular-sized envelope.

Gestures involve using body movements or facial expressions to communicate a message. Nodding your head up and down to indicate approval, side to side to indicate disapproval, or shrugging your shoulders to indicate uncertainty are examples of gestures used to communicate a message without speaking. Gestures are helpful in teaching a skill. For example, to teach a person how to recognize a quarter by pointing, the instructor states, "Show me the quarter." Then the instructor:

1. Places a finger on the quarter

The desired response is given away by using the gesture of placing the instructor's finger on the quarter. The chances of a correct response from the person with developmental disabilities is increased. Fading the gesture may include:

2. Placing finger 2 inches from the quarter
3. Placing finger 4 inches from the quarter
4. Placing finger 6 inches from the quarter
5. Giving the instructional command only

The gesture is less and less complete until no longer needed. The person with developmental disabilities is required to perform more and more of the desired behavior before being reinforced.

Physical assistance is the most common error-free learning strategy. In physical assistance, the desired behavior is taught by hand-over-hand assistance in the completion of the skill. The person with developmental disabilities is put through the behavior with the aid of the instructor, which is particularly helpful in teaching activities of daily living such as dressing skills. For example, to teach a person to put on his or her socks, the instructor:

1. Grasps the individual's hand and removes the sock with it.

This process ensures success for the person, who in turn is reinforced for the completion of the skill. Creating independence in the performance of the skill requires fading the assistance provided by the instructor. Fading procedures may include:

2. Guiding the person through the behavior with the instructor's fingertips
3. Tapping the person's hand to initiate the behavior and allowing the person to complete the behavior
4. Giving the instructional command only

Depending on the skill level of the person with developmental disabilities, the sequence of fading may change. For example, rather than following the process above, the instructor may write the fading procedures as:

1. Grasp the person's hand and remove sock.
2. Grasp the person's hand and remove sock to toes.
3. Grasp the person's hand and remove sock over heel.
4. Grasp the person's hand and remove sock to the ankle.
5. Grasp the person's hand and remove sock to midcalf.
6. Give the instructional command only.

Through the fading procedure employed, the person with developmental disabilities is required to perform more and more of the desired behavior.

Choosing the appropriate error-free strategy requires a detailed understanding of the person with developmental disabilities. In the same way some people in society learn information better visually, auditorially, or in combination, people with developmental disabilities will also show preferences for learning new skills. Instructors' experience with the person over time and in a variety of different situations using the different error-free strategies will reveal the learning preferences of the individual.

Consequences for Correct Responses

The instructor needs to determine, in advance of the instructional period, exactly what he or she is to do if the person demonstrates a correct response. The specific techniques, including what is said, are written. Writing these techniques enables the instructor to monitor the delivery of reinforcers. For each person with developmental disabilities, a reinforcement menu should be established that identifies each person's reinforcement preferences. These reinforcers serve as tools available to the instructor for increasing or maintaining behaviors. Reinforcers are varied throughout the instructional process. This ensures continued interest in the reinforcer and prevents satiation.

Consequences for Incorrect Responses

As with correct responses, the instructor determines his or her own responses in writing prior to the instructional period. Examples of instructors' techniques to handle incorrect response may include: stating "no" in a firm voice, turning the head for 3 to 5 seconds, or combining the two. Following the use of incorrect response procedures, the instructor presents the next trial.

Criterion Level of Acceptable Behavior for Movement Between Program Steps

Moving from one step to another in the task analysis or in the sequence of fading is an important aspect of instructional strategies. Waiting too long to move may create a dependency; moving too fast may create confusion. For most programs, three, four, or five consecutive correct responses are sufficient for program movement.

Materials

The specific materials needed for the implementation of the instructional strategy are identified. For example, if oversized pants are used for teaching dressing skills, the instructor identifies exactly the pants to be used. This ensures that all instructors use the same materials in their teaching sessions, allowing for consistency in the program. Other miscellaneous materials needed for the program are also listed, such as data sheets and a pencil.

Setting

Instruction should take place in the appropriate setting: dressing in a bedroom, shaving in a bathroom, and so forth. In addition, teaching should follow the natural flow of the day's events. Teaching dressing skills in the morning would be more appropriate than at midday or early evening. Identifying the setting establishes expectations for the staff. Without clarity identifying the setting, confusion among staff may occur. First shift may feel second shift is responsible for implementation of the objective, and vice versa.

Opportunities for Practice/Generalization

Finally, the instructor identifies opportunities to practice and to generalize the new skill. This aspect of instructional strategies is important. It provides the means by which to evaluate the chosen objectives. If no opportunities exist to practice or generalize the skill, then facility staff should question seriously the appropriateness of the objective. Multiple opportunities to use the new skill throughout the person's day should be available. These opportunities are defined in writing so that staff members remember to provide them.

Figure 3 shows a completed instructional form. Instructional forms are written for each objective that requires formal intervention from staff. Once written, staff determine if the skill is to be taught using forward or backward chaining methods.

Person's name: __John Smith__

Program implementor: __Tom Winner__

Program area: __Activities of Daily Living__

Instructional objective: __Given a command, John will wash his hands correctly 4__
__out of 5 times requested on 3 consecutive days.__

Instructional command statement: __"John, wash your hands."__

Task analysis: Sequence for fading cues:

1. Turn on water.   6. Rinse hands.   A. Grasp John's hands; complete the behavior.
2. Pick up soap.   7. Turn off water.   B. Guide John's hands with fingertips.
3. Rub soap on hands.   8. Dry hands.   C. Guide John's hands from wrist.
4. Put soap down.   D. Tap John's hands; John completes the
5. Rub hands together.   behavior.

Consequences: A. Correct response — __"Good hand washing."__

               B. Incorrect response — __State firmly, "No, John," plus ignore response by__
                                         __turning head 3-5 seconds.__

Criterion level of acceptable behavior for movement between program steps: __3 consecutive correct__
__responses__

Materials: __soap, towel, water, shirt, pencil__

Setting: __bathroom, kitchen__

Opportunities for practice/generalization: __In the morning; prior to meals.__

Date started: __1/4/85__

Date completed: _____

Figure 3. *Example of a completed instructional strategy form. Reprinted from Gardner, J. F., & Chapman, M. S. (1985). Staff development in mental retardation services: A practical handbook (p. 112). Baltimore: Paul H. Brookes Publishing Co.*

175

Forward chaining involves teaching the skill beginning with the first step in the task analysis coupled with the first step in the selected sequence of fading. The trials are presented until the criterion for movement between program steps is achieved. The instructor proceeds to the second step in the sequence of fading while remaining on the first task in the task analysis. Instruction continues until the person performs the first task of the task analysis independently. The training session then focuses on the second step of the task analysis. Figure 4 visually describes this process.

Backward chaining involves teaching the skill beginning with the last step in the task analysis coupled with the first step in the sequence of fading. In backward chaining, the instructor applies the full support of the selected error-free strategy for all tasks in the task analysis but is concerned with applying the sequence of fading with the last step. Trials are presented until the criterion for movement between program steps is achieved. The instructor then, providing total support for all tasks except the last, proceeds to the second step in the sequence of fading. Once the task is performed independently, the next to the last step becomes the focus of fading procedures. Figure 5 visually represents this process.

While the individual with developmental disabilities learns the skill faster using backward chaining, the training technique used generally has no effect on retention of the skill once learned.

Program Checklist

		Yes	No
1.	The facility employs one error-free strategy for each objective.	—	—
2.	Multiple opportunities exist to practice/generalize each skill being taught.	—	—
3.	Staff employ forward or backward chaining methods to teach a new skill.	—	—

Task analysis   **Sequence of fading**

1. Turn on water
2. Pick up soap
3. Rub soap on hands
4. Put soap down
5. Rub hands together
6. Rinse hands
7. Turn off water
8. Dry hands

1. Grasp hands and complete the behavior
2. Guide hands with fingertips
3. Tap hand to initiate behavior
4. Instructional command only

Figure 4.   Forward chaining method of teaching.

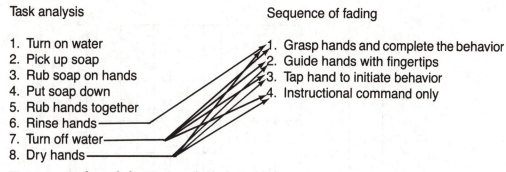

Task analysis

1. Turn on water
2. Pick up soap
3. Rub soap on hands
4. Put soap down
5. Rub hands together
6. Rinse hands
7. Turn off water
8. Dry hands

Sequence of fading

1. Grasp hands and complete the behavior
2. Guide hands with fingertips
3. Tap hand to initiate behavior
4. Instructional command only

Figure 5.   Backward chaining method of teaching.

Data Collection

Data collection is a critical component of the instructional process. Through analysis of the data, the instructor is able to determine the effectiveness of the selected intervention strategy. Data reveal successes and problems in the program. The instructor is able to use this information in determining changes needed in the program.

Figure 6 is an example of a data sheet for use in the instructional process. This form is designed to be used with the instructional strategy form identified in Figure 2. The data sheet enables the instructor to list critical elements of the instructional strategy without having to take the completed form into the teaching situation. Spaces are provided for the presentation of 10 trials. Pluses (+) for correct responses and minuses (−) for incorrect responses are scored as trials each time the instructional command is given. Figure 7 is an example of a completed data sheet.

It is rare that an instructional program is written that does not at some time throughout its implementation require modification and changes. If the person shows little or no progress, the instructor must respond. The instructor should evaluate the following as listed in order:

1. The reinforcer used
2. The task analysis
3. The sequence of fading
4. The assessment data

All of these elements are not changed at once. Rather, the instructor systematically searches for the problems in the instructional program. The instructor begins by changing the reinforcer. The question "Is it powerful enough to motivate the person?" is answered by selecting another reinforcer from the reinforcement menu and observing how it affects the person's performance of the behavior. If the performance improves, then the instructor has a clearer understanding of why he or she experienced difficulty and does not need to look be-

DATA SHEET

Person's name: _____

Instructional objective: _____

Task analysis:
1. _____
2. _____
3. _____
4. _____
5. _____

Sequence of fading:
A. _____
B. _____
C. _____
D. _____
E. _____

Date	Reinforcer used	Task analysis	Sequence of fading	Trials 1	2	3	4	5	6	7	8	9	10	Comments

Figure 6.   Data sheet for documenting program progress. Reprinted from Gardner, J. F., & Chapman, M. S. (1985). Staff development in mental retardation services: A practical handbook [p. 114]. Baltimore: Paul H. Brookes Publishing Co.

DATA SHEET

Person's name: _John Smith_

Instructional objective: _Given a command, John will wash his hands correctly 4 out of 5 times requested on 3 consecutive days._

Task analysis:
1. Turn on water. 6. Rinse hands.
2. Pick up soap. 7. Turn off water.
3. Rub soap on hands. 8. Dry hands.
4. Put soap down.
5. Rub hands together.

Sequence of fading:
A. _Grasp hands and com-plete the behavior._
B. _Guide hands with fingertips._
C. _Guide hands from wrist._
D. _Tap hands._
E.

Date	Reinforcer used	Task analysis	Sequence of fading	\multicolumn{11}{c}{Trials}

Date	Reinforcer used	Task analysis	Sequence of fading	1	2	3	4	5	6	7	8	9	10	Comments
1-4-85	Tokens	(1-7) 8	A	+	+	+								
1-4-85	Tokens	(1-7) 8	B	+	+	+								
1-4-85	Tokens	(1-7) 8	C	+	-	+	-	+	+	-	+			

Figure 7. Example of a completed data sheet for documenting program progress. Reprinted from Gardner, J. F., & Chapman, M. S. (1985). Staff development in mental retardation services: A practical handbook [p. 115]. Baltimore: Paul H. Brookes Publishing Co.

yond the reinforcer. If, however, the instructor changes the reinforcer and observes no change in performance, the instructor proceeds by evaluating the task analysis. The steps in the task analysis may be too big for the person, and more steps may need to be added. For example, the task "dry hands" may need to be broken down into the following additional steps:

1. Pick up towel in the left hand.
2. Rub back of right hand with towel.
3. Rub palm of right hand with towel.
4. Transfer towel from left hand to right hand.
5. Rub back of left hand with towel.
6. Rub palm of left hand with towel.
7. Put towel down.

If the instructor determines that the steps in the task analysis are sufficient and difficulties in the program continue, he or she reviews the selected sequence of fading. The instructor determines if the selected error-free strategy is appropriate or if the sequence of fading needs to be changed. For example, going from guiding the person's hand with fingertips to tapping the person's hand may be too large a step. Adding an additional step, guiding the person's hand with fingertips at the wrist, may be needed.

If the instructor continues to experience difficulty, he or she reviews the assessment data collected. The staff may have misread data. The identified objective may not be appropriate for the person at this time, or a critical prerequisite skill may be missing. The interdisciplinary team may need to consider substituting a new objective.

Program Checklist

		Yes	No
1.	Data collection is a component of each skill being taught.	___	___
2.	Instructional strategies are changed as staff encounter problems implementing programs.	___	___
3.	Data are used in making decisions about the appropriateness of instructional strategies.	___	___

Coordinating Instruction

The interdisciplinary team process focuses on the individual with developmental disabilities. Objectives are established to meet the individual's needs. Implementation of instructional strategies can be divided into two categories: those that require one-to-one instruction and those that can be implemented in groups. Most objectives are taught in group settings. Therefore, facility staff must "break out" all objectives into one of these categories in order to allocate its resources appropriately. To accomplish this, staff must look at the identified objectives for all individuals that make up a living or working unit and determine those that require one-to-one instruction and those that do not. This process involves:

1. Developing a list of all the objectives for the individuals that make up the living or working unit
2. Grouping objectives into categories—those requiring one-to-one training and those that can be taught in a group setting
3. Allocating staff resources and time to address one-to-one training
4. Reviewing the group objectives for similarities or grouping patterns
5. Defining group composition
6. Allocating staff resources and time for group interventions

Developing training stations is an effective means for coordinating instructional activities. In the living unit one or two staff members are assigned to training one-to-one objectives, while the remaining staff work with small groups. Individuals are rotated through each station assuring that all objectives are addressed.

Training by groups does not mean that all members of the group must have the same objective. Through the group process, the instructor is able to address multiple objectives. For example, one group may have four members. The group activity may focus on identifying emergency signs: exit, fire escape, and danger. For one individual, the objective may be to discriminate by pointing among the three signs. For another individual, the objective may be to follow a two-step command. For yet another member of the group, the objective may be to remain on task for 15 minutes. The instructor must be aware of the different focus each objective has and develop strategies for addressing all objectives in the group. The process may look like the following:

> The instructor presents the three cards to John and states, "John, point to exit" and "Bob, thank you for sitting quietly."
> The instructor presents two cards to Sam and states, "Sam point to exit and put the other card on the table" and "Bob, good watching."
> The instructor presents one card to Bob and states, "Bob, touch danger."

In this example multiple objectives are addressed through one activity. The instructor moves from one individual to another in the group and presents activities at their defined level.

Formal Versus Informal Instruction

The process described to this point addresses the formal process of providing instruction to individuals with developmental disabilities. Learning does not occur only in the formal process. Multiple opportunities exist throughout the day for informal training. Informal training may not involve objectives or data sheets but consistently seeks opportunities in the person's environment to enhance the skills of the individual. For example:

• Talking to the individual during dressing, bathing, mealtime, and so forth provides an informal opportunity for training socialization skills.
• Stopping on a walk to point out a cloud formation teaches awareness of the environment.
• Talking to the individual while pushing his or her wheelchair is an informal opportunity for auditory stimulation.
• Staff responding to an individual staring out the window by asking, "What are you looking at?" is an informal opportunity for socialization and receptive and expressive language environment.
• Rubbing the back of a person who is crying for no apparent reason is an informal opportunity for emotional development.

Advanced Consideration for Instructional Programs

Facility staff must continually evaluate the environment to determine its influence on the teaching/learning process. Many different factors may positively or negatively influence the person's performance. An awareness of these will increase staff effectiveness in teaching a skill. Examples to consider include:

• Work area height: Is the work table suitable for the person? Does it need to be lower? higher?
• Work area size: Is the work area suitable for the person? Does it need to be bigger? smaller?
• Lighting: Does the person perform better with direct or indirect lighting? Florescent or incandescent lighting?
• Is the room temperature suitable for learning?
• Does the person prefer materials presented from the left or right side? from top or bottom?
• Does the color of material make a difference?
• Does who is sitting next to the person make a difference?
• Does who provides the training make a difference?
• Does the time of day make a difference? Does the person attend better in the morning, afternoon, or evening?
• Is the person's clothing appropriate? too tight?
• Have any recent changes occurred in the person's medications? What are the side effects?

These and many other examples aid staff in understanding the person and the instructional process and in working toward increasing the effectiveness of teaching.

Program Checklist

	Yes	No
1. The staff identify strategies for group instruction.	___	___
2. Individualized objectives are taught in group settings.	___	___
3. Staff identify multiple opportunities for informal teaching.	___	___
4. Staff evaluate the environment for its positive or negative influence on the person's performance.	___	___

IMPLICATIONS

For Qualified Mental Retardation Professionals

The QMRP is responsible for ensuring that the intervention strategies produce outcome measures for each individual. On a periodic basis as defined for each individual, the QMRP reviews the assessment data for each objective and determines if progress is being made. The QMRP does not simply repeat notes made by the different facility staff but takes a broader look at all objectives and summarizes the effects of the total intervention program. Issues addressed in this review include:

- If the needs identified by the team for each individual with developmental disabilities are being addressed by the facility
- If movement exists within each objective toward greater independence
- If each staff person is contributing to the program efforts
- If changes need to occur in the implementation of an objective
- If the service needs of the individual not defined in an objective are being met (e.g., outside assessments)
- If the implementation of objectives are integrated throughout the individual's day.

The QMRP serves as the individual's advocate in the facility. In situations where progress is not being made, the QMRP intervenes and requests changes in the implementation strategy. Documentation of this process is critical since it provides a history of changes and modifications in the IPP designed to meet the individual's needs. Documentation demonstrates conclusively the efforts of the facility to address individual needs.

For Specialized Service Staff

Specialized service staff must ensure that their services and expertise are integrated throughout the day and shared with all staff. Specialized service staff operate within a transdisciplinary model. Different disciplines share expertise with each other and implement individual programs or staff training programs with more than a singular view of the person. For example, the occupational therapist might implement a communication goal while feeding an individual. Through the transdisciplinary model, a greater base of knowledge is available to both the individual with developmental disabilities and the direct care staff. Intervention strategies developed by specialized service staff are written for the direct care staff. They are easy to read, free of professional jargon, and focus on the routines and rhythms of the individual's day. Finally, the specialized service staff monitor the implementation of the intervention strategy to ensure that direct care staff clearly understand the program and are able to demonstrate its implementation.

For Quality Assurance Coordinators

The task for the quality assurance (QA) coordinator is to ensure that the designed intervention strategies result in skill improvement for each individual. Client outcome measures are stressed. This requires not only a review of the written programs and associated data but also the QA coordinator's direct observation of formal and informal teaching. The question, "Do staff know what to do?" is answered by observing staff in various situations. Staff should be able to demonstrate clearly the various components of the intervention strategy. In addition, the QA coordinator should observe high levels of staff-client interaction during informal situations. Staff knowledge of intervention programs should be apparent if disruptive, self-stimulatory, or aggressive behaviors occur. These behaviors should not be overlooked by staff but are addressed competently.

The QA coordinator's review of the record should reveal a clear, concise road map of activities and designed interventions. Evidence should exist of:

- The staff's understanding of the person through the assessment process that clearly demonstrates the individual's strengths, interests, and needs and is based on staff's direct observation of the person in different environments
- An effective interdisciplinary team process that results in objectives that maximize a person's interests and build on strengths to address needs
- Written intervention strategies that reflect the team process
- Data to support the implementation of the objectives
- A review process conducted by the QMRP that results in changes in approaches if necessary
- Different documented approaches tried before programs are discontinued

CONCLUSIONS

Active treatment is based on good teaching practices and competent staff knowing what to do in both formal and informal settings. Formal teaching is a planned, systematic process with predictable instructor behavior as the goal. In the formal process such things as task analysis, error-free strategies, sequence of fading, and consequences are determined in advance of the instructional period. In addition, opportunities to practice/generalize the new skill are also planned. If the facility staff experience difficulty defining these opportunities, then serious consideration should be given to the appropriateness of the chosen objective.

While the planning process is individualized, many objectives are addressed in small groups. Facility staff will need to develop procedures for addressing the implementation of objectives in small groups in addition to one-to-one training.

The informal teaching process is as important as formal teaching. Spontaneous interactions between staff and individuals with developmental disabilities provide additional opportunities to teach skills in a natural and informal manner.

Finally, facility staff must be able to prove with data that the skills and abilities of the person with developmental disabilities have improved because of the interventions provided by the facility. The new standards focus on client outcome measures. The facility must prove "but for" hypotheses (e.g., but for the services provided by the staff of the facility the individual with developmental disabilities would not demonstrate improved skills and abilities). This requires that all staff understand their role, the implementation of formal and informal teaching programs, and the contributions they make to the skill enhancement of individuals with developmental disabilities.

REFERENCE

Gardner, J., & Chapman, M. (1985). *Staff development in mental retardation services: A practical handbook.* Baltimore: Paul H. Brookes Publishing Co.

11
Monitoring and Evaluation

Solomon G. Jacobson

Monitoring and evaluation are used to determine if the potential of an individual with developmental disabilities is being realized by the programs provided by the intermediate care facility. Monitoring and evaluation help determine if demonstrated progress exists in meeting individualized goals as a result of programs and services provided to the individual. Measurable progress consists of demonstrated improvement in the individual's quality of life, including enhanced choices and visible evidence of well-being. Monitoring and evaluation ensure that the facility's systems, such as the individualized planning process and the programs used to implement the plan, are adjusted and changed to improve the individual's chances of successful progress.

Monitoring consists of collecting data on whether or not a service is provided and on whether or not a milestone, such as the achievement of an individual's objective, is met. Monitoring is a day-to-day event. Evaluation consists of determining if the process used to meet the objective was appropriate and efficient and, if not, to determine why not. It covers a longer time span than monitoring.

BACKGROUND

Monitoring Implementation of an Individual's Program

Individual monitoring is the daily review of implementation. Monitoring helps ensure accountability and contributes to quality assurance. The qualified mental retardation professional (QMRP) has the overall responsibility to monitor each individual's progress, but each staff person is individually accountable for his or her work with the individual. Monitoring ensures that programs are in compliance with regulations and with the standards set by the facility itself. In this regard the QMRP has the overall responsibility for ensuring that regulations are met, but all staff must be aware of regulations and monitor compliance. In addition to the QMRP, monitoring responsibilities are shared by supervisors who monitor direct care staff and department heads who monitor clinical staff.

In an intermediate care facility for the mentally retarded (ICF/MR), individual monitoring leads to stability and consistency in program implementation. The periodic checks on implementation ensure steady application of standards. Frequent feedback from monitor to staff allows immediate correction of deficiencies. Monitoring asks, "How are we doing today?"

Evaluating Individual Performance and Progress

Individual evaluation documents performance and progress. Evaluation provides knowledge of how staff efforts result in improved individual outcomes. Evaluation of each individual's progress measures attainment of his or her individualized goals. Evaluation of level of effort indicates the extent of the staff's contribution to meeting goals and can help determine if progress was achieved with most efficient use of resources. Individual evaluation asks, "How have we done so far?"

Evaluating Systems Through Individual Performance

This chapter focuses on evaluation of attaining the individual goals of those served by the ICF/MR. Beyond individual monitoring and evaluation is systems evaluation. An ICF/MR and similar habilitation programs, however, are based on meeting individualized goals. Their systems performance is derived from, and determined by, the aggregate of individual outcomes. In this case evaluating the "system" consists of examining those components that make up the delivery of individualized programs. Such components operating in a system include administrative procedures, staff development, equipment, and specialized assessments.

Essentially two types of systems evaluation exist: 1) process evaluation, which examines the procedure used in delivering services; and 2) outcome evaluation, which summarizes the accomplishments, or lack of them, of the human service program. In either case involving the users of the evaluation in its design is important. This ensures that useful questions are addressed and that the users will both cooperate in collecting the data needed for the evaluation and be interested in reading and using the findings.

How the completed evaluation is to be used should be among the first items to be considered. Evaluations should answer such questions as: "What is the measure of success achieved by the program?"; "What factors contributed to the success of the program?"; and "What must be changed to improve program operations?" Such questions must be posed before the evaluation is designed and data are collected. Otherwise, a good chance exists that the evaluation will satisfy few users and lead to few changes.

An early step in designing a systems evaluation is to set criteria for measuring program success. Two examples of criteria are effectiveness, which measures the consistency of actions with missions and goals, and efficiency, which measures the use of resources to get best results at the least cost.

Several types of systems evaluation instruments are available, including structured surveys, open-ended surveys, observations, and audits of documents and records. Whatever instrument is selected, it should be pretested before use. An instrument should be valid and measure what it is supposed to. An instrument should also be reliable and measure the same thing each time it is used.

To collect data for an evaluation, the establishment of an adequate procedure is important. This involves pretesting the collection instruments to ensure that the procedures are clear and understandable. Data collectors need to be trained in what to observe and how to enter properly the data they collect. Once the data are collected, they must be reviewed to determine if correctly entered. Editing data before they are used in analysis increases the utility of those data.

The next step is to select the type of analysis that will best answer the user's questions. Basically three types of analysis exist: 1) comparison of findings against internal or external standards, such as using the Health Care Financing Administration (HCFA) conditions of participation; 2) comparison of findings against performance of similar programs, such as comparing the percentage of individuals placed in supported employment among all ICFs/MR in the same region; and 3) comparison of findings against the program's past performance, such as comparing the percentage of individuals meeting their goals over several calendar years.

An analysis of the data describes "how" the system is performing. The art of evaluation comes in interpreting the data to determine "why" events and actions have produced the observed results. But no matter how technically superior the technique, an evaluation is useful only if it is used. Sharing the findings with users results in systems change based on careful analysis of the system.

Cautions in Implementing Systems Evaluation

Bradley (1984) points out that a major problem in evaluation of human service programs is the difficulty in determining if individual outcomes, such as movement to a less restrictive environment, are a result of the facility's service interventions. This is because many factors exist that influence the individual. For example, movement towards a less restrictive environment may be due to the maturity gained by the individual in the aging process or to the influence of family members, rather than to the intervention of facility.

In research, most proof comes through controlled experiments in which one group receives an intervention, and another comparable group does not. All things being equal, improvement in the first group is attributed to the intervention. This type of control is difficult in an ICF/MR, and many would find it undesirable since it denies choice to the subjects of the experiment.

As Bradley points out, "The evaluation research simply cannot fulfill the criterion for validity as required by the classical research model" (p. 51). She recommends that the best research design uses the goals and objectives set for the individual. Placing the emphasis on better measurement, rather than careful matching of control groups, is a desirable alternative to expensive experimental research designs.

Bradley recommends monitoring the results of the programs for each individual with developmental disabilities as a desirable alternative to systems evaluation. The objective in outcome monitoring should be to suggest to the provider or practitioner which techniques are relatively effective or ineffective in reaching certain objectives. Monitoring can point out possible areas for improvement or further study.

REVIEW OF THE STANDARDS

483.410(a) *Governing body*
483.430(a) *Qualified mental retardation professional*
483.440(f) *Program monitoring and change*
483.460(a–n) *Health care services*

The standards indicate that the governing body of the facility is ultimately responsible for the implementation of the active treatment program in the facility. The qualified mental retardation professional monitors each individual's active treatment program. The standards set forth requirements for program monitoring and change (483.440(f)).

The standards also detail the requirement for oversight review of behavior management programs by a specially constituted committee or committees. Finally, the standards cover the requirements for monitoring behavior management programs that employ time-out, restraint, or drugs.

The standards also set forth requirements for monitoring of health care services. The responsibilities of the physician, nurse, pharmacist, dentist, and laboratory personnel for periodic reviews and monitoring are described.

Monitoring and Evaluation as They Relate to the Active Treatment Cycle

Monitoring and evaluation for individuals are extensions of the active treatment cycle: individual assessment, interdisciplinary team meetings, setting goals and objectives, planning activities and programs, implementing these programs, and monitoring the implementation. Monitoring and evaluation, as conducted by the QMRP, feed information back into the active treatment cycle and ensure that the cycle is responsive to the needs and preferences of the individual.

Assessments

Assessments are used in the active treatment cycle to determine the program and treatment plan that is appropriate to the individual. A variety of assessment devices exist, and nearly all focus on the individual. No single assessment device is going to explain all the characteristics, needs, and preferences of the individual. The monitoring role of the QMRP is to ensure that the assessments reflect the individual and that consistency in interpretation and use of the assessments is present.

A variety of formal assessment instruments fall into three broad categories: 1) individual assessment instruments measure adaptive functioning, such as self-care; 2) environmental assessment instruments weigh characteristics of such settings as the residence or the work site; and 3) cognitive tests measure individual personality and intelligence.

In selecting assessment instruments, Doucette and Freedman (1980) suggest the following process:

Understand the characteristics of the situation.   In this step, determine what decisions or actions, such as plan development or progress measurement, and which client domains, such as self-care or communication, will be measured by the instrument and who will use the data. The characteristics of the population and the settings are also important considerations.

Examine the aspects of an assessment instrument that are relevant to the situation.   Start by listing the client domains, such as activities of daily living, requiring assessment and examine how comprehensively and precisely the instrument covers these domains. Determine if the instrument can be administered with relative ease and if the results are usable by facility staff. Finally, check out how the instrument was field tested. The instrument should be valid in that it measures what it purports to measure and inferences can be drawn from the instrument. The instrument should also be reliable in that consistency and stability of the scores exist if used by several observers.

Review and select the available assessments in terms of the dimensions.   Selection of assessment and measurement instruments requires patience. After determining the need and use of the instrument, several instruments should be examined to determine which ones work best in the particular program environment. In general, the more precise the data, the longer the instrument. Both clinical and direct care staff should discuss the trade-offs between ease of use and utility of the findings. Seek optimal, rather than perfect, instruments.

Collect the data according to standardized procedures. A good instrument will have been extensively field tested. Following the collection instructions carefully helps ensure that the data are both valid and useful. Continual training and reliability checks are needed to improve consistency over time and across settings. Those using the assessment might take shortcuts if they find the test is an imposition or make observations that are biased toward favored individuals. This danger is avoided by continuously checking the administration of the assessment and making sure that the results are being used effectively for the benefit of both individuals with developmental disabilities and staff members.

Less formal types of assessments that measure performance in specific program settings are also available. Assessments also determine strengths and needs and identify and reinforce the talents, energies, and preferences of the individual with developmental disabilities. These assessments still must be carefully considered, as discussed above. This ensures results that are accurate and useful as baseline data to show individual growth and progress and as documentation in the preparation of individualized plans through the interdisciplinary process.

Program Checklist

	Yes	No
1. Assessments are related to program environments.	—	—
2. The facility uses a variety of assessments to develop individual program plans.	—	—
3. Day and residential staff are trained to assess individual performance in program settings.	—	—

Interdisciplinary Team Meeting

At the interdisciplinary team meeting (ITM), the QMRP plays a special role. The QMRP must ensure that quality in both the process and product is present. In terms of the process, a good ITM has a lively discussion about the needs and preferences of the individual. At the meeting, information is shared, and discrepancies and conflicts are understood and resolved. The QMRP can lead or delegate, but his or her function is to ensure that the team comes to a resolution on the appropriate goals and objectives for each individual.

Goals and Objectives

The individual's goals and objectives are the product of the ITM. Here, the QMRP must ensure that the goals and objectives meet both the immediate needs and preferences of the individual, as well as meeting the long-range goals for placement and employment. As far as possible, the goals and objectives should be directed toward functional skills that assist the individual in meeting his or her long-term goals. The QMRP has the role of reviewing these goals against the information from the team and the knowledge gained by the QMRP through direct contact with the individual in order to ensure that the goals meet the quality standards set in governmental and facility guidelines.

Individual Plan

The individual plan turns the goals and objectives into a sequenced series of learning tasks and activities that will enable the individual with developmental disabilities to meet the goals. The QMRP must carefully review these plans, since they will form the basis for the program implementation that follows. The QMRP must monitor the procedures used to implement the goals and ensure that they are appropriate and acceptable for the individual.

Implementation

As in all other elements in the active treatment cycle, the implementation strategy is individual in nature and takes into account the functioning of the individual. In this stage the QMRP monitors the implementation of the individual's program through direct observation and review of individual data. If progress is made and an objective is met, the QMRP arranges for a new objective for the individual. If progress has not been made, the QMRP must intervene to increase the chances that progress will occur. But at all times, the QMRP must review the process to ensure that the individual's rights are protected and that his or her needs and preferences are being met.

Periodic Review

At the periodic review the role of the QMRP is to look at the total individual. Direct care staff and support staff have perspectives that are somewhat narrowed by their day-to-day concern and responsibility for the individual. Although each staff member should take the broader perspective (and many do), only the QMRP is required to take an overview.

Role of the QMRP in Monitoring and Evaluation

Throughout the active treatment cycle the role of the QMRP is to monitor the process and flag products or processes that are delayed or inadequate. The QMRP documents such things as missing reports,

incomplete data, and inadequate performance in an attempt to identify and remove barriers to active treatment.

The role of the QMRP is to ask questions. If an individual has
failed to make progress, the QMRP might inquire if a change has occurred in roommates, program, or medications. These must be examined to determine if they might inhibit progress. The QMRP should
advance the state-of-the-art in the facility on behalf of the individual
with developmental disabilities in order to ensure that maximum efforts are made to improve services to the individual and to move the
individual toward self-sufficiency.

Bradley (1984) points out that:

> Outcome monitoring generates information on the effect a program is
> having on its participants. This information can be expressed as the per-
> cent of clients who have reached a pre-determined service goal or goals, a
> reduction in particular problems, or a change in circumstances as a con-
> sequence of service. By definition, data on the outcomes of human
> development services are always related to a change in client status
> (p. 121).

Program Checklist

		Yes	No
1.	The QMRP coordinates the monitoring process.	——	——
2.	Goals and objectives are directed toward the ac-quisition of functional skills and the provision of support services.	——	——
3.	The QMRP checks to determine that the proce-dures are appropriate and acceptable to the indi-vidual.	——	——

Ensuring Effective Data Collection

Effective data collection is essential in monitoring and evaluating individuals with developmental disabilities served by an ICF/MR. Data
must be collected on the specific objectives in each individual's plan.
The exact nature of the data and the frequency of collection depends
on the objective. If the objective, for example, is to improve daily living skill, then data must be taken each time there is formal training
in the skill. Another example is the collection of data on the use of
positive reinforcements in encouraging appropriate behavior. In this
case, the number of reinforcements observed in a time sample (such
as 3:10 p.m. to 3:15 p.m. on Tuesdays and Fridays) is the interval for
data collection. In other cases, data are collected only if an incident,
such as an injury, occurs.

All data collected must be reduced to a report showing the results of the staff's efforts. Such reports include periodic progress
notes, incident and injury reports, and participation in group activities. Data in these reports can be compared with data from past re-

ports—such as the percentage of all objectives met in this quarter compared to last quarter, or they can be contrasted against set standards—such as the consistency in meeting staff ratio requirements. A uniform data base for individual monitoring and evaluation allows consistent interpretation of results and comparison of achievement among units within the facility or in other facilities.

Key to useful data are staff who know and care about the data (Patton, 1978). Showing how data are useful in making their jobs easier encourages staff to care about data. Those staff asking for the data must tell those collecting the data how the information is used. Even better, those collecting the data should be given the opportunity and means to use the data themselves. If, for example, front-line staff learn to interpret the data to determine when individual progress has been achieved, this shows success and builds staff esteem. If, on the other hand, the data indicates that the program is not working, staff can begin to think about changes they may suggest to the program staff who designed the program.

Staff should be instructed in how to collect data and reinforced for proper collection. Reinforce data collection by sharing results with the staff so that they see how data are useful in making day-to-day decisions about programs and activities. Ensure that data are collected properly by following these steps:

Set clear data collection elements. Data should be based on observable and measurable units of behavior or activity. The data collection forms should be clear, as detailed below, and instructions on the type and frequency of data collection must be clearly stated.

Train staff requesting the data. Do not assume that those staff persons needing data, especially the clinical staff, have any training in how to motivate other staff to collect data. Training should cover the following points:

- Techniques of data collection and analysis
- How to instruct and motivate staff to collect and use data
- How to train staff to identify the behavior or activity being recorded and when to record the data
- How the clinical staff will use the data and how direct care staff can use the data

Train staff collecting the data and their supervisors. Such instructions should cover how and why to collect data, the types of forms used, the analysis that will be performed on the data, and the uses of the data in working with individuals.

Have the supervisor check the data daily. The supervisor should review data entry to determine if the data are timely and accurate. For example, if frequency checks are made on the half-hour, was the last half-hour filled in? If the supervisor observed a behavior at 3:00 p.m., was it entered by staff for that time period? Are data filled in several hours or days in advance? If the data are correctly entered, the supervisor signs and dates the data sheet. If the data are incorrectly entered or are inaccurate, the supervisor informs the line staff person and suggests ways to improve the data collection procedures. If data collection continues to be inaccurate, the supervisor can request in-service training for the staff person or perhaps begin a progressive disciplinary procedure.

Have the specialized service staff member check the data regularly. On a regular basis, the specialized service staff member using the data should observe the staff person recording data and review the data entries to determine if the data are timely and accurate, and sign the data form to indicate that it has been reviewed. If the data lack validity or reliability, an in-service training session is given to the staff person or persons involved. Record all in-service training sessions.

Conduct a check of reliability on a regular basis. A good time to check data collection is about 2 weeks after it begins. This is because the effects of the training may be wearing off, and the motivation of the staff persons may be declining. The best way to cross-validate data collection is for two persons—such as the clinical specialist using the data and the direct line staff person collecting the data—to observe the individual with developmental disabilities during the same specified period, looking for the presence or absence of a targeted behavior or activity. The length of the dual data taking depends on the frequency of the behavior or activity observed. The data from both observers are then compared and interrater reliability is calculated and recorded.

Make corrections based on results of the data check. If the level of agreement between raters falls below a set standard, usually 80% agreement, corrective actions are needed, such as further in-servicing, further definition of the target behavior or activity, or a change in data collection procedure. Continue checking the data until agreement rises above the standard, and then spot check on a regular basis. Keep a record of all data checks.

Review data collection procedures when making reports. Whenever the QMRP or a clinical staff person prepares a progress report or review, he or she should certify in the report that the data used in preparing the report are correctly entered based on his or her review of: 1) the data entries, 2) the staff in-service training, and 3) the comments and signatures of supervisors and clinical staff. If the data are not deemed correctly entered, the staff member preparing the report should state what corrective actions, such as in-servicing or disciplinary actions, were recommended and followed.

Perform regular compliance checks by the QMRP. The QMRP should review data entries periodically and ascertain that: 1) data were collected, 2) daily supervisory reviews are completed, 3) regular reviews by the clinical staff were done, and 4) regular reliability checks were conducted. If deficiencies are present, the QMRP should discuss the problem with the supervisor and recommend such corrective measures as staff training.

Program Checklist

	Yes	No
1. A uniform data base for monitoring and evaluation is present.	—	—
2. The facility can demonstrate to staff how data enhance job performance.	—	—
3. Staff are trained in data collection and utilization methods.	—	—
4. Program coordinators check data daily.	—	—
5. The facility has procedures to check the reliability of data.	—	—
6. Program coordinators certify the correctness of data entries.	—	—

Preparing Monitoring and Other Data Collection Forms

A variety of forms are used in monitoring and evaluation. Many facilities use checklists to determine if programs follow the correct procedures. For example, a monitoring form may be used to check off if the assessments needed to prepare an individualized plan are done correctly and on time.

Any monitoring form developed or adopted by a facility should be pretested to ensure that it can be used effectively by staff and provide useful information. The following procedure is recommended for preparing new forms:

Draft the form. Prepare a draft version of the form (or a copy of an existing form), and write a statement answering these three questions: 1) Why is the form needed? 2) What is the purpose of the form? 3) How will the form be used when completed? The draft form and responses to the questions should be reviewed and approved by either the forms committee or by the department head.

Check the draft form. Fill out the draft form using existing data or going into the field and collecting the data. Answer these questions: 1) Does the form collect the information needed? 2) Is the form clear and easy to fill out? 3) Can the filled-in information be easily read?

Write instructions on how to collect the data. Draft a statement detailing, step by step, how the data collector should collect the data. Explain how to fill out *each* blank in the form.

Test the data collection form and instructions. Ask potential form users to fill out the form following the instructions. Ask them these questions: 1) Are the instructions clear? 2) Are any difficulties apparent in writing on the form? 3) Are any questions unclear? 4) How long did it take to complete the form? 5) Is the form seen as useful? 6) What improvements are suggested?

Revise the data collection form and set of instructions. Based on the field test, revise the form and instructions to simplify the procedure.

Prepare for analysis of the collected data. Draft a set of procedures for analyzing and using the resulting data in taking actions, tracking the findings over time, and filing the completed forms and reports.

Conduct a pretest of the form. Ask staff members to participate in a formal pretest as follows: 1) Instruct teams of two or more to take the draft form into an observation setting and fill in the form. 2) Question team members on the ease of completing the form and understanding the instructions. 3) Compare completed forms to test for interrater validity (do all team members score the same observation the same way?).

Attempt to analyze and use the pretest data. If the form is designed for direct individual use, such as employee assessment, take five forms and provide feedback to the concerned parties. If the data are also going to be reported upon as a group, take 20 forms, analyze the data, and draft a report including data tables and interpretation of the data. Answer these questions: 1) Can the data be used in one-on-one situations to provide feedback to concerned staff? 2) Can the data be used to answer questions about the group?

Make final revisions and introduce the form. Continue revisions until both the form and instructions are clear and usable. When introducing the form, plan in-service training that explains how to fill out the form and, most important, how the results are used by staff to improve programs or standards of living for individuals with developmental disabilities.

Using Videotaping in Monitoring and Evaluation

One use of videotaping in monitoring is setting up a video camera in a fixed location to record staff interactions with individuals with developmental disabilities. Such cameras soon become part of the furniture, and the results tend to reflect actual behavior. Staff can review the videotape and critique their interactions with the individuals they serve.

In a similar manner individual behavior or activities can be videotaped and used to monitor staff performance in data collection. For example, a 10-minute period of interaction can be videotaped, and staff can be asked to view the tape and record the number of reinforcers they observed being used. Results can be compared. If less then 80% of the raters agree about the number of reinforcers used, then either a better definition of reinforcers is needed or more staff training in observation is required.

Another monitoring use of videocameras is maintaining staff skill levels. If a staff member's use of a service intervention, such as a reinforcement technique, is taped immediately after it is learned, the tape can then be viewed by staff on occasion to determine if the techniques learned are still being used. Since staff easily slip back into poor habits, viewing of their own best performance is a form of self-monitoring.

Videotaping can also be used in evaluation. It can provide a visual record of a developmentally disabled individual's performance before and after a service intervention. For example, videotaping an individual at mealtime shows changes, over time, in his or her social behavior. In a similar manner staff competency in handling various situations can be recorded before and after training to demonstrate changes in staff competence over time.

Using Computers in Monitoring and Evaluation

Computers are useful in monitoring trends in program performance. For example, indexes and indicators based on individual data can automatically show if staff performance is above or below expectations. In this way problem areas are flagged. While computers are especially useful for aggregating well-defined and discrete data elements, they can also be used to aggregate qualitative information. This is done through coding comments and observations and using the results to supplement the quantitative data. Through the use of graphics, the computers can provide charts and graphs that identify trends, provide information on potential problems, and provide feedback on progress. Through the use of computer-generated reports, detailed monitoring and evaluation reports may be produced that give timely information to staff and program managers.

Monitoring and Evaluation in Widely Separated Locations

A special problem occurs when the facility has several ICFs/MR in widely separated locations. In this situation, QMRPs and area supervisors may have to increase time on each site to ensure that data useful in monitoring and evaluation are collected. If a computerized data collection program is used, the results can be sent through modems over telephone lines to a central location. In this manner a single QMRP can monitor several sites in scattered locations. Since most programs designed for data collection use specially prepared screens, the staff need very little knowledge of computers to use them successfully.

Program Checklist

	Yes	No
1. Monitoring forms are pretested.	—	—
2. Data are used to provide feedback to staff.	—	—
3. Videotaping is used to monitor staff consistency in program implementation.	—	—
4. Staff in decentralized locations utilize computers and modems to facilitate monitoring.	—	—

IMPLICATIONS

For the Individual

The individual with developmental disabilities should participate in monitoring activities. At the very least, staff should discuss with individuals the purposes of the monitoring activities. Where possible, individuals should be encouraged to monitor their own progress and to comment on services they are provided. In a similar manner staff should review the results of evaluations with individuals with developmental disabilities and inform them of progress made toward meeting their individualized goals.

For Qualified Mental Retardation Professionals

Monitoring the day-to-day implementation of individualized active treatment programs is the QMRP's most important role. The QMRP must immediately follow up to reinforce improvements and to make corrections as needed. Evaluation of individual progress is the QMRP's second most important role since it provides information on staff performance. If an evaluation fails to show progress toward individualized goals and objectives, the QMRP must take corrective action to improve the individual's program or adjust the system to perform better.

For Specialized Service Staff

If it is to be effective, monitoring of services to individuals must be shared by specialized service staff. They must monitor the implementation of specialized services to ensure that clinical, regulatory, and quality assurance standards are met. Clinical specialists need to review the data collected by the staff to ensure that documentation of individual progress is valid and reliable. The specialist must then act on the results of monitoring to correct any misapplication of disciplinary approaches by facility staff.

In addition, the clinician participates, from the perspective of his or her discipline, in the evaluation of individual progress based on specialized service interventions. The clinical specialist uses established standards to evaluate individual progress in areas of concern to his or her discipline in order to ensure that results of any evaluations are used to correct procedures and to lead to improved progress.

For Direct Care Staff

Data needed to monitor performance are collected by direct care staff in accordance with principles prescribed by the facility. Staff should be trained to examine the data on a daily basis to spot indicators that trigger the need to review the program for possible correction. Direct care staff should also participate in the evaluation of each individual's progress and work with other staff to examine data measuring progress in meeting individualized goals. Based on their knowledge of the individual with developmental disabilities and their use of the data, direct care staff should be active participants in any discussion on system changes or program changes needed to improve facility progress in meeting individualized goals.

For Quality Assurance Coordinators

The quality assurance (QA) coordinator also monitors the facility to determine the degree of compliance with regulations. Based on this review, the QA coordinator should educate the staff regarding their compliance with governmental regulatory standards. The QA coordinator will be interested in the monitoring activities of the facility and will want to know how information gained in monitoring is used to correct observed problems. In a similar manner the QA coordinator needs to look at the facility's assessments and evaluations of the individual to derive in-depth information on program performance. After examining the data to determine the progress made in meeting individualized goals, the QA coordinator prepares deficiency statements to identify those areas in the facility that need correction.

For Program Managers

Supervisors and other program managers use monitoring data to improve daily performance of their staff. Program managers must conduct daily site visits to make direct observation of staff activities. They must review data to flag areas needing immediate attention. Program managers also use assessments and evaluations to determine how to improve performance and to indicate if policy changes are needed. Using monitoring and evaluation data, program managers can determine if staff resources are used effectively and can identify systems and programs that must be changed to improve performance.

For the Family

Family members, guardians, and advocates share in monitoring service delivery. They should be asked by the facility to provide suggestions on how to monitor service delivery. If possible, they should participate in the actual monitoring of selected services. By making regular visits, family members can monitor such basics as the type of interaction between staff and individuals, the satisfaction level of the individuals, and the cleanliness of the facility. Certainly, family members, guardians, and advocates should review the results of assessment and evaluations to determine the impact of facility programs on the individual. They may be able to suggest appropriate ways to improve service delivery based on their reviews of the evaluation results.

For Trainers

The trainers' responsibility is to instruct staff on how to collect and use data. They should provide instruction on methods and techniques for collecting valid and reliable data and inform staff on how to use data to improve performance. The trainers should assist the staff in interpreting data from monitoring and evaluation. Trainers should be invited to participate in meetings designed to interpret data for use in improving systems and programs. Trainers should then disseminate findings to reinforce good performance and suggest corrections.

In turn, training efforts should be evaluated to determine that staff are learning new skills. Since staff must demonstrate competence in active treatment, training is best evaluated by continual tests of competency. When staff are trained and fail to demonstrate competence, the cause could be in the training, in the supervision, or in the staff member, but only careful evaluation can identify and resolve the problem.

CONCLUSION

Monitoring and evaluation provide factual information on the quality of services provided by a facility. Monitoring covers day-to-day compliance with the facility's policy and procedures. As a result of monitoring, information is given to staff on their compliance with governmental regulations and with the facility's standards for quality care. As staff measures their performance with governmental and facility standards, they can make the adjustments needed to improve the process and results of their services.

While monitoring ensures that services, on a day-to-day basis, are delivered appropriately, evaluation determines if the use of facility resources is appropriate and yields beneficial results. The data-based findings of evaluations provide empirical evidence of accomplishments or failings. Feedback from evaluations allows staff to maintain good performance and to improve below-standard performance.

In human services, staff rewards come in achieving demonstrated progress by persons with developmental disabilities. Staff feel a sense of pride in anticipating and performing at, or above, standards. If program managers reinforce proactive staff actions that result in obtaining or exceeding standards, staff morale should be enhanced. In human services, staff find gratification in observing and measuring real progress in individuals with developmental disabilities. In turn, through monitoring and evaluation, program managers are able to direct resources and design programs that efficiently meet individualized goals.

REFERENCES

Bradley, V. J. (1984) *Assessing and enhancing the quality of services: A guide for the human services field.* Boston: Human Services Research Institute.
Doucette, J., & Freedman, R. (1980). *Progress tests for the developmentally disabled: An evaluation.* Cambridge, MA: Abt Books.
Patton, M. Q. (1978). *Utilization-focused evaluation.* Beverly-Hills: Sage Publications.

III
SPECIAL
CONSIDERATIONS
AND CONCLUSION

12
The Community-Based Intermediate Care Facility for the Mentally Retarded

Nancy R. Weiss

Operators of small, community-based intermediate care facilities for the mentally retarded (ICFs/MR) face a variety of challenges. This chapter explores the challenges associated with the small facility as well as the implications of the 1988 ICF/MR standards for service delivery in community settings. The exploration covers methods for addressing these challenges and for overcoming the obstacles common to the operation of scattered-site programs.

Small facilities are characterized by more than simply the number of individuals served. Because they are small and freestanding, community-based programs offer the potential for full community integration. Living in integrated community settings allows individuals to take advantage of a broad range of resources and a variety of experiences. Small facilities potentially provide individuals the opportunity to live in integrated and normalized environments. These facilities offer residents the opportunity to become contributing members of their communities.

Traditional residential facilities are, for the most part, inwardly oriented. Services and resources required to meet the needs of residents and to run the physical plant are available within the structure of the facility. Small ICFs/MR, in contrast, are outwardly directed.

They utilize the resources in the community to meet the needs of individuals. Contacts with outside service providers, however, may create unique challenges. Staff and residents of small facilities have the responsibility of maintaining relationships with community members. Both community relationships and contractual arrangements for services must be well maintained to ensure community integration.

Large facilities provide a comprehensive array of services. For example, the services of a physical therapist, a dietician, or even an electrician or plumber are usually available within the facility. Food is prepared at a central location. Residents of these facilities generally attend on-grounds day programs, and the recreational services address the needs of large groups of individuals.

The inward orientation of large facilities provides administrators control over service delivery. They directly employ professional and support staff, while the group home administrator often contracts for those services.

In addition, the economies of scale enjoyed by large facilities often enhance accessibility to specialized service staff. For example, a facility serving 70 individuals with self-injurious behavior might hire a psychologist specializing in behavioral programming. An ICF/MR group home could not afford to employ such a specialist directly. Moreover, the small facility may have difficulty contracting with specialists on a part-time basis. Small, community-based facilities are often unable to locate dentists, dieticians, physicians, and other specialized service staff who are skilled in meeting the needs of individuals with developmental disabilities.

Successful community-based ICFs/MR provide high-quality, individualized programming; enhance community integration; and create a comfortable, responsive, and respectful environment. Facilities are successful when an individual's instructional goals are tailored to their strengths and interests, and teaching methods result in the successful achievement of new skills. Finally, the acquired skills should be usable in current and future environments.

Community integration does not occur simply because a program is located in a neighborhood setting. Attending the movie theatre, dining in local restaurants, shopping in neighborhood stores, and obtaining medical care within the community do not constitute full community integration. Community integration is achieved when individuals:

- Have the same number and types of community contacts as non-disabled citizens
- Have friendships with individuals who are not paid staff or volunteers
- Select program outcomes and activities
- Participate in community activities such as voting, neighborhood clean-ups, volunteer work, and civic groups

- Are provided the full range of support services to function as independently as possible
- Make friends outside the developmental disabilities community

REVIEW OF THE STANDARDS

The 1988 ICF/MR standards are far less prescriptive than previous standards. They focus on program outcomes rather than on specifying exact policies and procedures. The new standards do not distinguish between a large and small facility. All standards apply to both settings.

The orientation toward outcome offers more freedom to the service provider in achieving compliance. Small facilities, with contractual professional staff, for example, can now determine the process for meeting standards. This process may differ significantly from that used by a large institution. Both approaches will be acceptable, however, if they produce appropriate individual outcomes.

Rather than conforming to detailed regulatory processes, facilities can focus attention on ensuring that:

- Staff are competent.
- Individual's rights are protected.
- Instructional programs are well designed.
- Residents make progress toward functional objectives.
- Effective behavioral programming is designed and implemented consistently.
- Residents participate in a range of activities and achieve community integration.
- Individual's health needs are addressed.
- Physical environments are clean, safe, and attractive.

One regulation does distinguish between large and small facilities. Facilities serving fewer than 16 individuals do not require on-duty and awake staff on a 24-hour basis unless a physician has ordered a medical care plan, or individuals are aggressive or assaultive, or they present security risks. A medical care plan is required when an individual's needs require 24-hour licensed nursing supervision.

APPLICATION

Although each small facility is unique and each state approaches the ICF/MR program somewhat differently, staff face many common challenges. Different alternatives are available to address each of these challenges. The following solutions and approaches incorporate sound professional practice. They have practical application for both the new and long-term provider of ICF/MR services.

Facility Administration

In large facilities staff often have limited opportunities to influence management decisions. Large and formal organizations have well-established procedures. By comparison, staff in small agencies have opportunities to contribute to the development of policies and procedures.

The governing body selects the adminstrator, formulates or approves all policy, establishes mission and philosophy, and provides fiscal and managerial oversight. All staff should participate in the development of mission and philosophy statements. The mission statement formalizes the agency's purpose and priorities. The mission and philosophy statements guide decision making. The governing body and senior management review, revise, adopt, and distribute these guiding documents. The governing body of a new agency must adopt policies and procedures before initiating services.

Small agencies may be operated publicly or privately. They may be governed by a board of directors or by corporate officers. They may be proprietary or nonprofit operations.

A board of directors is generally responsible for the management of private agencies. Parents, advocates, volunteers, or political appointees serve on the governing body. The board benefits from representatives with particular skills and experiences such as attorneys, accountants, or real estate agents. Some boards of public agencies are composed of representatives of local municipal governments. Board members of both public and private agencies may have other commitments and will be able to devote limited time to fulfilling the role of board member.

Because of those time constraints, facility management and staff should provide orientation, training, and information to board members to enable them to make effective decisions. For example, facility staff can invite board members to housewarmings, send announcements of special occasions, and encourage informal visits.

The board of directors will consider issues from varied perspectives. The board should be viewed as an asset to the agency. Management staff should increase board awareness and understanding of the operation of the agency.

Record Keeping and Documentation

The maintenance of client records, documentation, and the protection of confidentiality deserve special considerations in small facilities. In larger facilities medical records staff generally manage record keeping. In smaller facilities maintaining client records and protecting confidentiality may become the responsibility of staff who lack the necessary training or experience. Unlike other duties, such as meal preparation, recreational supervision, and house operations, record keeping may be an unfamiliar task. The agency must train staff in maintaining records and confidentiality.

Training should also emphasize compliance with facility policy and procedures and the necessity of documentation. For example, if agency policy requires bed checks every half hour, staff must both perform and document the bed checks. The documentation confirms the activity took place and that the policy was followed.

Training should address the importance of clear and factual record keeping. All information in an individual's record becomes part of a legal document. Training should indicate that falsifying the record may result in legal penalties. Accurate records assist staff to make programmatic decisions. Decisions regarding the selection of objectives, revision of a program, achievement of an objective, and medication changes depend on accurate record keeping.

Accurate record keeping is encouraged by simplifying systems for charting. Formal charting, such as documentation of instructional programming, the use of reinforcers, or medication administration can be simplified by forms that are maintained in an accessible place. Records should be accurate and objective. They should be kept brief, clear, and pertinent.

Mistakes occur in the record-keeping process, and changes in schedules may take place. Staff must know how to report an error and how to document a schedule change. They must accurately document a mistake or change of plans rather than falsify a record for the purpose of producing documentation that appears correct. In-service training should provide clear guidelines on record keeping.

Finally, staff must understand the importance of maintaining confidentiality. Staff cannot reveal a resident's name or send a copy of a client's record without written consent. Concerns about confidentiality often develop in the small community-based program where staff interact daily with medical professionals, workers from other agencies, or members of the community. For this reason, staff training should identify strategies for maintaining confidentiality.

Program Checklist

		Yes	No
1.	Board members are provided with sufficient information to govern service delivery.	___	___
2.	Board members participate in facility activities and make informal visits.	___	___
3.	Staff receive training on record keeping and the maintenance of confidentiality.	___	___
4.	Records are accurate, brief, and pertinent.	___	___

Management of Services Provided Outside the Facility or Under Contract

Services can be provided by agencies other than the ICF/MR through a written agreement. The ICF/MR facility must ensure that the purchased service meets required standards of quality. Small agencies usually contract for the service specialists such as physicians, nurses, social workers, physical therapists, occupational therapists, speech pathologists, or pharmacists. Specialists employed under contract are rarely as available or flexible as are staff who are employed directly. Contractual specialists often are employed elsewhere on a full-time or part-time basis. They may choose contract work because this arrangement affords them greater flexibility and autonomy. For these reasons, they may be less willing or less able to work certain hours or perform certain duties than are directly employed staff.

Many community residential agencies contract for day program, sheltered workshop, or supported employment services. These services are needed to meet the needs of the individual. Staff must ensure the coordination between the day and residential programs. The ICF/MR should promote opportunities to discuss and exchange information about program planning, progress, and modification.

Contracting for services allows access to a full range of professional services. In addition, it allows the residential provider to maintain a focused mission rather than diversifying and attempting to provide all services to all individuals.

The written agreement with the outside service provider must address the expectations of both parties. The agreement should also specify the process to resolve potential conflicts between agencies.

In some instances service needs of individuals may exceed those routinely provided by an outside agency. For example, more detailed documentation than the physician would usually provide or more rigorous training than normally provided by the day program may be required. These additional requirements should be specifically addressed in the written agreement.

The ICF/MR management is responsible for the quality of the physical environment, whether the facility is owned or leased. The lease or rental agreement should specify responsibility for upkeep and repairs. The agreement should also designate responsibility for physical modifications that might be necessary. Finally, when appropriate, the facility management should negotiate a long-term lease to provide stability in residential settings.

Protection of Individual Rights

Protecting the rights of individuals is particularly important in community settings where staff work autonomously. In scattered-site programs managers find that constant supervision or frequent oversight is more difficult to maintain. In these settings each staff person must know relevant agency policy and internalize the principles that guide respectful treatment.

All individuals with developmental disabilities should be encouraged to exercise their rights as citizens. These include the right to vote, the right to self-advocate, the right to due process, the right to participate in community affairs, and access to the training necessary to exercise these rights. These are particularly relevant in community settings. Staff should be trained to assist individuals to participate as contributing members of their communities. Staff should train individuals to manage their own finances to the degree to which they are capable. Individuals need adequate opportunities to spend money in the manner they choose.

Active participation of parents, legal guardians, and advocates promotes rights. Families are often geographically closer when the individual with developmental disabilities lives in a community setting rather than in an institution. Staff should establish ways for families to become involved in the facility. Some parents might prepare a special dinner; others may participate in a recreational activity or join an advisory committee. Some families may only maintain phone contact. All levels of involvement should be encouraged.

Some parents may have concerns about their child moving to a community residence. They may worry about the risks of community living or about the longevity of the placement. They may feel uncomfortable when their child moves to a new home in a different neighborhood. Staff should make an effort to understand the complexity of the parent-child relationship. Staff can build parents' confidence over time by providing quality services supporting the individuals' relationships with families.

Program Checklist

	Yes	No
1. Written contracts with outside agencies and specialized service staff are available.	___	___
2. Contracts detail the services to be provided.	___	___
3. Written policy and procedures on client rights are available on-site.	___	___
4. Staff can state agency policy regarding the protection of individual rights.	___	___
5. Participation of parents and advocates is actively encouraged.	___	___

Staffing

Community-based programs encounter special situations in facility staffing. Unplanned staff absences creates critical coverage problems. A small agency experiences a crisis if several people are unable to work. Staffing problems can be minimized by maintaining a list of trained substitutes.

In small facilities the total number of staff is limited. Therefore, all employees need to be flexible. Administrators and specialized service staff must sometimes provide direct service during staff shortages. Staff must be prepared to perform a variety of different duties and responsibilities when necessary.

Flexibility is promoted by performing other jobs on a periodic basis. Administrators may choose to make this a regular requirement. In-service training policy may require each direct care worker, administrator, and specialized service staff to assume the role of another worker for a few days each year. For example, an administrator may work the night shift in a group home, a day program instructor might work at the group home, and a group home worker might "shadow" the psychologist for a few days. In this way each team member will develop an appreciation for the contribution of the others. Such role changes may be initially disruptive but are an effective method for building a supportive and cooperative team.

The number of facility staff depends on the number needed to provide comprehensive active treatment services. No standardized ratio of staff to individuals served will guarantee quality care. ICF/MR standards require sufficient numbers of direct care staff to implement individual program plans. Minimum ratios may not adequately address the need for high-quality, individualized programming.

Staff training is sometimes difficult to provide in the small facility. A large pool of employees at large facilities allows the scheduling of regular orientation and in-service training. A small agency may not have enough employees to provide coverage while others participate in in-service training. Small agencies generally will not have enough new employees starting at the same time to make classroom style orientation training practical.

Administrators must be creative in designing staff training. For example, training workbooks, quizzes on sections of the policy/procedure manual, or videotapes of previous training sessions may aid in training. Newer workers can be paired with more experienced staff to learn procedures. The trainer/staff member should document the training provided.

Policy should designate minimum training requirements before staff can work alone. These might include CPR, first aid, response to emergencies, medication administration, special medical procedures and treatments, implementation of behavior programs, and a review of the policies that pertain to individual rights, abuse, and mistreatment.

Staff reinforcement and recognition are important in the small facility. The facility should be committed to salaries for these individuals that reflect the importance of their jobs. Because of frequent staff turnover, periodic performance reviews and salary increases, however modest, should be provided. For example, the successful completion of policy manual quizzes or training on instructional programming might lead to a salary review. Workers become more valuable as they acquire needed skills and are able to work more autonomously.

In addition to pay increases, a variety of methods to reinforce good work are available. They include:

• Personally thanking the good worker
• Mentioning exceptional performance at a staff meeting
• Writing a short memo with a copy to the individual's personnel file
• Noting in the house log that the holiday decorations looked great or that the picnic was a success
• Publishing special recognitions in an agency newsletter
• Recognizing a worker of the month
• Offering to work for an employee on his or her birthday or during a shift of his or her choice

---

Program Checklist

	Yes	No
1. Staffing ratios are sufficient to provide active treatment services.	___	___
2. A variety of staff training methods are employed.	___	___
3. Minimum training requirements for new staff are specified.	___	___
4. Staff complete minimum training requirements prior to working.	___	___
5. Supervisory staff employ a staff reinforcement system.	___	___

Maintaining the Focus on the Individual

Small community-based providers are challenged to focus on each person's individuality. Staff sometimes find it easier and more efficient to provide group services rather than services focused on the needs of individuals. The ICF/MR standards emphasize individual strengths, needs, and service requirements. Promoting choices, quality staff-client interactions, balancing the need for risk taking with the need for protection from harm, and community participation maximize social integration and individuality.

No direct correlation exists between small size and high quality. Wide variation among facilities that serve the same numbers of individuals is evident. Some facilities promote community participation while others provide few opportunities for growth, self-determination, or community integration.

Staff should support and encourage individuals to make choices. Supervisors should reinforce this behavior in each worker. When providing services to groups of individuals, staff often rely on routines and schedules. These assist staff to address objectives and to provide recreational activities. Opportunities for making choices should be introduced into the schedule wherever possible. If staff consider making choices a goal, they will be able to identify opportunities to do so.

In larger facilities, opportunities to make decisions such as whether to take a bath or shower, what to eat, what to wear, or whether to participate in activities are often limited. Some individuals with developmental disabilities may need encouragement to express themselves and express their preferences. Decision making may need to be formally taught and practiced.

The opportunity for making choices is not limited to individuals with verbal skills. All individuals regardless of degree of disability have interests and preferences. Staff can notice facial expression, verbalizations, and when the individual is most alert and making eye contact to indicate preferences. Staff are able to determine preferences and interests of nonverbal individuals through careful observation.

Disruptive behaviors may be an attempt to communicate or a critique of services. The message communicated by the behavior should be considered before attempting to change the behavior. The individual may be expressing boredom or frustration, asking for attention or physical contact, requesting to participate in an activity, or to be relieved of a task. For example, an individual who often screams while performing prevocational tasks may be expressing either boredom or frustration with the complexity of the task. Staff should give this individual the chance to try alternative work activities. The interdisciplinary team should consider a new program that is more responsive to the individual's strengths and interests.

Staff should note the patterns of behavior. Observation of when behavior problems are likely to occur can indicate the individual's choices and preferences. When staff respond to individual preferences, they reinforce the behavior and indicate that they value individual preferences.

The number and types of staff-resident interactions is another indicator of quality. Staff often interact only minimally with residents. Informal social contacts are frequently brief and impersonal. Warm and genuine informal interactions stress individual importance. Facilities should encourage staff to spend unstructured time with residents and to use informal opportunities for teaching. The number and quality of informal interactions will increase when they are a valued, integral component of the program.

Another indicator of quality is the balance between the principles of normalization and the right to risk. Reasonable judgment must be exercised. The importance of individual choice and the availability of a breadth of experiences must be balanced with the right to protection from harm. Staff may face this tension daily. Difficult choices arise in the following dilemmas:

• Should an individual who has seizures bathe privately?
• At what point should an individual walk to the store unattended?

- What should staff do when they disapprove of an individual's purchase, for example, a pornographic magazine or a BB gun?
- When and in what form should adults be able to express their sexuality?
- How should staff handle their own discomfort about homosexuality?
- Should an individual be allowed to dress in clothes that are not age appropriate or that call undo attention to himself or herself?

Often no right or wrong answers are apparent. Management should assist staff to feel comfortable discussing these issues and support employees as they strive to find the best solutions.

Finally, community integration is an indicator of quality. Community-based facilities offer not only the opportunity for community presence, but also for community integration. Community integration means attending church with a neighbor or participating in an aerobics class at the YMCA. Community participation reinforces individual value and a sense of importance.

Participating in community activities gives individuals a chance to meet other members of the community and to establish friendships with people who are not paid caregivers. Community participation communicates that the individual's choices are valued. It also indicates to the community that people with developmental disabilities have preferences and interests and can contribute to their community.

Facilities should make community integration an important goal. The degree of community integration can be measured by tracking:

- The range of different activities individuals participate in during the day
- The number of activities people take part in by themselves or with just one other person with developmental disabilities
- The number of group activities individuals participate in that are not planned specifically for individuals with developmental disabilities
- The number of contacts residents have with individuals who are not paid staff, volunteers, or family members.

Program Checklist

	Yes	No
1. Individuals are supported and encouraged to make choices throughout their day.	___	___
2. The environment and activities reflect preferences of individuals.	___	___
3. The message communicated by the behavior is considered before an attempt is made to change the behavior.	___	___

Program Checklist—*continued*

		Yes	No
4.	Staff interactions with residents are warm and genuine.	—	—
5.	Staff consider the right to risk in encouraging community activities.	—	—
6.	Staff pursue community integration as a goal.	—	—

IMPLICATIONS

For Qualified Mental Retardation Professionals

The qualified mental retardation professional (QMRP) is responsible for the coordination and review of quality services. In some facilities the head counselor or house manager is the QMRP. In this case the QMRP is familiar with the residents and facility operations and can promote programs that respond to individual needs. The limitation of this model is that the house manager/QMRP may be unable to monitor objectively and critique the program. For this reason social workers and case managers are often assigned the QMRP role. Although the social worker/QMRP may be more objective in viewing the performance of the facility, he or she may not be as thoroughly familiar with the needs of the individuals served as the house manager.

When the house manager/QMRP sees a problem, he or she can correct it. The social worker/QMRP, being outside the direct chain of command, will be dependent on the house manager to correct deficiencies. Neither model is free of limitation.

For Specialized Service Staff

Facilities frequently encounter difficulties locating qualified specialized service staff to work with individuals with developmental disabilities. Sometimes these individuals may need additional training in providing services in nonclinical settings. A dietician, for example, who has hospital or nursing home experience may find menu planning that encourages choices a new and difficult task. Specialized service staff should understand the normalization principle, the importance of skill development, and the necessity for choices.

Small facilities may need additional procedures for specialized contractual employees. Interdisciplinary team meetings should be scheduled to maximize participation by specialized service staff. When attendance at these meetings is not possible, specialized service staff can participate through written reports.

For Direct Care Staff

Maintaining a staff of committed direct care workers can be one of the most difficult jobs of the small ICF/MR administrator. Small agencies are often limited in the compensation they can offer. Satisfaction, however, comes in working for an agency that is small enough to allow each staff member the opportunity to recommend improvements and make a difference.

The administrator should recognize that the direct care staff position requires a high level of responsibility and autonomy. Backup systems should be provided to support individuals working at scattered-site facilities.

For Quality Assurance Coordinators

Quality assurance (QA) coordinators should note opportunities for choice making, informal interaction, reasonable risk taking, and community integration. These can be found in recreational activities that are responsive to individual interests and instructional programming that is responsive to individuals' strengths and interests. QA coordinators should look for staff interactions that are spontaneous, warm, and respectful.

Occasionally, procedures that support the principles of choice making and reasonable risk taking may not be readily apparent to QA coordinators. In these instances the administrator or other program staff should discuss the procedures with the QA coordinator.

CONCLUSION

The challenge for the small community-based agency is to meet standards while creating an environment that responds to residents' needs, respects individuals and their rights, and assists individuals to live more independently. Quality instructional programs are individualized, responsive to strengths and interests, and result in documented progress.

The outwardly directed nature of small facilities and the scattered sites over a wide geographic area make managing service delivery complex. Staff must be well trained in agency policy and procedure. Staff should understand the agency's mission statement and act to ensure that services are responsive to individual needs, interests, and preferences. Formal and informal interactions between staff and individuals with developmental disabilities should reflect respect and concern.

Smaller ICFs/MR do not necessarily provide higher quality. Quality is determined by the facility's ability to attract, train, and maintain skilled staff. Quality is maximized by the staff's ability to focus on the needs of the individuals and to promote community participation. Small facilities do not achieve community integration simply by being located in neighborhoods. Community integration is significantly enhanced by participation in activities with nonhandicapped individuals.

Superior programs are characterized by the promotion of choice making, the quality of staff-resident interactions, the balance between risk taking and protection from harm, and full community integration. Excellence is determined by outcomes. Success in the operation of the small community-based ICF/MR is best demonstrated through the progress, achievements, and satisfaction of the individuals served.

13
Quality Assurance

Solomon G. Jacobson

Although federal regulations set standards for intermediate care facilities operations, they do not guarantee quality. Quality is ensured only if all components of an operation work together with one purpose: service to the individual with a developmental disability. Even if all federal standards, except one, are met, a facility cannot ensure that quality services are provided to consumers. Quality occurs when individuals gain skills and behaviors, when staff take pride in their work, when providers and advocates praise the facility, and when individuals with developmental disabilities are obviously pleased with the quality of their lives.

Until recently federal standards focused on such items as record keeping and physical plant. Many facilities would comply with the paperwork requirements, but this seldom had much to do with good quality care. Regulatory minimum standards tended to become the maximum performance level for some providers. Paper compliance was the norm.

More recently regulatory standards have moved from paper compliance with standards toward measuring the outcomes of the service. This is an important distinction. As outcomes become the focus of attention, facilities are placing greater emphasis on gaining results.

In the past emphasis was on such easily measurable and important aspects as food temperature, minutes of meetings, and width of hallways in residential settings. Now standards are also concerned with the impact of food service on consumer well-being, the results of meetings on improved service, and the livability of the residential environment. Quality assurance (QA) coordinators are asked to observe individuals with developmental disabilities more closely and measure the outcomes of the services they are provided.

Unfortunately, some facilities are reactive in their response to regulations. They are very concerned about being ready for surveys, but tend to prepare for the past reviews. The trauma of past deficiencies tends to concentrate a facility's attention on correcting these before the next survey.

Quality agencies are proactive and try to anticipate what future surveys will require. They try to understand the intent behind the standards. For example, they may reason that the increased federal interest in outcomes will lead to an emphasis on evidence of progress. The proactive facility will carefully document the skill level of all clients and continue the documentation to show client progress. When the facility is surveyed, it will be able to demonstrate progress. Quality means delivering services that go beyond the federal regulations and follow the facility's vision of excellence.

BACKGROUND

Purposes of a Quality Assurance System

Quality services for persons with developmental disabilities are based on knowledge and implementation of state-of-the-art program practices. This requires access to information, the dissemination of that information, trained and skilled staff, and information feedback systems. State-of-the-art in-service delivery is dynamic and changing.

Licensing and certification standards and regulations tend to be static and unchanging. They are best applied to input and formalized process measures that change little over time. They measure the capability or potential to provide quality services, but they do not measure actual performance. Licensing and regulation efforts to maintain minimum program standards may prevent programs from maintaining less than minimum program standards, but they do not form a base from which to launch superior programs.

The provider must assume the responsibility for deciding the level of quality service that will be delivered. This decision is independent of the regulations or standards that will be applied to the program. This provider decision requires a knowledge and commitment to the values and habilitation methods that exist in state-of-the-art service delivery. The values and the habilitation methods evolve over time. The state-of-the-art in 1990 is quite different than it was in 1985 or 1980.

In an important review of the state-of-the-art, Bradley (1984) provided general principles of quality assurance and included five fundamental purposes that must be served by a quality assurance system in an organization (p. 11):

1. The ability to ensure the capacity of providers of human services to offer acceptable levels of service
2. The ability to ensure that client services conform to generally accepted standards of good practice
3. The ability to ensure a commitment of resources (inputs) produces a reasonable level of service (outputs)
4. The ability to ensure that the services provided have the intended effect
5. The ability to ensure that the limited supply of services is provided to those clients most in need

Bradley identified three basic elements in quality assurance techniques (p. 12):

1. *Standards and measures*—the expected levels of provider competency or performance and the indicators used to gauge their achievement
2. *Monitoring and evaluation*—the actual measurement of service provider competence and performance and the communication of this information to the quality assurance organization
3. *Control mechanisms*—those procedures and techniques involved in initiating corrective action or any action necessary to bring actual competency or performance in line with what is expected

Measurable Components of a Human Service System

Any human service system, as explained by Donabedian (1980), consists of four measurable components of quality assurance: 1) Resources (or inputs) are the basis for production. Some examples include staff time, equipment, and shelter. 2) Next are the procedures (or processes) that produce the results. Facility procedures include such processes as assessments, planning, training, rehabilitation, and employment services. The use of resources in a process yields both short-term effects and long-term impact. 3) An effect (or output) might be the individual's attainment of an objective or the improvement of the residential environment. These are the direct results of the use of resources in a process. 4) A long-term impact (or outcome) is more difficult to measure but includes such things as the individual's movement toward a less restrictive environment or the improvement in the individual's quality of life. This system may be seen in Figure 1.

In order to determine if resources produce desired services and results, consistent measures of the costs of the resources and the results of the services must be used. According to Bradley, the cost measures should capture as many of the resources consumed in serving the individual as possible, while the output measures should capture the bulk of the products or services received by the users. In

Resources are INPUT into the system
(Resources include personnel hours, physical plant, equipment)

↓

Plans and procedures are used to PROCESS these resources
(Plans and procedures include individualized habilitation plans [IHPs],
administrative policy, and staffing schedules)

↓

Programs and services are the immediate OUTPUTS
(Programs and services include group activities, work activities,
recreation, socialization, training, and therapy)

↓

Long-range beneficial changes are the desired OUTCOMES
(Long-range beneficial changes include meeting IHP goals,
individual growth and development, and improved health status)

Figure 1.   Systems diagram of human services.

long-term programs, such as residential services, use of cost per time
interval (day, month, or year) is recommended by Bradley, while in
short-term programs, such as a summer recreational program, the
cost per period of service is most effective. In services given occasionally to the individual, such as physical or occupational therapy, the
cost per case or episode should be used (Bradley, p. 40).

Standards for Evaluating Quality Services

Services delivered to individuals can be judged by their accessibility,
adequacy, and acceptability. An *accessible* service can be available to
an individual when he or she needs the service. In addition to remov-
ing physical barriers to accessibility, services also remove such administrative barriers as inconvenient hours. An *adequate* service
meets, at least, minimum professional and regulatory standards in
providing for the specific needs of the user. An *acceptable* service
meets the recipient's personal needs for dignity, privacy, and choice.

The entire service delivery system can be judged by its effectiveness, efficaciousness, and efficiency. A service delivery process is *effective* if it meets its intended purpose. For example, in a campaign to
prevent flu, all individuals with developmental disabilities receive
shots. The process is *efficacious* if the service is effective and the results are ultimately beneficial to the user (i.e., the flu shots actually
prevent an outbreak of flu in the facility). Finally, the process is efficient (also called cost effective) if the service was both effective and
efficacious at the least expenditure of scarce resources (i.e., the flu

shots were delivered by the county health service at no charge to the facility).

Using Functioning to Measure Individual Progress

In quality assurance systems designed to ensure that the services provided have the intended effect, Bradley warns against assuming that changes in behaviors and capabilities are easy to measure by using single-dimension measures. While some changes are simple to measure, such as placement in a residential setting, most of the service user's problems are too complex to measure by a single measure. Instead, she advocates the use of measures in four interrelated areas of functioning (p. 47):

1. *Social adaption*—covering interpersonal skills, activities of daily living, household work, and so forth
2. *Vocational/educational performance*—including work and education
3. *Self-care*—activities such as bathing, dressing, and feeding oneself
4. *Mobility*—the ability to travel from place to place

Several quality assurance techniques are suitable for intermediate care facilities for the mentally retarded (ICFs/MR). One such system—outcome monitoring and evaluation—is discussed in chapter 11. Two techniques are discussed here: self-assessment and client tracking. While Bradley points out that self-assessment has limited scientific value, it has useful operational value, as described in a self-assessment manual quoted by Bradley (p. 115):

1. It alerts staff to problem areas of which they were previously unaware.
2. It provides a systematic method for documenting problems and reasons for change.
3. It facilitates discussion of service delivery issues among staff.
4. It provides baseline data as measures for evaluating changes and documenting progress in services and programs.

Information Feedback

Case tracking uses regularly reported client data to track client progress and identify problems. If predetermined standards are set, case tracking can report exceptions to norms, which allows managers to take action to correct those failing to meet standards and to reinforce those exceeding standards. Both case tracking and exception reporting rely, according to Bradley:

> on a large volume of data which is best managed by computers and can be a component of a general management information system. Computers have proven to be a particular asset in human service quality as-

surance systems. In addition to case tracking and exception reporting, computers process data that are indicative of service quality such as length of stay for inpatients, use of medications, client pre- and postservice status, and level of functioning. (p. 128)

REVIEW OF THE STANDARDS

483.410(d)	*Services provided under agreements with outside sources*
483.420(a)	*Protection of clients' rights*
483.420(c)	*Communication with clients, parents, and guardians*
483.430(a)	*Qualified mental retardation professional*
483.430(b)	*Professional program services*
483.430(d)	*Direct care (residential living unit) staff*
483.430(e)	*Staff training program*
483.440(a)	*Active treatment*
483.440(d)	*Program implementation*
483.440(f)	*Program monitoring and change*
483.450(a)	*Facility practices—Conduct toward clients*
483.450(b)	*Management of inappropriate client behavior*
483.460(a)	*Physician services*
483.460(c)	*Nursing services*
483.460(e)	*Dental services*
483.460(i)	*Pharmacy services*
483.460(k)	*Drug administration*
483.460(n)	*Laboratory services*
483.470(a)	*Client living environment*
483.470(h)	*Emergency plans and procedures*
483.470(i)	*Evacuation drills*
483.470(k)	*Paint*
483.470(l)	*Infection control*
483.480(a)	*Food and nutrition services*
483.480(c)	*Menus*
483.480(d)	*Dining areas and service*

No standards specific to quality assurance exist. Rather, the standards form the basis for developing a quality assurance system. The standards set forth by the Health Care Financing Administration set minimum regulatory requirements. In addition, the standards allow the facility to determine how it will meet the standards. Facilities have the opportunity to both set quality standards higher than the required minimums and establish their own process for meeting the quality assurance standards.

APPLICATION

The role of quality assurance is to set facility standards higher than those set by minimum regulatory standards. Quality assurance is systems oriented and attempts to improve all elements of a facility's operation:

- While not mandated by the regulations, quality assurance requires facility policy statements to guide the delivery of quality services.
- Quality assurance requires procedures in place to provide quality services.
- Quality assurance requires methods to monitor, evaluate, and correct the procedures and skills used to deliver quality services.
- Quality assurance requires skills of facility staff and practitioners sufficient to provide quality services.

In addition to the above, quality assurance requires a commonsense approach. The facility staff need to ask themselves constantly such commonsense questions as these:

- Would you be satisfied if you were an individual with developmental disabilities living in your own facility?
- If not, what would you change?
- How do you know that your services are as good as they can be?
- What more can you do to improve services, provide greater choices, and lead individuals to a less restrictive environment?

How to Design a Quality Assurance System

A logic lies behind a quality assurance system for an intermediate care facility for persons with mental retardation. This logic is based on the assumption that the ICF/MR has overall responsibility for ensuring that community-based services, such as a day program, meet the user's needs. Given this assumption, the logic of a quality assurance system flows as follows:

Facility and community services are centered on the needs of the individual with developmental disabilities. The facility's value base is the foundation for quality assurance. The mission statement indicates how values are to be implemented. In this statement quality services based on the needs of the individuals must be a goal. Throughout the facility staff actions must be consistent with the values and goals covered in the mission statement. Where actions deviate from values, facility staff need to intervene. An example of this is the facility that has "respect for individuals" as a value, yet some staff may refer to and treat these individuals as "the kids." Another example is the facility that values staff "get up and go," yet fails to reward or recognize initiatives.

Facility and community services are available, adequate, and appropriate in order to meet the user's measurable needs. As covered in Chapter 8, assessments of user's needs are a vital base for designing the type of services required to meet the individual's life and career goals. An initial step is to determine if the needed service is available at the time it is needed by the user. Such a service must also be adequate to meet the needs of the individual in terms of meeting basic standards. The mere availability and adequacy of a service, however, does not make it appropriate for each user. In order to be appropriate, a service must meet the individual's needs and preferences. For instance, a facility may have excellent work activities, but they may not be appropriate for elderly consumers who want to engage in retirement-related activities.

Facility and community service standards are set to measure services and outcomes. Using the federal regulations as a base, each facility should set its own standards for quality assurance. Each standard and its interpretive guideline can be taken as a starting point. The facility should feel free to make the standard stricter and the guideline more explicit. Additional standards may be drafted to ensure that services are appropriate and acceptable and lead to measurable outcomes. Using the example from above, the facility may want to draft standards for elderly consumers that respect their right to voluntarily remain in, or withdraw from, vocational activities.

The provider decision concerning level of quality is made specific by defining program indicators. The program indicators answer the question, "How do we know our level of quality is present?". They identify for staff those elements of quality viewed as important and ensure continued attention to these elements in the day-to-day provision of active treatment services. Most staff can identify concrete program indicators for a given level of quality service. The first element of the indicator is a performance standard such as:

- Direct contact staff are implementing the IPPs for all individuals with whom they work.
- All individuals with developmental disabilities are informed of their legal rights and responsibilities.
- The program coordinator observes the implementation of an individual's program at least once a week.

Performance indicators can be developed to cover all aspects of active treatment within an agency. They define acceptable levels of staff behavior that ensure the provision of active treatment services. They may range from the shared values in service delivery, to strategies for implementing individualized program plans, to the manner in which the grounds are maintained.

Facility and community service staff are indoctrinated and trained on quality assurance measures. Staff need to know that quality is a valued part of the facility's mission. Using several means to indoctrinate staff is best: posters, training sessions, audiovisual presentations, and clearly written policy and procedure statements. Modeling quality service by the executive director and managers is vital to any adoption of higher standards by facility staff. Supervisors are responsible for educating staff on day-to-day quality standards. Staff development specialists can create curriculum to emphasize the procedures and techniques for ensuring quality. For example, staff should be familiar with federal and facility standards and trained in how to conduct trial audits to determine if their unit meets these standards.

Facility and community services are monitored by qualified mental retardation professionals to ensure that outcomes meet standards. As discussed in Chapter 11 on client monitoring and evaluation, the qualified mental retardation professional (QMRP) has the responsibility to provide the day-to-day oversight needed to ensure that services meet the needs of the individual user. The QMRP ensures that assessments, planning, goal and objective setting, and program implementation and modification are done according to facility and federal standards. The QMRP reviews assessments, participates in selected goals and objectives, assists in the design of programs, and reviews the program and data collected about the programs to ensure that the individual is receiving appropriate services. Such follow-up is essential in quality assurance. It indicates to staff that quality assurance is a serious management concern and reinforces the assurance standards.

Facility and community service providers use sanctions and rewards to ensure quality service. Sanctions are essential for quality assurance. A sanction can be either positive or negative and is a control mechanism. If the QMRP discovers deviations below the facility standards, corrective actions are necessary. Sanctions can come in the form of private discussions, informal notes, formal letters, in-service training, and, if serious, progressive disciplinary actions. The QMRP and supervisor must emphasize that they are more interested in improvement than in punishment. Staff must know, however, that consequences will follow poor performance.

Since the ultimate beneficiary is the individual with developmental disability, sanctions should be effective. Peer pressure might be used. For example, if an interdisciplinary team is required to take up the slack caused by the poor performance of a single staff member, the team may try to assist or pressure that staff person into improving his or her performance if needed. Negative sanctions should be applied immediately. The actual sanction, though, should be done in private to encourage improvement. On the other hand, positive rewards for compliance encourage quality services and should be made openly. Public recognition of those providing exemplary services will encourage and instruct others to do likewise. Such incentives as commendation letters, write-ups in facility newsletters, recognition luncheons, or special trips all provide strong and positive reinforcement to staff providing quality services.

Program Checklist

		Yes	No
1.	The facility's value base is evident in the mission statement.	___	___
2.	Services meet individual needs and preferences.	___	___
3.	The facility establishes its own standards for quality assurance over and above federal requirements.	___	___
4.	The senior staff visibly demonstrate a commitment to quality assurance.	___	___
5.	The facility identifies sanctions and rewards to promote staff commitment to quality assurance.	___	___

How to Set Up a Quality Assurance Operation

Quality assurance is the job of the entire ICF/MR staff. In an effective system, staff members check each other's work and make useful suggestions on improvement. A formal quality assurance system, however, requires some specialized staff work. The functions of a quality assurance system are to set standards for compliance, review the performance, and suggest corrective actions. These functions, while shared by all staff, should be coordinated by designated staff members. In a large facility, a quality assurance office may be needed to gather the data to maintain quality standards. Here are the suggested steps:

Quality assurance staff prepare measurements for each standard. As discussed above, the federal standards are only the basis upon which each facility must set its own standards. The role of the quality assurance staff is to determine how best to measure outcomes that meet the facility's standards. What are the long-term goals for the ICF/MR and for each individual with developmental disability? These must be measurable. For example, long-term goals may include improvements in the ICF/MR safety record and increased integration of individuals in community activities and in supported employment positions. Some of these goals may be set at zero deficiency levels, such as reducing falls to zero, while others may be set at a percentage, such as ensuring that 60% or more of recreational activities are done in integrated settings.

Quality assurance staff determine methods to systematically review and sample performance. Incident reporting is a basic method used to review staff performance. Injury reports provide quantitative measures of staff competence. A facility should require that all injuries, however minor, be reported along with information on the circumstances. These data provide a daily check on the safety and well-being of the individuals with developmental disabilities. Quality assurance staff can investigate each incident and follow up on corrections. In addition, the quality assurance staff need to check on staff performance. At random, staff should be asked to demonstrate such skills as interacting competently with individuals with developmental disabilities, proper transfer techniques for nonambulatory individuals, and ability to enter data correctly in the records. Results of these random checks are useful for determining the performance level in each ICF/MR and for providing compensatory training as needed.

The performance standards can be used to establish a checklist to review and monitor the day-to-day performance of staff. Supervisory and management staff conduct walk-about surveys of the facility on a defined schedule that ensures each program area is reviewed frequently. Data are collected on the staff's compliance with identified performance indicators. The data can be computerized and reports generated for use by supervisory and management staff for providing feedback to staff. Feedback is important for continued growth and development and for achieving the standards of active treatment desired by the agency. Feedback results in sanctions for unacceptable performance and an established reward system that enable staff to achieve the desired outcomes.

Through a system of quality enhancement such as performance indicators and walk-about surveys, management staff are able to allocate resources and predict future agency performance in a formal survey. Analysis of the aggregate data enables management staff to identify trouble spots within the facility. Furthermore, data kept on the time of completed walk-about surveys enable staff to identify the time of day most difficulties arise in a given area. For example, the data reveal that 60% of the times surveyed between the hours of 6 p.m. and 8 p.m. all residents were engaged in age-appropriate activities in building X. The established criteria for this performance indicator is 100%. Observing this trend, management staff are able to allocate resources to ensure compliance with the identified performance indicator. Further analysis will aid in determining if the lower rating is the result of insufficient staff, insufficient materials, ineffective staff values, supervisory training, or the need for in-service training in program implementation. Through this system management staff are better able to accurately allocate needed resources.

Quality assurance staff follow up and help correct below-standard performance. Both the incident reports and the staff competency checks allow quality assurance staff to follow up on deficiencies. In many cases a memorandum to the appropriate supervisor is all that is required to improve services. If repeated problems are present, the quality assurance staff may have to report the situation to relevant department heads and request a timely response on how the deficiency was corrected. Since quality assurance should be a shared responsibility among all staff at the facility, quality assurance staff should avoid taking direct action, but rather remind staff of the need to adhere to facility standards for performance.

Quality assurance staff suggest improvements in the system to improve service delivery. Using data from incident reports and performance samples, quality assurance staff can determine patterns and suggest preventive measures. An investigation comes first. For example, if incident reports show that a large portion of falls occur at bedtime on weekends, the reasons could be many: inadequate staffing levels, lack of attention by staff, lack of competency in the staff, increased activity among the individuals with developmental disabilities, or diligent reporting of each incident by the weekend staff. Once quality assurance staff have investigated these reasons, they can suggest measures that will prevent falls in the future.

Quality assurance staff motivate all facility staff toward higher levels of quality performance. If only quality assurance staff are concerned about quality, a facility will always be below standard. All staff have to make quality performance a priority. This can be done by involving staff in setting standards, reviewing data on performance, and suggesting changes to improve service delivery. A campaign to involve systematically all facility staff in the day-to-day work of quality assurance will do a great deal to ensure that quality is built into the facility's operation. If staff are punished for poor performance, they will seek ways to avoid punishment, but this does not guarantee that performance will improve—only that staff is motivated to find new ways to disguise poor performance. If staff are rewarded for excellence, they will strive for excellence.

Program Checklist

	Yes	No
1. Quality assurance standards are measurable.	___	___
2. The facility randomly determines staff performance and provides compensatory training as needed.	___	___
3. Quality assurance staff analyze data and issue reports that are meaningful to all staff.	___	___

How to Use Computer Programs in Quality Assurance

Computers are extremely useful in quality assurance. Computers can combine the data needed to document delivery of quality services. Data bases can be developed to cover such items as incidents, training, monitoring visits, and medications. Progress reports by residential setting, for example, are possible using results from these data bases. Computers are also useful in providing readable and updated individualized habilitation plans. For example, typewritten task analysis instructions and behavior modification plans are more readable than handwritten notes. Many software programs can speed the generation of quality assurance reports and graphics.

The computer is useful in all four stages of a system: inputs, process, outputs, and outcomes. In the first case, as Bradley points out (pp. 131–133), "The inputs to human services are easily stored in computer systems. Generally, such data as client numbers, client demographics, staff numbers, staff complement, staff qualification, and units of service per client are typically collected system-wide by public agencies to monitor quality."

Second, process information, such as the delivery of services, can be tracked on a computer. For example, the hours of therapy provided to an individual with developmental disabilities and the number of recreational activities enjoyed by the individual can be easily tracked on a computer. If these hours or numbers fall below the amount prescribed by the individual's plan, the computer can flag such exceptions for immediate corrective action.

Third, the immediate results, or outputs, of the service delivery system, such as "the number of clients at a certain functioning level who have completed a particular activity" (Bradley, p. 132) can be easily kept in a computer data base. Finally, long-term impact or outcomes can also be measured on a computer. The movement of individuals with developmental disabilities to a less restrictive environment or into competitive employment are such outcomes. Using a computer allows facility staff to measure and ensure quality at every point. This is critical to the well-being of the individual.

If a facility is introducing the use of computers, Bradley suggests some factors that contribute to the successful design and implementation of a computerized quality assurance system (p. 137):

- Adequate resources, design, and implementation time is necessary for the success of computerized systems. The complexity of human services warrants the initial use of consultants during development time.
- Simplicity of system design encourages success. System design must produce information useful for management functions. In many cases this requires the translation of complex concepts into simple measurable instruments.
- Input from clinical staff and management personnel during development and implementation can counteract much of the fear associated with computerization. It can also generate enthusiasm and positive valuable participation on the part of the staff.
- Gradual implementation of the system helps to identify problems while at the same time acclimating staff to its use.
- The design and use of a good, understandable operational manual further enhance the utilization and acceptance of computers for quality assurance.
- Prompt feedback of computer data maintains staff cooperation

while strengthening the computer's effectiveness. Overall, staff knowledge of the benefits and uses of computerized systems will further the utility and success of such systems as a method to monitor and improve the quality of services.

Program Checklist

	Yes	No
1. The computerized quality assurance system is based on simple reporting forms.	___	___
2. The facility designed the computerized system with input from staff.	___	___
3. The quality assurance system yields data that enable staff to improve their performance.	___	___
4. The quality assurance system is field tested prior to implementation.	___	___

IMPLICATIONS

For the Individual

Since quality assurance is based on the individual's needs and preferences, individuals must be encouraged to act as informed consumers and to make their views known about service delivery. Staff need to be trained in how to interpret the concerns and preferences of individuals. This will allow individuals to make knowledgeable choices among alternative services and to plan a role in determining standards for quality services.

For Qualified Mental Retardation Professionals

The role of the QMRP is to monitor quality services on a day-to-day basis. The QMRP leads the staff in developing individualized habilitation plans that meet standards of quality services. Every day the QMRP reviews the implementation of plans to ensure that quality is maintained and moves rapidly to correct problems. If the services endanger the user, the QMRP intervenes directly. Otherwise, the QMRP works with staff supervisors and managers to correct problems in service delivery that inhibit quality services.

For Specialized Service Staff

In order to develop quality services, specialized service staff must meet the standards and requirements of their respective discipline. They can do this by regularly attending conferences to keep up with the state-of-the-art in their field and by taking and passing tests of competence as required by their discipline. The specialized service staff, in a quality program, interpret techniques from their discipline in a manner that is understandable and applicable by program staff. It is the specialist's role to assist other staff in implementing quality services. Along with other staff, the specialist participates in setting facility or community program standards to reflect quality services.

For Direct Care Staff

This is the staff that implements quality services. They must understand the need for quality services and know how to deliver it. This means the facility and community program must provide sufficient in-service training and reinforce the learning through practice and frequent updates, announcements, flyers, and other means. Staff should receive promotions or demotions based on standards of quality services. This is possible if the facility and community programs used by the facility have performance competency indicators that are based on quality standards and are clearly detailed. Then promotions, rewards, or, if necessary, reprimands can be based on these performance competencies.

For Quality Assurance Coordinators

The quality assurance (QA) coordinator should view individual outcome, not paper compliance, as key to a successful survey. The QA coordinator should look for evidence that individuals are making choices, improving the quality of their lives, and moving toward least restrictive environments. If such outcome measures fail to meet quality standards, then the QA coordinator should audit records to determine the causes of the problem. The role of the QA coordinator is then to educate facility and community program executives on how to improve quality services. The QA coordinator provides useful feedback that enables facility and community program executives to take concrete actions to improve service quality. If deficiencies are evident, the QA coordinator must follow up to determine if plans of correction are implemented. In general, the QA coordinator should encourage the facility to set and maintain standards that are higher than those set by regulation. If this is the case, the QA coordinator should be flexible and supportive as the facility works to implement its quality assurance system.

Whereas an executive may look for trends in services, the quality assurance specialist must act quickly and decisively to correct even a single incident if it indicates a decline in quality services. Immediate follow-up must be made to correct any failure to meet quality standards. Detailed documentation must be kept by the specialist to ensure that corrections are made and standards maintained. The specialist must anticipate areas of potential concern and act to forestall any diminishment of quality services. The quality assurance specialist understands that prevention and early intervention are keys to quality assurance. Working with the trainers and the program managers, the quality assurance specialists provide information on how to attain and sustain quality services in the facility and in community programs. Probably the most important role of the quality assurance specialist is to motivate all staff to attain, maintain, and then exceed the standards set by the facility.

For Program Managers

Supervisors must emphasize quality care to their staff and implement performance competencies in evaluating staff. Managers should provide on-the-spot corrections, adjustments, and modeling to emphasize importance of quality services. Performance standards for program managers should emphasize quality outcomes, and rewards or sanctions should be based on how effectively the staff under their control deliver quality services. Promotion of managers should be directly related to the productivity of staff in meeting quality standards.

For Family and Concerned Parties

As a prime support for the individual in the facility, family members and other concerned parties must stay informed about the needs and preferences of the individual. The consumer advocate should articulate these needs only as a supplement, not a substitute, for the individual's expression. The advocate should participate in setting standards for quality services. In this regard the advocate should review and comment on standards adopted by the facility and community programs, as well as suggest additional standards to improve quality of care.

For Trainers

Staff development specialists are the main resource in equipping staff to provide quality services. Trainers must design campaigns to promote quality service delivery. Emphasis should be placed on the variety of ways—visual, audio, written, and so on—to help staff understand and implement quality services. By developing curriculum in each subject, trainers place emphasis on quality control through standardization of service delivery. Trainers need to provide staff with monitoring and evaluation tools that can be used to ensure delivery of quality services. Trainers must exercise their own form of quality control and evaluate staff performance to determine if learning occurred as a result of training.

CONCLUSIONS

Quality assurance measures enable all staff to predict the outcomes of formal surveys. Critical to any agency, no surprises should occur in the formal survey process. Adequately monitored by walk-about surveys or mock formal surveys, management staff are better able to plan the deficiencies of the agency. Since deficiencies will be found during any survey process, management staff should strive to ensure deficiencies in the right areas. For example, an agency may be cited for lack of adequate numbers of direct care staff. This is far different and less significant than being cited for staff not knowing how to implement programs. Although the agency may not have adequate numbers of staff, that staff should be able to effectively demonstrate implementation strategies, appropriate staff-resident interaction, behavior management programs, and so forth.

Through such efforts data enable management staff to advocate appropriately for additional funding and/or resources that may be needed in the provision of active treatment services. In addition, the effect of implementing new programs, changing staffing ratios, or utilizing new materials is directly measured through quality assurance measures and subsequent data collection efforts.

The role of management is vital to the successful implementation of a quality assurance process. The values, expectations, and direction of the agency as stated in its mission statement provide the impetus for the quality assurance process. The leadership provided by management ensures it becomes a reality. Management staff must become an active part of the quality assurance process. This includes participating in the design of performance indicators, criteria statements, walk-about surveys, and mock formal surveys. In addition, utilizing the data as a means for feedback may assist in ensuring that staff place the same degree of importance on active treatment as the management staff.

Finally, management staff establish consequences for both desirable and undesirable staff behaviors. Desired norms are established and reinforced each time they are observed. Equally important, undesired behaviors are confronted and corrected.

Quality should be "Issue One" for all staff. Pride in delivery of quality service should be instilled in staff through daily reminders about its importance. Staff should be encouraged to recognize how they contribute to quality of life for individuals with developmental disabilities, and quality services should be recognized and appreciated. Both individual staff and teams of staff should be acknowledged for performance that exceeds facility or community program standards. Staff should be encouraged to celebrate achievements in meeting quality standards.

Quality must be incorporated in the organizational culture. Executives should be expected to maintain high standards and to reward staff for quality performance. Quality performance means that individuals are in the least restrictive environment, are integrated into community activities, and are attaining a good quality of life. Rewards and recognition for maintaining and exceeding quality standards should be given freely, and negative sanctions should be minimized. In a facility or community program, several clues indicate that quality services are important: staff actions and language will reflect internalized values; documented evidence that staff practice quality services will be present; and staff will articulate and demonstrate a commitment to quality care.

REFERENCES

Bradley, V.J. (1984). *Assessing and enhancing the quality of services: A guide for the human services field.* Boston: Human Services Research Institute.
Donabedian, A. (1980). *The definition of quality and approaches to its assessment.* Ann Arbor, MI: Health Administration Press.

14
Medicaid Reform, Quality Enhancement, and Program Development

James F. Gardner

In 1971 Congress transferred the intermediate care facility (ICF) program to Title XIX Medicaid of the Social Security Act. The legislation added to the existing ICF program authority for Medicaid funding to pay for "care for the mentally retarded in public institutions which have the primary purpose of providing health or rehabilitation services and which are classified as intermediate care facilities" (Lakin, Hill, & Bruininks, 1985, p. 1). Section 1905 of the amended Social Security Act stated that in addition to meeting the standards of an ICF, the ICF/MR would (Lakin et al., 1985, p. 2):

1. Provide health and rehabilitation services to mentally retarded persons
2. Provide a program of active treatment
3. Provide assurances that federal spending would not supplant previously allocated state funding

The ICF/MR program grew dramatically during the 1970s and 1980s. From a 400 million dollar program that accounted for 8% of Medicaid long-term care expenditures in 1975, the program grew to 3.6 billion dollars and 28% of all Medicaid long-term expenditures by 1982 (Lakin et al., 1985). Because of the open-ended nature of the Medicaid program, states were attracted to the ICF/MR as a means of maximizing federal dollars for state residential facilities (Fernald, 1984). The central position that the ICF/MR occupied in the financing of residential care raised questions about the appropriateness of the ICF/MR service model (Fernald, 1984).

Concerns also arose over the changing nature of the Medicaid program. The federal-state Medicaid program was intended as the main mechanism for financing health care services for poor people. By the early 1980s, however, a program of health services for the poor had become the largest public financier of both long-term care for the elderly and disabled and residential care for persons with mental retardation (National Study Group, 1983). The National Study Group on State Medicaid Strategies in 1983 noted that AFDC families who represented 66% of the Medicaid caseload accounted for only 25% of the program cost. The aged and disabled, accounting for 27% of the caseload, were responsible for 72% of the program expenditure (National Study Group, 1983).

The study group identified three primary groups of Medicaid recipients (National Study Group, 1983, p. 6):

1. Low-income individuals and families
2. Functionally impaired elderly and disabled individuals
3. Mentally retarded and developmentally disabled people

The study group also noted that "Medicaid reform must: 1) explicitly consider how to balance appropriately the medical and non-medical service needs of each of the three target groups, 2) specify the primary delivery system most appropriate to client need, and 3) identify the linkages between health care resources and other non-health resources" (National Study Group, 1983, p. 18).

In addition to the larger concerns with the direction of the Medicaid program, specific criticisms of the ICF/MR program model have focused on size, its medical orientation, and the social segregation of the program from the community. Since the late 1970s efforts have steadily progressed to move Medicaid funding beyond the ICF/MR as a large residential facility.

The first effort consisted of proposals to certify small, less than 15-bed facilities as ICFs/MR. States such as Minnesota, New York, Michigan, and Texas led in the development of this model (Lakin et al., 1985). Other states with different residential facility needs, financing, or historical development were more cautious. In the early 1980s the cost of complying with the ICF/MR standards and the appropriate life safety codes pushed the per capita cost beyond an acceptable limit for some states (Gardner, 1986).

In an effort to curb the rising costs of the Medicaid program, Congress included in the Omnibus Budget Reconciliation Act of 1981 a Home and Community Based Waiver that gave the Secretary of the Department of Health and Human Services the authority to waive specified requirements in the law to permit states to finance community services through Medicaid. The waiver required that persons served in the community would qualify for care in the ICF/MR. The waiver was intended to reduce overall Medicaid expenditure by providing nonmedical services outside skilled nursing facilities and ICFs/MR. The reasoning was that home health aide, homemaker, respite, case management, and other community services would generally cost less than the cost of nursing home care (DHHS, 1984; Gardner, 1986; NASMRPD, 1982, 1985).

The utilization of the waiver to underpin community program expansion was limited because the waivers were granted only to defined and limited numbers of people, were tied to complex financial formulas, and were given at the option of the Department of Health and Human Services.

The potential for the waiver and the need for Medicaid reform were, in part, the impetus for the introduction of the Community and Family Living Amendments in 1984 by Senator John Chafee. The original Chafee legislation proposed to redirect federal Medicaid funds from long-term facilities to community-based programs over an extended period. The primary aim of the legislation was to reverse the financing incentives for supporting large Title XIX facilities. The bill would have phased out Medicaid support to residential facilities serving more than 10 nonelderly disabled adults. The Chafee bill would have entitled those individuals to receive a wide range of home-and community-based service.

The Chafee bill has evolved over time. The current Senate version of the original Chafee bill, "The Medicaid Home and Community Quality Services Act of 1989," and a companion House bill, "The Medicaid Community and Facility Habilitation Amendments of 1989," were introduced in the Senate and House respectively in February 1989. While important differences exist between the two bills, the intent is similar. The current Medicaid reform legislation proposes to extend further Medicaid financing to a range of family and community-based services for people with developmental disabilities.

In a review of the current ICF/MR program, Lakin, Hill, White, Wright, and Bruininks (1989) note that ICF/MR services do not meet the objective of the 1987 Developmental Disabilities Act of offering "persons with developmental disabilities the opportunity, to the maximum extent feasible, to make decisions for themselves and to live in typical homes and communities where they can exercise their full rights and responsibilities as citizens." They conclude that Medicaid Title XIX "needs substantial reform to adequately serve persons with developmental disabilities" (Lakin et al., 1989, p. 155).

Quite probably, some features of the new program will remain similar. The services will be provided within the context of the Medicaid program, and the federal government will maintain some regulatory and disciplinary control over it. Despite whatever financing and regulatory mechanisms are constructed, the program issues in developmental disabilities will remain the same.

The design of service programs that has prompted the need for Medicaid reform will continue to rest on the basic principles of individualization, legal rights, and social integration. Emphasis on quality enhancement and positive approaches to behavior management have also increased.

PROGRAM REFORM

Innovation in the design and provision of services to persons with developmental disabilities continues to flourish at the local community level. With or without Medicaid reform, programs based on the support services model, positive behavior management, and quality enhancement will guide the direction of future service delivery.

The Support Services Model

The central principle of the support services model is that where one lives or works depends upon the presence of necessary support services (Davis & Trace, 1982). Proposed reforms in Medicaid legislation would allow greater financial support for services in the community. This incremental approach to putting together packages of services that allow persons to live and work in the community is replacing the one where the full range of services must be offered at a central location.

The support services model is also important because it emphasizes the possibility of social and environmental adaptation rather than providing an exclusive focus on the limitations of the individual with developmental disabilities. The exclusive focus on the individual creates the disability. The support services model recognizes that the determinant of disability is societal and that social and environmental supports can allow people with disabilities to function ably in the society.

An exclusive focus on the particular dysfunction of the individual creates social situations that force the inability or diminished ability to become paramount. Claire Liachowitz argues, for example, that disability is "a complex construct dependent upon personal attributes other than physical [or mental defect], and upon elements of the social environment" (Liachowitz, 1988, p. 108). The lack of an ecological approach to disability that recognizes the importance of social and physical environments "results in various social constructions that force handicapped individuals into a position of deviance" (Liachowitz, 1988, p. 5). Absent the necessary supports to compensate for the diminished ability, socially created imperatives force deviancy on individuals.

Thomas T. H. Wan presents a disability model that consists of three sets of factors (Liachowitz, 1988, pp. 7–8):

1. Disabling conditions
2. Host factors such as education, occupation, race, age, and gender
3. Environmental factors such as patterns of industrialization, poverty, and broad based support services

The support service model provides more opportunities for change than does an exclusive focus on dysfunction alone.

The support service model is tied closely to the form and function paradigm that Phillipa Campbell and William Bricker developed in the first edition of *Program Issues in Developmental Disabilities*. At that time they pointed to the difference between the form of a behavior and the function of a behavior. They noted that normally developing individuals with intact motor and sensory processes exhibit specific forms of behavior in an orderly sequence. Thus infants sit, crawl, and then walk. In a similar manner verbal speech evolves through a number of developmental forms. Both the developmental model and the continuum of service model were premised on the belief that people with developmental disabilities had to progress through the forms of a behavior and graduate through a service delivery system (Campbell & Bricker, 1980).

The support service model focuses instead on the function of behavior. If the individual cannot drink from a cup because of limited hand-to-mouth coordination, and little change is likely, then the focus should shift from the individual to environmental and social supports that can serve the function. Special equipment or an attendant can solve the problem of drinking. Likewise job coaches can enable people to work, and in-home family support workers can keep families together.

Positive Behavior Management

The emphasis on positive behavior management represents more than a preference for shaping behavior through positive reinforcement rather than aversive conditioning. This is certainly important and consistent with humanistic values and individual rights. In addition, the emphasis on the positive approach indicates that people with developmental disabilities have motives and reasons for their behavior.

In the mid 1970s much of the emphasis on behavior management stressed the consequences or reinforcement that followed a behavior. The typical staff development programs taught reinforcement schedules and types of reinforcers, while sophisticated staff carried stop watches and hand counters. Not a great deal of attention was placed on the antecedents or causes for the behavior. The underlying belief was that people with developmental disabilities did not have or could not articulate a reason for strange and often challenging behavior.

The emphasis on a positive approach to behavior management acknowledges that behavior serves a purpose for the individual. The individual may or may not be directly aware that the behavior takes place for a reason and produces a desired consequence. These patterns may be learned over time.

In the traditional behavior management approach, most of the intervention was placed on the manipulation of the consequences of the behavior. The positive approach to behavior management also stresses the manipulation of the antecedent conditions or the environmental reasons for the behavior. It also stresses the need to teach new skills so that people gain greater control and consistency in their lives.

Quality Enhancement

Whenever Medicaid reform legislation is enacted, an increased concern for regulation and compliance will result. The design and management of a licensing, certification, and regulation program will contain both federal and state elements. Program providers will have to meet the requirements as do the ICF/MR providers at the time (NASMRPD, 1989).

The continuing expansion of community-based services will also focus attention on quality enhancement. In the past an unspoken but common belief that community presence was evidence of quality may have been evident. Experience has demonstrated, however, that community programs require organized quality enhancement programs to maintain public confidence.

Economic and demographic trends into the next century will create significant pressure on community programs. The number of qualified persons in the work force seeking entry level positions in community programs is limited. This labor shortage can result in turnover, staff shortages, and increasing costs associated with recruitment, training, and supervision.

The labor shortage is accentuated by the low salaries paid to staff in some community programs. Starting salaries and yearly increases do not match those in other sectors of the economy. Retaining experienced and competent staff will remain a difficulty for many agencies.

Finally, many community-based programs will search for new methods of management and administration for decentralized, small programs in the community. The demographics of the labor market and the required level of staff competence suggest that supervisors will function as on-line mentors and teachers for new direct service staff.

Quality assurance can best be provided through the coordination of a variety of methods. These include (Bersani, 1988):

1. Certification for programs participating in the Medicaid program such as ICFs/MR
2. Accreditation for programs by independent, third-party organizations such as ACDD or CARF
3. Licensure of programs by the state agency
4. Citizen monitoring of programs by persons with disabilities, families, and advocates

Each of these quality assurance methods provides benefits. They can be used in different combinations and in different sequences.

No matter which method is employed, a difference between the development of quality programs and meeting regulatory requirements should be found. Quality programs require a sound value base, access to the latest advances in education, medicine, the behavioral sciences, rehabilitation, and proven systems for staff development and management. Quality programs generally meet regulatory requirements. Programs often attempt, however, to meet regulatory requirements by complying with all the regulations without designing and implementing good programs.

Quality enhancement and program development are long-term strategic activities that encompass values and assumptions about people with disabilities and that address the organization's mission statement. Approaching quality enhancement as a strategic undertaking should greatly increase the probability of compliance with regulations and standards. However, attempting to meet regulations and standards without a strategic framework minimizes the quality enhancement outcome.

The linkage between Medicaid reform, quality enhancement, and program development suggests that habilitation programs develop a strategic framework for quality enhancement and program development that includes:

1. Strategic planning
2. Organization development
3. Staff training and development
4. Internal monitoring and evaluation

Strategic Planning

Strategic planning is the process of determining what an agency is going to be in the future. Strategic planning includes an examination of the values and assumptions about people with disabilities, a listing of the threats and opportunities in the outside environment, and the strengths and weaknesses of the organization. Strategic planning results in the formulation of the mission statement of the organization.

Strategic planning and quality enhancement both focus on the "should" and the "ought" rather than the "is." The key questions for the strategic planner begin with the individual and move on to the organization's mission. The questions are:

• What does the individual want to do in the future?
• Where does the individual want to work and live in the future?
• How can the organization assist the individual to achieve future goals?
• What is the organization going to be in the future?
• With what level of quality will the organization operate?

Basing the strategic vision on individual needs results in a mission statement and values that link individual need and organization outcome. Without that connection to the individual the organization can fall prey to becoming more efficient and effective at accomplishing the wrong outcomes. The linkage between individual need and organization outcome addresses the quality assurance question of whether the individual's needs are being met.

Organization Development

Organization development refers to the management of planned change in an organization. French and Bell (1984) discuss organization development as an undertaking that is planned, organization wide, and directed from the top in order to increase organization effectiveness. Organization development activities stress the individual motivation, goal setting, problem solving, and team building. The activities are undertaken to assist work groups to manage work against a set of expectations (Golembiewski, Proehl, & Sink, 1982). Organization development efforts proceed on the assumption that employees are guided by internalized meanings, values, and habits.

The focus on quality enhancement also rests on staff commitment to meanings and values connected with the provision of services to people with developmental disabilities. The dedication to quality enhancement can develop as an outgrowth of the organization development activity within an agency. In addition the organization development effort can increase the skills and abilities of the interdisciplinary teams that play a prominent role in the quality enhancement program.

Staff Training and Development

Quality enhancement and program development require a focused program of staff training and development. In fact, staff training and development can be considered a component of organization development. Staff development ensures that all employees are aware of the organization's mission, its values and assumptions about people with disabilities, and the level of quality to which the organization aspires. Staff training ensures that staff are provided with the skills and abilities to meet the expected levels of quality.

Like quality enhancement, staff training and development is a long-term strategic commitment. Expectations for employee performance must be established, stated, and restated. All new employees go through a process of training and development. The key variable for quality assurance is whether that training and development is actively managed by the organization in conformity to a set of values and assumptions about people with disabilities or whether the process takes place in the informal organization.

Internal Monitoring and Evaluation

As indicated in Chapter 11, monitoring and evaluation determine whether the agency demonstrates progress in meeting the goals established for individuals provided services. Monitoring and evaluation serve a strategic function of ensuring that the organization remains responsive to individual needs.

Because of the day-to-day aspects of monitoring, the strategic focus of evaluation is often overlooked. The result is that monitoring becomes an end in itself, and compliance with a large number of individual performance standards becomes all encompassing. However, the purpose of monitoring is to enable the agency to answer the question of "how well did we do today?" The larger evaluation question determines if the organization is fulfilling its mission based on the empirical evidence of accomplishments or failings.

CONCLUSION

As values, technology, and financing strategies have evolved in the field of developmental disabilities, changes have taken place in the Title XIX Medicaid ICF/MR program. Future changes are possible and may include provisions that address the support services model, a stress on the positive approach to managing behaviors and a concern for quality enhancement.

The management of quality enhancement programs must proceed with a strategic focus on the mission of the organization and the outcome for the individual and the connection between the two. Quality enhancement is a process for guaranteeing the mission of the organization and specific outcomes for the individual. The goal of the quality enhancement program is to meet these two strategic goals. Compliance with standards and regulations measures goal attainment. Providers of service, individuals with developmental disabilities, and federal and state agencies should continue to recognize the important distinction between the goals and the performance indicators in a quality enhancement program.

REFERENCES

Bersani, H. (Aug. 1988). Quality assurance: Beyond minimal compliance. *DD Highlights.* Tucson, AR: CART.

Campbell, P., & Bricker, W. (1980). Programming for the severely/profoundly handicapped person. In J. F. Gardner et al. (Eds.), *Program issues in developmental disabilities: A resource manual for surveyors and reviewers* (pp. 127–153). Baltimore: Paul H. Brookes Publishing Co.

Davis, M. J., & Trace, M. W. (1982). *The support model: A new approach to providing a continuum of service.* Unpublished manuscript, Ellsworth Community College.

Department of Health and Human Services, Health Care Financing Administration, Office of Research and Demonstrations. (1984). *Report to Congress: Studies evaluating Medicaid home and community-based care waivers.* Baltimore: Health Care Financing Administration.

Fernald, C. D. (1984). *Too little too late: Deinstitutionalization and the development of community services for mentally retarded people. Executive summary and recommendations concerning Medicaid: ICF/MR.* Charlotte: University of North Carolina.

French, W., & Bell, C. (1984). *Organization development: Behavioral science interventions for organization improvement* (ed. 3). Englewood Cliffs, NJ: Prentice-Hall.

Gardner, J. F. (1986). Implementation of the home and community-based waiver. *Mental Retardation, 24*(2), 18–26.

Golembiewski, R. T., Proehl, C. W., & Sink, D. (1982). Estimating the success of OD applications. *Training and Development Journal, 36*, 86–95.

Lakin, K. C., Hill, B., & Bruininks, R. (Eds.). (1985). *An analysis of Medicaid's intermediate care facility for the mentally retarded (ICF-MR) program.* Minneapolis: University of Minnesota.

Lakin, K. C., Hill, B. K., White, C. C., Wright, E. A., Bruininks, R. H. (1989). Longitudinal patterns in ICF-MR Utilization, 1977–1989. *Mental Retardation, 27*(3), 149–158.

Liachowitz, C. H. (1988). *Disability as a social construct: Legislative roots.* Philadelphia: University of Pennsylvania Press.

National Association of State Mental Retardation Program Directors, Inc. (1982). *An update on the Medicaid home and community care waiver authority.* Alexandria, VA: Author.

National Association of State Mental Retardation Program Directors, Inc. (1985). *Federal administrative constraints on state Medicaid outlays for MR/DD recipients.* Alexandria, VA: Author.

National Association of State Mental Retardation Program Directors, Inc. (1989). *Federal Medicaid reform legislation: Optional approaches to assuring the quality of title XIX-funded community services for persons with developmental disabilities.* Alexandria, VA: Author.

The National Study Group on State Medicaid Strategies. (1983). Restructuring Medicaid: An agenda for change. *Summary report of the National Study Group on State Medicaid Strategies.* Washington, DC: The Center for the Study of Social Policy.

Index

Page numbers in *italics* indicate figures; those followed by "t" indicate tables.

P·A·U·L·H·
BROOKES
PUBLISHING Co

ISBN 1-55766-029-8